Off the
Beaten Path®

new mexico

3 1559 00171 7493

Help Us Keep This Guide Up to Date

Every effort has been made by the author and editors to make this guide as accurate and useful as possible. However, many changes can occur after a guide is published—establishments close, phone numbers change, hiking trails are rerouted, facilities come under new management, etc.

We would love to hear from you concerning your experiences with this guide and how you feel it could be improved and be kept up to date. While we may not be able to respond to all comments and suggestions, we'll take them to heart, and we'll make certain to share them with the author. Please send your comments and suggestions to the following address:

The Globe Pequot Press
Reader Response/Editorial Department
P.O. Box 480
Guilford, CT 06437

Or you may e-mail us at: editorial@GlobePequot.com

Thanks for your input, and happy travels!

INSIDERS' GUIDE®

OFF THE BEATEN PATH® SERIES

Off the

SEVENTH EDITION

Beaten Path®

new mexico

A GUIDE TO UNIQUE PLACES

RICHARD K. HARRIS

INSIDERS' GUIDE®

GUILFORD, CONNECTICUT
AN IMPRINT OF THE GLOBE PEQUOT PRESS

The prices and rates listed in this guidebook were confirmed at press time. We recommend, however, that before traveling, you call establishments to obtain current information.

Note: Please be aware that a second telephone area code is in the offing for New Mexico to augment the state's sole existing code, 505. Specific information regarding the new code was not available at press time.

INSIDERS' GUIDE®

Copyright © 1991, 1994, 1997, 2000, 2002, 2004, 2005 by The Globe Pequot Press

Text design by Linda Loiewski
Maps created by Equator Graphics © The Globe Pequot Press
Art on page 69 by Daisy dePothod; all other art by Carole Drong
Spot photography throughout © Barry Slaven/Index Stock

ISSN: 1536-6189
ISBN: 0-7627-3532-5

Manufactured in the United States of America
Seventh Edition/First Printing

For all who have
been—or will be—
enchanted by New Mexico.

NORTH
CENTRAL
NEW MEXICO

Taos

SANTA FE
AND
TAOS REGION

Los Alamos

Gallup

Santa Fe ★

Las Vegas

NORTHWESTERN
NEW MEXICO

Albuquerque

CENTRAL
NEW MEXICO

NORTHEASTERN
NEW MEXICO

Roswell

SOUTHWESTERN
NEW MEXICO

SOUTHEASTERN
NEW MEXICO

Las Cruces

Contents

Acknowledgments

This book benefited from the input of several members of the Tourism Association of New Mexico as well as the advice from members of the Old West Country organization. Also, many of the state's chambers of commerce, convention and visitor bureaus, and the New Mexico Department of Tourism provided key leads. In addition, *New Mexico Magazine, Southern New Mexico Magazine,* the *Albuquerque Journal, Albuquerque Tribune, Crosswinds, Local Flavor, La Cocinita,* and *Weekly Alibi* proved invaluable as research tools. Also, the Internet emerged as the most efficient information-gathering tool, second only to the telephone and my truck. Thank you to the many readers who have written and e-mailed their suggestions on places to include in future editions. But mostly I'd like to thank my family and friends for providing support and patience during this ongoing project and for giving up months of weekends to go "on the road" in the Land of Enchantment.

Introduction

Renowned New Mexico artist Georgia O'Keeffe once said, "If you ever go to New Mexico, it will itch you for the rest of your life." Millions of folks from all over the world have come to know exactly what she meant. The people, the culture, the landscape, the climate—New Mexico just gets under your skin and takes hold. Whatever form it takes, the New Mexico mystique is a powerful force to reckon with. It may hit you when you're hiking among the ruins of an ancient civilization, strolling along the narrow streets of Santa Fe, or just silently soaking up the smells and sounds of the forest. Frequently, visitors become so seduced by the Land of Enchantment that they're compelled to make it their home. When asked why, they can't always explain it. But on a broad scale it has a lot to do with space and freedom and pure light. The ever-present blue skies and spectacular sunsets are also addicting.

Tucked into the southwestern United States, New Mexico itself is essentially off the beaten path. Our state is often confused with Arizona on maps and is even mistaken for the country of Mexico. But most residents cherish this anonymity and obscurity about the place they call home. New Mexico's wide-open spaces, unique history, rich cultural diversity, and endless natural wonders combine to create an ideal atmosphere in which to escape and explore—or even get lost, if that's what you're after.

This is by no means a comprehensive guidebook to New Mexico; there are plenty of good ones around. Rather, it's a selective guide to the state's out-of-the-way treasures—some well known, some not—all of which are unique and offer something special to the adventurous traveler. Geographic diversity and vastness are paramount in New Mexico's 121,330 square miles. The state will delight you with its hidden charms as you explore its ghost towns, quaint bed-and-breakfast inns, quirky cafes, ancient Indian ruins and present-day Indian pueblos, isolated museums, and all the breathtaking scenery you can bear.

While satiating your wanderlust in our expansive state, remember that although New Mexico is the fifth-largest state in area (after Alaska, Texas, California, and Montana), it ranks thirty-sixth in population—a scant 1.8 million people, of whom approximately a third reside in the Albuquerque metropolitan area. The point: lots of space, few people. Because everything is so spread out, plan some time to get around and always carry a detailed, current map. (Call the New Mexico Department of Tourism, 505–827–7400 or 800–545–2070, for a free one.)

As one of the youngest states in the continental United States (it didn't achieve statehood until 1912, though it boasts the oldest capital in the nation,

Santa Fe), New Mexico is a land of ancient civilizations. The Anasazi Indians, ancestors of the state's present-day Pueblo Indians, first occupied parts of New Mexico more than 1,000 years ago, and the state is still very much a home to Native Americans. There are nineteen autonomous pueblos (communities on the Indian reservations) inhabited by the different tribes of New Mexico's Pueblo Indians, and part of the Navajo Nation—the largest Indian reservation in the United States—lies in northwestern New Mexico. Native Americans and their rich culture remain a vital part of life in most of our state.

Though several pueblos are included as entries in this book, many are not. It's important to realize that the pueblos and other Native American lands do not exist for tourists. However, many pueblos welcome visitors and even host such events as feast days, arts and crafts shows, and ceremonial dances that are open to the public. Keep in mind that the reservations are sovereign nations with their own laws and policies (and languages, though most American Indians now speak English), and so call ahead before you venture out. A list of the Indian pueblos and tribes of New Mexico begins on page 201. An aside is appropriate here. During the past several years Indian tribes across the United States have opted to enter the seemingly lucrative field of operating gaming casinos. New Mexico tribes are no different in this respect. And while many, if not most, of New Mexico's tribes now operate casinos, I have opted not to include such information in this edition. If you are interested in such gambling opportunities, however, rest assured that you'll see the often elaborate casinos (and/or their billboards) that have, for better or worse, cropped up along New Mexico's highways.

A strong Hispanic heritage also exists in New Mexico. The Spanish first came to New Mexico with Coronado's expedition in 1540, and the first Spanish colony was established near San Juan Pueblo in 1598. Later, additional Spanish settlers came north on El Camino Real ("The Royal Road" connecting Mexico City to Santa Fe). The Spanish influence took hold, and Hispanic traditions and culture are very much inherent in New Mexico. This heritage is responsible for New Mexico's designation as the oldest wine-growing region in the United States, starting with the missionaries' vineyards in the 1600s. Though a few of the state's many modern wineries are included in this book's narrative, refer to pages 201–02 for a complete list.

New Mexico is also a land of newcomers. Anglo settlers didn't begin arriving until the opening of the Santa Fe Trail in 1821. Later, the railroad connected New Mexico to the population centers of the East. During the early part of this century, Anglo settlers from the East, seeking a remedy for tuberculosis and other ailments, headed to New Mexico's dry climate on their doctors' advice. Many of these latter-day pioneers subsequently made their fortunes here.

New Mexico has held an allure for artists since the turn of the twentieth century. The northern New Mexico community of Taos is a picturesque arts enclave; Santa Fe is firmly established as an art capital of international prominence; and, more recently, Albuquerque too has become known as a major art center. Despite the concentration of galleries in these three cities, small towns throughout the state also offer quality museums and galleries just waiting to be explored.

People often travel the world over without visiting places that have a lasting effect on them, but after your first visit to New Mexico, expect to feel the urge to come back. It was Georgia O'Keeffe's itch, and soon it will be yours as well.

A Note about the Seventh Edition

Much has changed in New Mexico since this book was first published in 1991, though, of course, more has remained the same, which is fortunate for those of us who like our state pretty much the way it is. Revised editions, such as this book, not only allow information to be updated but also permit the addition of new attractions not included in any previous edition. A good way to begin experiencing New Mexico is from cyberspace with a visit to the official Web site of the New Mexico Department of Tourism at www.newmexico.org. Come on, surf the high desert of the American Southwest, where the vibes are cool and the sun always shines.

Climate Overview

A clue to New Mexico's climate: Before "Land of Enchantment" became the state slogan, New Mexico went by the nickname "the Sunshine State," based on the fact that every part of New Mexico receives at least 70 percent sunshine year-round. However, as with most states, New Mexico's weather depends on the region and season.

Autumn weather is the most pleasant and predictable, usually sunny and mild. Early spring, while often quite warm, usually brings strong, dusty winds. June is the hottest month, often reaching the upper nineties, with late July through August bringing the state's cooler monsoon season, when brief afternoon thunderstorms are common. Keep in mind that even during summer it can get quite cool during the evenings, often requiring a sweater or jacket, especially in communities at higher elevations, which tend to be cooler throughout the year. Winter is a mixed bag because, while it is usually sunny and relatively mild, the state does receive snowfall, which ranges from less than 2 inches annually in the lower Rio Grande Valley to as much as 300 inches in the mountains of north central New Mexico.

Key to restaurant prices (price per average entree):

Inexpensive: Under $8   Expensive: $15–$20
Moderate: $8–$14   Very expensive: More than $20

Helpful Information

NEW MEXICO TOURISM

New Mexico Department of Tourism, 491 Old Santa Fe Trail, Santa Fe, NM 87501; (800) SEE–NEWMEX (800–733–6396); www.newmexico.org

USEFUL WEB SITES

State of New Mexico, www.state.nm.us
New Mexico State Parks, www.emnrd.state.nm.us/nmparks/
New Mexico's National Parks and Monuments, www.nps.gov/
Ski New Mexico, www.skinewmexico.com/
New Mexico museums and other cultural offerings, www.nmculture.org/
(Note: Other useful Web sites are scattered throughout this edition.)

MAJOR NEWSPAPERS

Albuquerque Journal,
P.O. Drawer J,
Albuquerque, NM
87103; (505) 823–3800;
www.abqjournal.com

Albuquerque Tribune,
P.O. Drawer T,
Albuquerque, NM 87103;
(505) 823–3653;
www.abqtrib.com

Santa Fe New Mexican,
202 East Marcy Street,
Santa Fe, NM 87501;
(505) 983–3303;
www.sfnewmexican.com

Las Cruces Sun-News,
256 West Las Cruces Avenue,
Las Cruces, NM 88005;
(505) 541–5400;
www.lcsun-news.com

Farmington Daily Times,
P.O. Box 450,
Farmington, NM 87499;
(505) 325–4545;
www.daily-times.com

Gallup Independent,
500 North Ninth Street,
Gallup, NM 87305;
(505) 863–6811;
www.gallupindependent.com

Roswell Daily Record,
2301 North Main Street,
Roswell, NM 88201;
(505) 622–7710;
www.roswell-record.com

PUBLIC TRANSPORTATION

Amtrak,
214 First Street SW,
Albuquerque, NM 87102;
(505) 842–9650, (800) 872–7245;
www.amtrak.com

Greyhound,
300 Second Street SW,
Albuquerque, NM 87102;
(800) 231–2222;
www.greyhound.com

Albuquerque International Sunport,
2200 Sunport Boulevard;
Albuquerque, NM 87106;
(505) 244–7700;
www.cabq.gov/airport

Fast Facts about the Land of Enchantment

- Area (land): 121,336 square miles; rank: 5
- Capital: Santa Fe
- Largest city: Albuquerque, population city, 464,000; metro, 737,000 (2002)
- Number of counties: 33
- Highest elevation: 13,161 feet, Wheeler Peak
- Lowest elevation: 2,840 feet, Red Bluff Lake, along the Texas border south of Carlsbad
- Population: 1,829,146 (2001); rank: 36
- Statehood: January 6, 1912; the 47th state
- Nickname: Land of Enchantment
- State Song: "O, Fair New Mexico"
- State Motto: Crescit Eundo ("It grows as it goes")
- State Flower: Yucca
- State Tree: Piñon
- State Grass: Blue Grama
- State Bird: Roadrunner
- State Fish: New Mexico Cutthroat Trout
- State Animal: Black Bear
- State Vegetables: Chile and Beans
- State Fossil: *Coelophysis* dinosaur
- State Insect: Tarantula Hawk Wasp
- State Gem: Turquoise
- State Cookie: Biscochito (or bizcochito)
- State Poem: "Asi es Nuevo Mexico" by Luis Tafoya
- State Ballad: "The Land of Enchantment" by Michael Martin Murphy

FAMOUS NEW MEXICANS

- Buffalo Bill Cody, showman famous for his Wild West Show
- Black Jack Ketchum, notorious train robber
- Gen. John (Blackjack) Pershing, cavalry officer in the 1880s
- Gen. Douglas MacArthur, World War II hero
- Ralph Bunche, Nobel Peace Prize winner
- Manuel Lujan Jr., secretary of interior during the George H. W. Bush administration
- Miguel Trujillo, Isleta Pueblo activist who campaigned to win Indians' right to vote
- Ezequiel C. de Baca, nation's first Hispanic governor
- Ernie Pyle, renowned World War II correspondent
- Conrad Hilton, founder of the Hilton Hotel chain
- Ernest Thompson Seton, author, naturalist, artist, cofounder of the Boy Scouts
- Harrison J. Schmitt, astronaut, moonwalker, former U.S. senator
- Clyde Tombaugh, astronomer who codiscovered the planet Pluto
- J. Robert Oppenheimer, head of Manhattan Project, which developed atomic bomb

Traditional Foods of New Mexico

Some of the most enjoyable moments during any vacation are mealtimes, especially when you find yourself someplace with a unique cuisine. New Mexico is one such place. The traditional food of New Mexico—*la comida de Nuevo México*—is centered around the crops that American Indians were growing in this area when Spanish explorers arrived in the late 1500s: corn, beans, squash, and chile (always spelled with an "e" on the end in New Mexico).

New Mexico cuisine is very different from the Tex-Mex cuisine of our neighbor to the east, where chile is spelled "chili," and rather than denoting a vegetable (the chile pepper), it connotes a spicy bean-and-beef concoction. New Mexican cuisine can be as basic as a plate of red or green chile enchiladas, which can be found almost anywhere in the state, or as elaborate and experimental as an entree of piñon-laced corn crepes filled with chipotle chiles and topped with squash blossoms, which could only be found in a trendy Santa Fe bistro.

While dishes such as enchiladas or posole (a chile-infused hominy stew) are omnipresent in New Mexico restaurants, they can be time-consuming to prepare at home. Therefore, scattered throughout this edition are several simple recipes for some favorite traditional (and adapted) New Mexico dishes and accompaniments—everything from green chile stew to a classic margarita. I hope you enjoy this little taste of the Southwest!

- Robert H. Goddard, developer of world's first liquid-fuel rocket
- Edgar D. Mitchell, Apollo 14 astronaut
- Nancy Lopez, Hall of Fame golfer with LPGA
- Al, Al Jr., and Bobby Unser, famous race-car-driving family
- Don Meredith, former Dallas Cowboy
- Trent Dimas, Olympic Gold Medal–winning gymnast
- Sam Donaldson, ABC News anchor

Southwestern New Mexico

This rugged region of the state is often referred to as Old West Country. Its wild-and-woolly past echoes in the remains of ghost towns, museums, and the memories of many old-timers. Mining and ranching have traditionally dominated the landscape and have given residents their fiercely independent nature.

This is also the only region in New Mexico that borders a foreign country—our state's namesake to the south, Mexico. In southwestern New Mexico you'll find the nation's first designated wilderness area, the Gila National Wilderness, as well as our state's largest lake, Elephant Butte Reservoir. And on a more somber note, this region was the site of the world's first nuclear bomb explosion.

Also in this region—especially in Grant and Catron Counties, which contain the majority of the Gila National Forest (which in turn contains the aforementioned Gila National Wilderness)—visitors will discover what naturalists have long known: There are upward of 400 bird species that call this region home, whether seasonally or year-round, making this area a birder's paradise. And counted among these species are many types of colorful, enchanting hummingbirds, which continue to fascinate both old and young alike.

SOUTHWESTERN NEW MEXICO

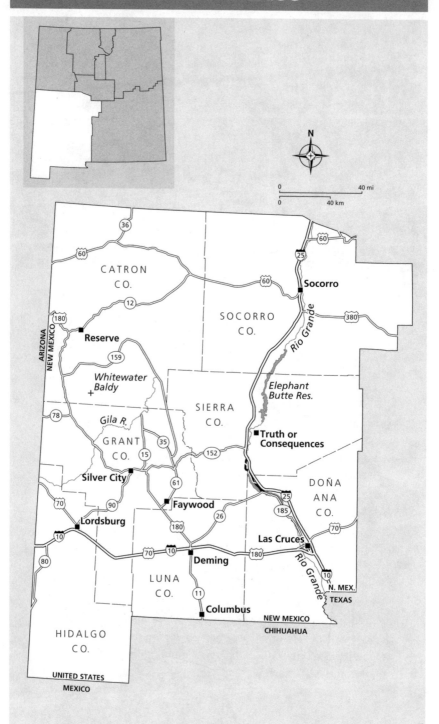

Socorro County

As you approach the ***Very Large Array*** (VLA, for short) from the east, you'll start to see a pattern of massive white dishlike objects interrupting the grassy plains of the horizon. As you get closer, the picture focuses a bit—"Looks like rows of huge sci-fi ray guns aimed at distant otherworldly enemies," you muse. But at this point, little do you know that the Plains (of San Agustin) are alive with the sounds of outer space.

You can't get more basic or accurate in the naming business than whoever came up with the name of this oft-photographed, high-tech haven:

The Very Large Array is a very big deal. Really. The VLA is an astronomical observatory used to study not only our solar system but also distant galaxies at the edge of the universe. Consisting of twenty-seven dish-shaped antennas (each 82 feet in diameter) that are connected to form a single radio telescope, the VLA is the most powerful of its kind in the world. And visiting astronomers from all over the world come here to study the universe. (The acclaimed sci-fi blockbuster *Contact,* starring Jodie Foster, was filmed here.)

In the unstaffed visitor center, a nine-minute video orients you to the history of the VLA, after which you can check out displays in the museum dedicated to radio astronomy. Next, take the walking-tour trails on the grounds of the VLA. One of the first

newmexicotrivia

Created in July 1850, Socorro County is New Mexico's oldest county.

stops is the "Whisper Gallery," where two dishlike structures face each other about 50 feet apart. Have a friend stand at one while you stand at the other. By whispering into a small ball attached to the dish by a string, the two of you

Very Large Array

can communicate clearly. On a minute and simplified scale, the structure illustrates how the VLA works.

To get to the VLA, drive about 20 miles west of Magdalena via U.S. Highway 60, turn south onto Highway 52, and then take a right onto Highway 166 to the visitor center; (505) 835–7000. It's open daily, 8:30 A.M. to sunset, and there's no admission charge. Guided tours are offered on weekends in June through mid-August.

Clear on the other side of Socorro County, in the small community of San Antonio, you'll find the Owl Bar Cafe & Steak House, commonly known as the **Owl Cafe.** Serving customers since 1945, the Owl Cafe is a watering hole with a reputation—for its green chile cheeseburgers, that is. (Keep in mind that green chile and red chile refer to the peppers that are used extensively in New Mexican cooking. New Mexicans also use "chile" with an "e" for the bean or meat concoction that gringos spell "chili.") New Mexicans traveling in these parts make a point to pass through San Antonio around lunchtime just to get their daily chile fix at the cafe.

newmexicotrivia

Chile peppers are New Mexico's top cash crop, and New Mexico ranks first in the amount of chiles produced and acreage planted, double that of its nearest rival, California.

Choose one of the many booths to get a good view of the old wooden bar that runs the length of the dining area, or, better yet, prop yourself on a barstool as a vantage point from which to count up all the "wise ones" that constitute the cafe's owl-deco motif. The bar was saved from a fire that destroyed the town's A. H. Hilton Mercantile Store in the early 1940s. It was in Hilton's San Antonio hotel that his son Conrad began as a baggage carrier, only to end up starting one of the world's largest luxury hotel chains years later.

The Owl Cafe is ¼ mile east of Interstate 25 on U.S. Highway 380, near the intersection with Highway 1, about 10 miles south of Socorro; (505) 835–9946. It's open daily except Sunday from 8:00 A.M. to 9:30 P.M. (or 10:00 P.M., if they're busy).

Though you won't find many owls at the 57,191-acre **Bosque del Apache** ("Woods of the Apache") **National Wildlife Refuge,** if you time your visit for late fall or winter you're sure to spot lots of migratory birds in this sanctuary along the Rio Grande. Bring plenty of film—and a telephoto lens if you have one—to join the ranks of international photographers who are drawn by the beauty of the *bosque* and its birds.

Established in 1939 as a "refuge and breeding grounds for migratory birds and other wildlife," the refuge also provided winter habitat for greater sandhill

Snow geese landing at Bosque del Apache

cranes. In 1941, only 17 cranes visited the refuge, whereas their number is now as high as 17,000.

There's a visitor center that can fill you in on what to expect on the driving or walking tour. The migratory patterns of different bird species are highlighted, and you can put your back against the wall, spread-eagle, in the "How Big Is Your Wingspan?" display to see how you measure up to the feathered ones. Then there's the Birdcall Game, in which you listen to a recorded call and try to match it to a list of birds.

The self-guided, 15-mile tour loop is available for driving, cycling, and walking, and takes you through the birds' habitat in the *bosque*. Here's where you get a close view of snow geese, sandhill cranes, peregrine falcons, bald eagles, and the rare whooping cranes, along with 290 other bird species. If you forget to pack your binoculars, the visitor center rents them, $5.00 for four hours, $10.00 for eight hours.

Each year during the third weekend in November the refuge hosts the Bosque Fall Festival. It celebrates the wildlife of the Middle Rio Grande Valley and the return of the snow geese and cranes. The festival includes bird-related demonstrations as well as wildlife arts exhibits and area tours.

Bosque del Apache is 8 miles south of Highway 380 (at the Owl Cafe) on Highway 1; (505) 835–1828. There's no admission fee at the visitor center, but there's a $3.00-per-car charge for the tour loop. Visitor center hours are 7:30 A.M. to 4:00 P.M. weekdays and 8:00 A.M. to 4:30 P.M. weekends. The tour loop is open daily from one hour before sunrise to one hour after sunset.

And if you're a serious birder who just can't get his or her fill on only a day trip to the *bosque,* book a room at the ***Casa Blanca Bed and Breakfast Guesthouse*** in San Antonio. Less than 10 miles from Bosque del Apache, the

1880s Victorian country farmhouse is owned by innkeeper Phoebe Wood. Whether you're into birds or not, a stay at Casa Blanca is a relaxing experience away from the noise of the city.

During fall and winter, guests enjoy the warmth of a wood-burning stove in one of three guest rooms—all with private baths—and, in warmer times, avail themselves of the rural serenity of Casa Blanca's large veranda surrounding the front of the home. In addition, the bed-and-breakfast has two sitting areas, one with a piano, and a large selection of books and board games.

Casa Blanca is a couple of blocks from the Owl Cafe, at 13 Montoya Street in San Antonio; (505) 835–3027. Rates range from $70 to $100, double occupancy. Pets are negotiable. The inn closes during the summer.

One of the least accessible and most eerie places in New Mexico is open to the public only twice a year. The *Trinity Site,* ground zero to the world's first nuclear explosion, is located in a remote part of the usually off-limits White Sands Missile Range deep in southeastern Socorro County. Following more than two years of research and development in Los Alamos (see Los Alamos County entry in North Central New Mexico chapter), the Manhattan Project culminated in the detonation of the bomb at 5:29.45 A.M. on July 16, 1945. The

FAVORITE ATTRACTIONS/EVENTS IN SOUTHWESTERN NEW MEXICO

Very Large Array,
Socorro County
(505) 835–7000

Bosque del Apache National Wildlife Refuge,
Socorro County
(505) 835–1828

Mogollon Catwalk,
near Glenwood
No phone

Gila Cliff Dwellings National Monument,
north of Silver City
(505) 536–9461

Gila Bird and Nature Festival,
May, Silver City
(505) 538–9700

Great American Duck Race,
August, Deming
(888) 345–1125

Hatch Chile Festival,
Labor Day weekend, Hatch
(505) 267–5050

Hillsboro Apple Festival,
September, Hillsboro
(505) 895–5686

Whole Enchilada Festival,
September, Las Cruces
(505) 526–1938

Festival of the Cranes,
November, Bosque del Apache National Wildlife Refuge
(505) 835–0424

blast was seen across a radius of 160 miles, which included Albuquerque and Santa Fe, and windows were shattered in Silver City, 120 miles from the site.

Most signs of the blast have been removed; even the 1,200-foot-diameter, 8-foot-deep crater resulting from the blast has been filled in, though part of the blast area at ground zero has been left intact for display purposes. A fence encloses much of the ground-zero area. Small pieces of Trinitite, the fused silica rock formed by the extreme heat of the blast, still litters the site, and folks say it's radioactive enough to fog photographic film. A black lava monument erected in 1965 and a National Historic Landmark plaque dedicated by the National Park Service in 1975 are about all that remain.

"Open house" tours are held on the first Saturday of April and October. For information on the Trinity Site tours, call the White Sands Missile Range public affairs office (505–678–1134).

Catron County

In the nation's most lightning-struck region sits **The Lightning Field** by American sculptor Walter de Maria. You can't just drop by for the show, though: All visits are overnight affairs and require reservations. *The Lightning Field* is large-scale environmental art created by de Maria and completed in 1977. The work, which was commissioned and is maintained by the New York–based Dia Center for the Arts, is composed of four hundred 15- to 20-foot shiny steel poles placed in a grid measuring 1 mile by 3,330 feet. The tips of the poles form an exactly even plane, like a bed of nails for some evil giant. During thunderstorms the poles act as lightning rods, creating a dazzling light show.

The adventure starts in the town of Quemado, where, after meeting with the caretaker early in the afternoon, you're taken for a forty-five-minute ride on dirt roads to a visitor cabin. You, along with any other visitors, are then left until late the next morning. During the day, take the two-hour hike to the field to get a closer look at the rods and wander among them; as long as there's no lightning, you're safe. Otherwise, you can safely view the lightning strikes as long as you stay outside the perimeter of the field.

Because late summer is prime time for thunderstorms, a visit in late July or August gives you the best chance for a spectacular show. The field is also attractive during other times of the year, however, because the shiny rods provide shows of another sort with the help of sunshine or, on a clear night, moonlight.

Visiting season is May 1 through October 31. For more information and to make reservations, call (505) 898–3335. For comprehensive information and to make reservations on-line, visit the Dia Center's Web site at www.lightning field.org. A one-night stay costs $110 (minimum) per person, which includes meals and transportation to and from Quemado. (*NOTE:* During July and August, rates go up to $135, which still does not cover the center's actual cost of operations; therefore, additional contributions are appreciated.) Despite the high adventure of viewing the lightning field, keep in mind that it is fine art on a grand scale; no photographs are permitted.

As New Mexico's most sparsely populated but geographically largest county, Catron County contains the bulk of the three-million-acre Gila National Forest. In this region you'll find ***Mogollon,*** set in a narrow valley flanked by canyon walls along Silver Creek. For about sixty years after its great gold strike of 1878, Mogollon earned a reputation for lawlessness as the Mogollon Mountains continued to give up millions of dollars' worth of gold, silver, and copper.

A Glimpse of Southwestern New Mexico: Impressions of the Gila

Every time I go hiking in the Gila Wilderness, my awe at the vastness of the place grows. It was the nation's first designated wilderness area, and together with the adjoining Aldo Leopold Wilderness, it makes up the largest roadless area in the lower forty-eight United States. There's no vantage point from which you can view the whole 3.3-million-acre expanse. I've never hiked across the Gila Wilderness from boundary to boundary, nor do I know anyone who has, and I'm not sure how long such a trek would take. A Forest Service ranger I met along the trail one day told me it takes him a week to patrol the major hiking routes on horseback. Yet I can unmistakably sense the immensity of the wilderness when I'm there. It's the same feeling as standing at the rim of the Grand Canyon on a pitch-dark night: You can't see it, yet somehow you know it's there.

Part of it is the variety of the terrain. Depending on which of the three forks of the Gila River you choose to hike up from the trailhead at Gila Cliff Dwellings, you can find thickets lush with desert vegetation, primeval ponderosa pine forests, steaming hot springs, slot canyons that run for miles between vertical rock walls so close you can reach out and touch both sides at once, and many other natural wonders. It's a land so big and wild that countless predatory beasts range across it, including bears, mountain lions, coyotes, and even the only free-roaming wolf pack in the Southwest. Deer leap out of the bushes and startle you. Sitting on the river bank, you can see trophy-size fish gliding through the crystalline water; in fact, one species of trout is found nowhere else in the world except the Gila Wilderness.

One way to see the true size of this wilderness is to drive completely around its perimeter. From Socorro, take Interstate 25 south past Truth or Consequences, then Highway 90 west to Silver City. Go north on Highway 80 to Reserve and take Highway 12 to the intersection with Highway 60 not far from the Very Large Array radio telescope. By the time you make it back to Socorro, you will have traveled nearly 400 miles.

Perhaps because of its inaccessibility, neither territorial troops nor the Apache warriors Victorio and Geronimo could tame this onetime headquarters of Butch Cassidy and his crew.

Today Mogollon is only semighostly: A handful of residents live here, and the old buildings are only slightly marred by the presence of facades built for the 1973 Western *My Name Is Nobody,* starring Henry Fonda. Mogollon is, however, still one of New Mexico's best-preserved ghost towns. During the summer, a couple of residents open shops for the trickle of visitors who venture into these parts.

Mogollon is located about 9 miles east of U.S. Highway 180 (about 37 miles south of Reserve) on Highway 159—a very narrow, cliff-hugging road with many hairpin turns. (It is paved, though.) If you're feeling adventurous and you have the time, keep going past the town and into the Gila National Forest and Mogollon Mountains for exquisite backcountry hiking and camping. Roads and trails are generally well marked, but take a USDA Forest Service map, available at the general store in Glenwood, for more precise exploring expeditions.

About 3½ miles farther south on U.S. Highway 180, you'll come across the tiny village of Glenwood. Here you can explore one of the truly awesome sites in New Mexico: the ***Mogollon Catwalk.*** Plan this outing in late fall or early winter, during the week if possible, to avoid seeing another soul. You can't find a better site for a picnic.

Set in the beautiful Whitewater Canyon just outside Glenwood, the Catwalk trailhead is covered with stately old sycamores and cottonwoods. The perfectly clear Whitewater Creek rushes alongside the trail, completing the pristine setting. The canyon was a favorite hideout for Apaches and desperados, including Butch Cassidy, in the 1880s.

The initial rocky trail soon turns into the Catwalk, a narrow metal walkway (with a sturdy rail) that hugs the sheer rock wall of the gorge as it winds along the creek up the canyon for about 1 mile past the gorge. Though the gorge is 100 feet deep (and the canyon walls rise 1,400 feet), the Catwalk stays about 20 feet above the river. The point is that a walk on the Catwalk is exciting and visually stimulating, but it's not scary. The Catwalk is well maintained for safety.

The Catwalk got its start as the result of pipelines that were laid through the canyon in 1893 to provide water for a mill that serviced nearby gold and silver claims. Because the lines needed continual maintenance, the workers who had to walk along the suspended pipes referred to them as the catwalk. Today you can even see parts of the old pipelines.

The Mogollon Catwalk is located about 5 miles from U.S. Highway 180 in Glenwood (40 miles south of Reserve), at the end of Highway 174 (well marked with signs), also known as Catwalk Road. There are no set hours, admission charges, or phones.

The best place to stay in Catron County is the **Silver Creek Inn.** This bed-and-breakfast, in the scantily populated ghost town of Mogollon, may be the quietest place you've ever slept. The building was constructed in 1885 as a hotel and general store and is one of the few examples in New Mexico of a two-story adobe structure. The present owners have renovated it with contemporary Southwestern flair, including a terra-cotta tile roof and Santa Fe Territorial–style redbrick trim. You'll want to arrive early enough to spend some time relaxing on the enclosed patio with its waterfall and sweeping, curved exterior staircase. Room rates range from $115 to $165 and include both dinner and breakfast. The inn only accepts adults age twenty-one and older, and no pets—the owners explain that the ghosts scare them. Contact: (866) 276–4882; www.silvercreekinn.com.

For dining within walking distance, you'll find the **Blue Front Bar and Cafe** (505–539–2561). The food is great—especially the hearty breakfasts and smoked barbecue on weekends—and reasonably priced.

Grant County

Silver City is the largest community in Grant County and home of Western New Mexico University. As its name implies, mining played a key role in the town's history. Billy the Kid also figures into Silver City's past—he spent part of his childhood here before moving on to establish his notoriously lawless career.

Unlike most of New Mexico's old mining towns, Silver City survived the boom-bust pattern of the industry to become Grant County's trade center and county seat. At the turn of the twentieth century, the town capitalized on its dry climate to become a haven for people with tuberculosis. This delightful climate, with its four distinct seasons, continues to attract new residents, particularly retirees.

newmexicotrivia

The grave of Billy the Kid's mother, Kathrine Antrim, is located in Silver City.

Take a stroll down Bullard Street (around Broadway Street) near the city's center to check out its historic downtown district. You'll find an eclectic mix of shops and cafes, including the famous Buffalo Bar, housed in architecturally significant, late-1800s buildings. Like Las Vegas, New Mexico, up north (see San Miguel County entry in the chapter on Northeastern New Mexico), Silver City's inner core is enhanced by a choice selection of Victorian homes. During the past few years, Silver City has become somewhat of a budding artists' colony, and, as such, there are now contemporary art galleries and even an espresso bar.

One of the city's finest examples of Victorian architecture is now the home of the **Silver City Museum.** But this unusual brick structure was originally the home of mining magnate Harry Ailman, who had it built in 1881. Later it served as the city hall and as a fire station before becoming a museum in 1967. This is the place to start investigating Silver City's rich history, from the prehistoric Mogollon Indians who inhabited the area, through the mining days, to the present. The museum sponsors special, long-running exhibits, such as "More Than Civilizers: Women of Silver City, 1870–1910." Visitors can even climb to the top in the museum's cupola, built for ventilation, and get a 360-degree view of the town.

The Silver City Museum is located at 312 West Broadway; (505) 538–5921. It's open Tuesday through Friday from 9:00 A.M. to 4:30 P.M. and weekends from 10:00 A.M. to 4:00 P.M. There's no admission charge.

Another local museum worth a visit is the **Western New Mexico University Museum.** Housing the largest permanent exhibit of prehistoric Mimbres pottery and culture in the United States, the museum also features other pottery, ancient tools, jewelry, and historic artifacts from the archaeologically significant Casas Grandes site in northern Mexico.

The museum is located in Fleming Hall, 1000 West College Avenue, on the WNMU campus in Silver City; (505) 538–6386. It's open Monday through Friday from 9:00 A.M. to 4:30 P.M. and Saturday and Sunday from 10:00 A.M. to 4:00 P.M.; closed school holidays and Christmas break; free admission.

The most distinctive lodging in the Silver City area can be found at the newly and extensively renovated **Bear Mountain Lodge,** a bed-and-breakfast located on 178 acres bordering the Gila National Forest. The lodge was originally constructed in 1928 as the Rocky Mountain School (reputedly a place for delinquent boys), with later incarnations as a country club and a dude ranch before being purchased by the late Myra McCormick, legendary birder and avid conservationist, who ran the lodge for forty-one years. Before her death in 1999, McCormick bequeathed her lodge and her land in trust to the Nature Conservancy. After spending a significant sum transforming the rustic lodge into Southwestern chic, the conservancy now operates the lodge, which offers eleven luxuriously appointed rooms, each with a private bath and locally hand-crafted mission-style furnishings. Despite the extensive renovations, the lodge retains its historic charm and integrity, as evidenced by the hand-hewn beams, striking pine staircase, stone fireplaces, and hardwood floors throughout. The lodge employs a staff naturalist to provide information to guests about area flora and fauna; and guests are allowed to tour the conservancy's nearby Gila and Mimbres River preserves. As more than 300 species of birds are found here, don't forget your binoculars—but leave the kids at home, as children age nine and younger are not allowed.

To get to Bear Mountain Lodge from Silver City, head north on Highway 180 (Highway 180 takes a right turn at Mr. Ed's Do-It Center and becomes Fourteenth Street in town); turn right (north) on Alabama Street, which becomes Cottage San Road; head north about 2¾ miles; and the road to Bear Mountain Lodge is marked to your left. Rates range from $115 to $200 per room per night (which includes breakfast), with a two-night minimum stay (inquire about single-night availability); (505) 538–2538; (877) 620–2327; www.bear mountainlodge.com.

An economical as well as historical lodging option can be found down-town at the **Palace Hotel.** Established in a former bank building, which was built in 1882, the hotel originally opened in 1900 as a modern showplace. Restored to its former elegance in 1990, the hotel offers eighteen guest rooms and suites and a complimentary continental breakfast served in the skylit garden room upstairs.

You'll find the Palace Hotel at 106 West Broadway; (505) 388–1811; www.zianet.com/palacehotel. Rates range from $38 to $62 per room per night, double occupancy.

You'll have to explore the back streets of Silver City to find **El Paisano,** in a residential neighborhood at 802 East Fifteenth Street. This friendly, local-favorite eatery has thrived in its obscure location since 1975. Your quest will be rewarded with generous portions of some of the best Mexican food north of the border, including tostadas covered with refried beans and guacamole on your choice of yellow or blue corn tortillas. Or try the chile rellenos (stuffed green chile peppers) filled with diced chicken. An all-you-can-eat salad bar comes with all meals, as do traditional sopapillas and honey for dessert. It's open Monday through Saturday from 11:00 A.M. to 9:30 P.M.; (505) 538–5803.

Just north of Silver City, on the edge of the Gila National Forest, the village of **Pinos Altos** ("Tall Pines") is a prime spot for any off-the-beaten-pather. Though Pinos Altos's mining history dates from 1803, it was a later gold discovery by three Forty-Niners from California in 1860 that led to the establishment of Pinos Altos as a mining camp. Roy Bean operated a general store here with his brother before moving to Texas to become "the law west of the Pecos." During the past few years, several of the town's old stores have been replaced by modern shops.

Pinos Altos's points of interest include the **Hearst Church,** the Buckhorn Saloon, the Pinos Altos Opera House, and the Pinos Altos Museum. The small

Hearst Church

though architectually interesting (Southwestern Gothic?) Hearst Church was built in 1898 with money donated by Phoebe Hearst, whose late husband, George (father of newspaper tycoon William Randolph Hearst), had left her mining interests in Pinos Altos. The adobe, stone, and wooden-shingle church, originally called the Gold Avenue Methodist Episcopal Church, now houses the Grant County Art Guild gallery. It also contains the hearse that carried the body of Pat Garrett (killer of Billy the Kid), along with other horse-drawn vehicles. The building is open only during summer weekends and holidays, from 10:00 A.M. to 5:00 P.M.

With its faded whitewashed facade, the **_Buckhorn Saloon_** is one of the West's finest old bars, distinguished by 18-inch-thick adobe walls and rustic timbers. Stepping through the old watering hole's doors at dusk is like stepping back a hundred years. The saloon glows with soft lighting and smiling people clustered around the bar and small tables. The Buckhorn now also has a fine restaurant, serving burgers, steaks, and seafood as well as vegetarian dishes.

On closer inspection, two perennial bar patrons aren't even real—they're realistic-looking mannequins. Indian Joe keeps his seat at one end of the bar; though occasionally a newcomer offers to buy him a drink, he has yet to acknowledge the offer. Debbie DeCamp, the other mannequin, keeps an eye on the saloon entrance from a balcony; she's based on a young woman who lived in Pinos Altos at the turn of the twentieth century and met an untimely death during a brawl. A friend, the story goes, wrote the following "memorial" over the door to Debbie's room:

> *Shed a tear for Debbie DeCamp,*
> *Born a virgin and died a tramp.*
> *For 17 years she retained her virginity.*
> *(A real good record for this vicinity.)*

The Buckhorn is open daily except Sunday. Bar opens at 3:00 P.M. and dinner is served from 6:00 to 10:00 P.M. It's located on Main Street in Pinos Altos; (505) 538–9911.

Next door to the Buckhorn you'll find the ***Pinos Altos Opera House,*** which presents melodrama theater every Friday and Saturday at 8:00 P.M. from late January to Thanksgiving. Call (505) 388–3848 for reservations.

The ***Pinos Altos Museum,*** just across the road from the Buckhorn, is located in the rear of the Log Cabin Curio Shop. The tin-roofed log cabin was the county's first private schoolhouse, built around 1866. The museum's holdings include an extensive collection of Indian arrowheads and equipment and furnishings from the area's mining heyday.

The shop and museum are open daily from 10:00 A.M. to 5:00 P.M.; (505) 388–1882.

Pinos Altos is located about 6 miles north of Silver City, just off Highway 15. Be aware that in Pinos Altos most of the roads are dirt but are in good condition unless there's been a lot of rain.

Deep within the Gila National Forest but less than 40 miles farther on Highway 15, you'll find the rather hidden ***Gila Cliff Dwellings National Monument*** (505–536–9461; www.nps.gov/gicl). It's dedicated to preserving and celebrating the ancient Pueblo Indians of the Mogollon culture, who inhabited the area for about a hundred years starting around 1280. These cliff dwellers were approximate contemporaries of the Anasazi Indians, who lived in New Mexico's northwestern region. Similar to the Anasazi, the Mogollon Indians mysteriously disappeared, and archaeologists have been puzzled ever since the dwellings were discovered. Drought, disease, and tribal wars top the list of theories.

A visit to the park involves a healthy mile's hike along a trail that ascends some 200 feet up the canyon walls to the cliff dwellings. The dwellings themselves are tucked into caves in the cliff and are made of adobe and timber. Most visitors are extremely quiet when walking among the rooms of the dwellings, partly because the caves' acoustics amplify voices but also because

Pinos Altos Opera House

they're showing respect for the people who lived here so long ago. On the edge of the Gila National Wilderness, and along the Gila River, the monument is a peaceful and beautiful place for a hike.

The Gila Cliff Dwellings are open daily from 8:00 A.M. to 6:00 P.M. Memorial Day through Labor Day and from 9:00 A.M. to 4:00 P.M. (visitor center, 8:00 A.M. to 4:30 P.M.) the rest of the year. Admission is $3.00 per person for anyone age twelve or older, or a $10.00 family rate. (*NOTE:* The park is actually in Catron County but is accessible only through Grant County. Also, the signs along Highway 15 near Pinos Altos claiming the drive to the monument will take two hours seem greatly exaggerated—at least in good weather!)

In conjunction with a visit to the Gila Cliff Dwellings, consider a stay at the **Wilderness Lodge and Hot Springs,** a bed-and-breakfast inn located nearby in the tiny valley community of Gila Hot Springs, which is adjacent to the east fork of the Gila River. The century-old lodge building was originally a school-house located in Hurley, a small town southwest of Silver City. In the 1960s the building was dismantled, moved, and reconstructed on its present site. A shady front porch with seating spans the imposing lodge, which is run by innkeepers Dean and Mary Bruemmer. Inside, guests will find ample room as well, as there's a large country kitchen and a two-bedroom suite with private bath on the first floor; upstairs are five nicely appointed guest rooms, which share a

Hot Springs Pool

bath, and a large common area with book and video libraries. Delicious home-baked breads and muffins and a wonderful homemade granola accent the ample breakfast offerings. (Dean's the talented baker here, having once worked for Myra McCormick at the aforementioned Bear Mountain Lodge.)

The highlight of a stay at the Wilderness Lodge is a soak in one of its two beautifully sculpted rock pools, which are fed by natural hot springs and located in an enchanting patio area across the driveway from the lodge. Herbs and other flowering perennials grow between the boulders lining the pools' perimeters, and some of the fragrant mint plants have "escaped" to the edges of the adjacent *acequia,* or irrigation ditch, which flows with clear water warmed by the hot springs. A soak at sunset provides stunning vistas of the bluffs above the Gila River and the mountains of the Pinos Altos Range in the distance.

Rates range from $58.00 to $85.00 for double occupancy, plus $8.00 for each additional person and $5.00 for "well-behaved" pets. To get to the Wilderness Lodge, take Highway 15 north of Silver City approximately 40 miles to the village of Gila Hot Springs, turn right on Access Road (¼ mile south of Doc Campbell's trading post), then left on Jackass Lane. The lodge will be down the lane on your left; (505) 536–9749; www.gilanet.com/wildernesslodge.

If you're just visiting the area for the day, consider a soak at the village's namesake, ***Gila Hot Springs,*** just up the road a bit from the Wilderness Lodge. Four shallow, natural-looking pools are filled with geothermal water that continuously falls out of a pipe into the first pool. The water flows from pool to pool and eventually drains into the nearby Gila River. It's quite a lovely spot though not totally isolated, as it's visible from the nearby dirt road. The springs are on private land (though there are no adjacent buildings), and there's an honor-system pay station near a small parking area; $2.00 per person for adults; no phone.

Heading southeast of Silver City toward Deming you'll find *City of Rocks State Park.* This relatively flat park is filled with vertical rock formations, some as high as 50 feet, resembling the monoliths at Stonehenge. The rocks are the result of erosion on the remains of volcanic eruptions that occurred millions of years ago. Because you can climb on the rocks, as well as hide behind them, this park is a natural playground for kids of all ages. Picnic and camping facilities are available. The park is located 31 miles southeast of Silver City via U.S. Highway 180 and Highway 61; (505) 536–2800. It's open daily from 7:00 A.M. to 9:00 P.M. Admission is $4.00 per vehicle. Camping is available for $10.00 per night for "dry" campsites and $14.00 per night for sites with electricity and water hookups.

If you're planning to spend the night in the vicinity of City of Rocks, the most tantalizing option (and just about the only one) is *Faywood Hot Springs,* where you'll find four cabins and a carpeted tepee. The cabins are recently built, one-bedroom units, each with a sleeping loft, a kitchenette, and a screened-in porch. Best of all, rates include unlimited use of the public pools and one free hour in a private pool. Nonguests pay $10.00 a day for adults and $5.00 for children to use the public pools—one clothing-optional and another where bathing suits are required. Private pools and hot tubs cost nonguests $10.00 per person per hour for adults, $5.00 for children, with a $20.00 minimum charge. Cabins cost $80.00 a night, and the tepee costs $35.00 a night, both with additional charges for more than two people. Faywood Hot Springs is located a short distance south of the entrance to City of Rocks on Highway 61; (505) 536–9663; www.faywood.com.

While in the Gila region, check out beautiful *Lake Roberts* along Highway 35, about 3 miles east of its intersection with Highway 15. It's quite nice by New Mexico lake standards, meaning the shoreline is somewhat wooded and meandering—very nice for canoeing! Regardless, if fishing or other water sports do bring you here, consider a stay at *Spirit Canyon Lodge and Cafe,* located near the southeast end of the lake. Along with the adjacent cafe, the lodge is run by Fran Land, a retired university professor from Chicago, who says escaping to the Southwest to open the inn and cafe was her response to a midlife crisis.

The homey lodge features comfortable rooms with king- or queen-size beds and private baths. A hummingbird observatory and bird feeding attract human nature lovers. The cafe seems to have become a favorite of locals. The emphasis here is not necessarily on innovation—the breakfasts, lunches, and dinners are mostly limited to popular standbys—but in their accomplished execution. In addition to tasty burgers, sandwiches, and salads, the menu also includes steaks, catfish, herbed chicken breast, pork chops, fried shrimp, and a veggie plate. And, prices are quite reasonable. On Saturday the cafe serves special home-style German meals.

Lodging rates are $55 for double occupancy. Spirit Canyon Lodge and Cafe is located at 684 Highway 35 at mile marker 22; (505) 536–9459; www.spirit canyon.com.

Less than 10 miles east of Silver City along Highway 152, you'll come across the impossible-to-miss *Santa Rita Mine.* Regardless of how you feel about the environmental impact of such an open-pit operation, its size and scope are hard to ignore. Currently run by the mega-mining concern Phelps Dodge Corporation, the mine's dimensions are 1½ miles long by 1 mile wide by 1,800 feet deep, and it produces 300 million pounds of copper annually. As one of the oldest operating mines in North America, the site was originally mined by Native Americans and later by colonial Spaniards before the modern era of mechanized mining began; it's been an open-pit operation since 1910.

Visitors are allowed to view the mine only through a chain-link fence from above; no one is allowed in the pit itself. The stair-step design through the multicolored bedrock—required for trucks to remove the ore—looks somewhat like an inverted version of the ancient Aztec and Mayan ruins in southern Mexico and Central America. The parking and viewing areas are clearly marked; no phone; no fee.

Hidalgo County

Texas and Oklahoma may have their panhandles, but New Mexico's got its boot heel and Hidalgo County is it. Closer to Tucson, Arizona, than to Albuquerque, most of this area is desolate, although cattle ranching and, more recently, vineyards have made their imprint on the land.

The largest town is Lordsburg, but perhaps the most unique place is *Shakespeare,* a ghost town 2½ miles southwest of Lordsburg.

Originally settled in the 1850s as Mexican Springs, a stage stop on the Butterfield Overland Trail, Shakespeare was named in 1879 by mine promoters to honor the bard and perhaps improve the town's fortunes. The town was the site of a couple of mining hoaxes, including the Diamond Swindle of 1870—when the area was seeded with diamonds to attract investors—before a real silver boom hit in 1879, only to fizzle some fifteen years later. Shakespeare's last hurrah came with a second silver strike in 1907. The silver played out in the 1930s.

Because the town has been privately owned since 1935, it has been protected from weekend ghost-town looters, and the admission charge goes toward further preservation and restoration. It's accessible to the public only through guided tours that include the interiors of several buildings. One of these structures, the Stratford Hotel, is said to have briefly employed Billy the Kid as a dishwasher.

To get to Shakespeare, take the Main Street exit off Interstate 10 in Lordsburg, turn south, and follow the signs. Tours are held at 10:00 A.M. and 2:00 P.M. on the second Saturday and Sunday of the month from May through December; on the third or fourth weekend of April, June, August, and October, historical reenactments are staged. Call (505) 542–9034 to verify the current year's dates. The admission charge is $3.00 for adults and $2.00 for children ages six to twelve ($1.00 higher for reenactments).

Luna County

Luna County's primary community is **Deming,** known for its pure air and fast ducks. Yes, ducks. Deming is home of the world-famous Great American Duck Race (888–345–1125; www.demingduckrace.com), held annually on the fourth weekend in August. Thought up more than fifteen years ago in a bar as a way to create more interest in the area, the duck races have captured international media coverage for Deming. More than just a duck race, the "fowl event" includes a parade, a golf tournament, a chile cookoff, a hot-air-balloon rally, several sporting tournaments, and even a "Duck Queen" contest. It has also become one of New Mexico's most well-attended events.

Deming's more than ducks, though. The city's also home to the impressive **Deming Luna Mimbres Museum.** Located in the three-story, 1916 red-brick National Guard Armory building, the museum has about 25,000 square feet of exhibition space. There's a bit of everything here, as evidenced by the many "theme rooms," including the Military Room, the Quilt Room, the Doll Room, and the Tack Room. The museum also depicts life in the Southwest, focusing on ranching, railroading, and mining. The Mimbres Room showcases examples of centuries-old Mimbres Indian pottery. The pottery's distinctive, black-on-white geometric designs are known for the way they mismatch animal body parts.

The museum is at 301 South Silver in Deming; (505) 546–2382. It's open Monday through Saturday from 9:00 A.M. to 4:00 P.M. and Sunday from 1:30 to 4:00 P.M. There's no set admission charge, but nominal contributions are expected. Across the street the museum has renovated an old "customshouse" into another space that showcases the area's border-town past.

Most parks make a big deal about leaving everything as you found it and strictly forbid visitors to take anything with them when they leave. But at **Rockhound State Park,** located on the west side of the Little Florida Mountains, "taking a little of the park" is encouraged. That's right—visitors may each take up to fifteen pounds of rocks with them per visit. You'll find all kinds and colors here, including varieties of quartz crystals, agates, and opals. Even after years of rock hounds carrying away mementos of their visit, old-timers say it's hard to tell that the place is any different than it was years ago. Plan to spend a lot of time staring at the ground here, and while you're on the lookout for your personal gems, watch out as well for loose rock and inconspicuous drop-offs.

newmexicotrivia

The state of New Mexico shares 175 miles of border with the country of Mexico in Hidalgo, Luna, and Doña Ana Counties.

Rockhound State Park is off Palomas Road via Highway 11, southeast of Deming; (505) 546–6182. It's open daily from 7:30 A.M. to sunset. There's a $4.00-per-vehicle admission charge. Camping is available: $10.00 per night for "dry" campsites and $14.00 per night for sites with electricity and water hookups.

STATE PARKS IN SOUTHWESTERN NEW MEXICO

Caballo Lake/Percha Dam State Park,
18 miles south of Truth or
Consequences,
(505) 743–3942

City of Rocks State Park,
28 miles northeast of Deming,
(505) 536–2800

Elephant Butte Lake State Park,
7 miles north of Truth or Consequences,
(505) 744–5421

Leasburg Dam State Park,
15 miles north of Las Cruces,
(505) 524–4068

Pancho Villa State Park,
in Columbus,
(505) 531–2711

Rockhound State Park,
14 miles southeast of Deming,
(505) 546–6182

If you drive 32 miles south of Deming on NM 11, you'll reach the Mexican border at the little town of **Columbus.** Although it's so far off the beaten path that most of its inhabitants are Border Patrol officers and their families, its solitude has attracted a number of former Santa Feans. The occasional visitor is surprised to find that the community has a gourmet cafe, a large art gallery, and a nice bed-and-breakfast inn (Martha's Place; 505–531–2467). Mariachis from the neighboring Mexican town of Las Palomas play on the town plaza most weekends.

Columbus is best known for having been invaded during the 1916 Mexican Revolution by insurgent leader Pancho Villa and 1,000 of his men in a ferocious battle that left 160 Americans and Mexicans dead. It was the only time the continental United States has ever been invaded by a foreign army. The incident is recounted in the **Columbus Historical Museum,** located in a former railroad depot in the center of town. The free museum is open daily from 10:00 A.M. to 4:00 P.M. September through April; the rest of the year Monday through Friday from 11:00 A.M. to 2:00 P.M. and Saturday and Sunday noon to 5:00 P.M.; (505) 531–2620.

Also worth visiting is the large cactus garden in **Pancho Villa State Park,** featuring thirty varieties of desert succulents. The sixty-acre park has picnic facilities and old army vehicles that were used by General John Pershing in the U.S. retaliation for Villa's raid. The park is always open. Admission is $4.00 per vehicle; (505) 531–2711.

Sierra County

Sierra County is home to New Mexico's largest body of water, **Elephant Butte Lake.** It's named for a huge gray rock formation, or butte, that rises from the water and resembles an elephant. Near the lake you'll come across the city of **Truth or Consequences.** The city changed its name from Hot Springs to Truth or Consequences in 1951, following an open challenge over the airwaves from the popular radio show of the same name to honor its tenth anniversary. As a reward for the name change, the show pledged the city an annual festival during which the show would be broadcast. The show, along with its later television incarnation, has long since ended, but the annual Truth or Consequences Fiesta is still going strong. Ralph Edwards, former host of the show, had not missed the event for almost a half century when he retired from his annual appearance in 1999.

Truth or Consequences (often "T or C," for short) is popular for its many therapeutic hot springs (from which the community got its first name). In fact, there's a contingent of folks who'd like to change the town's name back to Hot

Springs (some old-timers and newcomers alike use "T or C–Hotsprings" as part of their return address), but after several ballot defeats through the years, the name Truth or Consequences seems destined to endure for this scruffy little community, which continues to attract retirees and "snowbirds"—those seniors who like to winter where it's warm. Since the late 1990s, however, the town's relative isolation, eclectic residents, and funky desert aesthetic have become part of its appeal for younger "regulars" from Albuquerque and Santa Fe, as well as for visitors from around the globe.

newmexicotrivia

Sierra County, home to Elephant Butte and Caballo Lakes, boasts more water than any other county in New Mexico.

The ancient Mimbres Indians of southern New Mexico—who, like the Anasazi of northern New Mexico, are the ancestors of present-day Pueblo Indians—sought out the area's natural hot springs more than 1,000 years ago for the water's sacred, healing powers. And though much has changed through the centuries, the healing waters remain—but now they come with scientific mineral analysis. There are currently eight bathhouses in Truth or Consequences that offer soaks for as little as $4.00, which is quite a bargain when compared to the pricier hot springs options in northern New Mexico. One such bathhouse is the historic and evolving *Marshall Hot Springs Spa and Resort.*

Originally established in the late 1920s, "the Marshall," as it's locally known, was rescued, after years of deferred maintenance and lack of vision, by Jane Ehrenreich (who formerly ran a popular vegetarian restaurant in Guatemala for eleven years). Jane bought the place in 1998 and began renovations to transform the Marshall into her vision of a healing center and spa.

Boasting natural flowing pools, as opposed to "pump and drain" tubs used by several of the local hot springs establishments, the Marshall exudes unpretentious New Age New Mexico at its laid-back best. A private soak in one of their tubs is quite a treat, especially with the knotted rope dangling above the center of the square cement pool, playfully perfect for stretching tired muscles. A dimmer switch and peaceful Native American flute music playing low in the background complete the truly sensory experience.

With several years' hard work, Jane has lovingly renovated much of the two wings of the old on-site motel (which were once cabins used by workers during the construction of nearby Elephant Butte Dam, circa 1912), creating seven unique guest rooms, most with private baths and kitchenettes. In addition, a large studio space has been created, which is used for classes such as belly dancing, qi gong, and yoga, as well as for various retreats; and the bath-house, which also has been expanded, contains a very nice gift shop featuring handcrafted jewelry among other exquisite and sensory items.

Lodging rates range from $55.00 to $80.00 per night; soak rates range from $4.00 to $8.00, depending on duration (guests receive unlimited complimentary soaks); massage rates are $45.00 an hour, $70.00 for 1½ hours. You'll find the Marshall, along with the other free-flowing hot springs near downtown T or C, at 311 Marr Street (at Pershing); (505) 894–9286; (877) 894–9286; www.marshall hotsprings.com.

Another unique choice nearby is *Riverbend Hot Springs,* the only out-door soaking option in T or C. On the banks of the Rio Grande, Riverbend offers a variety of lodging accommodations—private suites and rooms, dormi-tory-style rooms, and campsites including large tepees—and is also an American Youth Hostel. The communal tubs, which are filled twice per day, morning and evening, for Riverbend guests, have a nice view of Turtleback

Ted Turner's Buffalo

The second largest private land-owner in New Mexico (only Henry Singleton of Beverly Hills, California, owns more), media mogul Ted Turner owns the 360,000-acre Armendaris Ranch in southwestern New Mexico as well as other big ranches in the northeastern and central parts of the state. Turner is not in the cattle business, though. Instead, he raises American bison (commonly called buffalo). Of the estimated 250,000 bison in North America, Turner's herds total 170,000 head—a remarkable number when you consider that a century ago there were only 1,500 bison left alive.

Turner's ranches process about 10 percent of their bison for meat each year, and the herds still increase in size due to the beasts' high birthrate. Buffalo is one of the healthiest red meat choices around, with two-thirds the fat and one-half the calories of beef. In fact, it's leaner than chicken or most fish. Don't look for it in your local supermarket any time soon, though; most buffalo meat is sold to natural and gourmet food stores and to restaurants throughout the West.

The federal government subsidizes the comeback of the bison by buying surplus meat. Each year, about $6 million is spent on buffalo meat. (What is done with it is a mystery.) Of that sum, more than $5 million goes to Turner. Lest you think that paying a multimillionaire to butcher excess meat sounds like a boondoggle, though, keep in mind that Ted Turner is also an active environmentalist. Each year he donates a sum roughly equal to his bison subsidy to organizations supporting green, or environmental, issues.

Mountain. A few years ago Riverbend completely renovated its tubs and constructed two new beautiful ones separate from the original soaking area. The new tubs are more private and have great views of the river and the mountains, especially during sunset, when, if you're lucky, you'll see ravens playfully soaring in the updrafts off Turtleback Mountain. If you're not staying at Riverbend, you may still book a private day-soak there. Communal tubs cost $6.00 per hour per person; private tubs cost $10.00 per hour per person.

Riverbend Hot Springs is at 100 Austin Street near the city park; (505) 894–6183; www.nmhotsprings.com. Lodging rates are $12 to $24 for camping, $18 to $36 for dorm rooms, and $42 to $55 for private rooms and suites (some with full baths, private entrances, and kitchenettes). You can rent an unfurnished tepee for $12 a night.

At 501 McAdoo Street is the plush and greatly hyped **Sierra Grande Lodge and Spa.** As T or C's answer to Santa Fe chic, the beautifully and meticulously renovated 1920s apartment building seems more than a little out of place amid the otherwise dusty, rough-and-tumble, anything-goes nature of downtown T or C. Sierra Grande offers luxury guest suites, therapeutic massage, skin-conditioning body wraps, anti-aging facials, and other holistic treatments, in addition to the geothermal mineral springs for which the area is known. The resort recently added a gourmet restaurant, which specializes in Mediterranean-Southwestern fusion cuisine, including vegetarian options made with fresh, locally grown ingredients. Lodging rates range from $65 to $425. For reservations, call (505) 894–6976; www.sierragrandelodge.com.

Near the town's center, you'll find **Geronimo Springs Museum,** named after a spring frequented by Geronimo, the famous Apache war chief. The spring itself has been incorporated into a very playful and colorful sculpture by noted New Mexican artist Shel Neymark of Embudo. The warm spring water meanders through the sculpture, which is accented by landscaping and seasonal plantings.

The museum is one of those community types for which residents have donated a broad assortment of artifacts from the area's past. The museum is laid out according to four categories: the Historical Past, Natural Resources, Ralph Edwards and the Fiesta, and the Cultural Heritage Room. This last space really takes visitors by surprise, with its floor-to-ceiling murals of famous locals painted by noted muralist Delmas Howe, who was born in Truth or Consequences. The room also contains four bronze statues of other famous New Mexicans, each sculpted by Hivana Leyendecker, an accomplished native New Mexican artist.

The museum is located at 211 Main Street across from the post office; (505) 894–6600. It's open Monday through Saturday from 9:00 A.M. to 5:00 P.M.

Admission charges are $2.00 for adults and $1.00 for children ages six to eighteen or $5.00 for a family; youngsters age five or younger get in free.

Southwest of Truth or Consequences, the village of **Hillsboro** is the quintessential one-horse town. Established in 1877 as the result of a gold discovery in the hills surrounding Percha Creek, Hillsboro is perfect for just pulling off the main street and strolling around town. You'll find several shops, a couple of cafes, an old saloon, and the **Black Range Museum.** This small historical museum is across from a public picnic area on the east side of the village. Hours vary widely, seasonally, but you may call ahead for an appointment, (505) 895–5233. Suggested donation is $2.00 for adults and $1.00 for youths ages twelve to eighteen. Kids age eleven or younger are free. Hillsboro is the kind of place where all the townspeople and merchants know one another and where a few well-cared-for "community" dogs take naps in the middle of Main Street. Steeped in mining history, the town is an enchanting, slow-paced marvel that has lured more than its share of artists and writers to become residents.

Speaking of enchanting, the **Enchanted Villa Bed & Breakfast** (505–895–5686) has a home along Hillsboro's main street. Run by innkeeper Maree Westland, this large, bright, whitewashed home was designed by Maree's great-aunt in 1941 as a romantic retreat for English nobleman Sir Victor Sassoon. The two-story inn's five large guest rooms all have lots of well-positioned windows for maximum light, and there are antiques and oak floors throughout. All rooms feature king-size beds and private bathrooms. Rooms cost $50 a night, which includes a full, hot breakfast.

Up until the late 1990s, the **Hillsboro General Store's Country Cafe** was the only place to eat in town. Continuously open since 1879, the store had survived boom and bust while variously serving as a post office, stage stop, telegraph office, soda fountain, and phone company. The place phased out its "general store" function in the late 1990s and now concentrates on serving up hearty breakfasts and lunches daily (and dinners on Saturday only), featuring soups, sandwiches, burgers, and a few New Mexican selections. Though the store no longer stocks the necessities of a rural household, it has adopted a gift-shop function, and the ambience of the old general store remains in the period decor and glass display cases. The cafe is located at 100 Main Street; (505) 895–5306.

More recently another excellent dining option has appeared on the scene in Hillsboro's historic barbershop next door to the S-Bar-X Saloon on Main Street, appropriately named the **Barbershop Cafe.** A modern pastel paint job and an outdoor seating area contrast this eatery with the aforementioned one, and the food is a bit more innovative as well. The fare is loosely billed as California Cuisine, with a diverse selection of burgers and sandwiches, such as the popular Chicken on Focaccia and Eggplant Parmesan Sandwich. Everything is made from scratch on the premises, including all breads, buns, pies, and other scrumptious desserts. Entrees change nightly and feature such diverse influences as Italian, Greek, and Asian.

The Barbershop Cafe is open daily except Monday for lunch. Dinner is also served Thursday through Saturday; (505) 895–5283.

If you're lucky enough to be traveling through Hillsboro on a weekend, make sure to stop into the studio of ***Gregory A. Gaylord, Clockmaker*** (505–895–5331; www.zianet.com/clockmaker). Located in the old Pole Barn next to the Black Range Museum, Gaylord's shop features his handcrafted fine clocks in addition to antique timepieces he's restored. Because Gaylord's clocks are particularly popular with high-end buyers—including celebrities, whose identities Gaylord prefers not to publicize—his work often takes him to Santa Fe and Tucson during weekdays, which means his shop is only open Saturday and Sunday from 9:00 A.M. to 4:00 P.M.

Hillsboro is 30 miles from Truth or Consequences: 12 miles south on Interstate 25 and then 18 miles west on NM 152.

Nine miles farther west on Highway 152, you'll enter the Black Range of the Mimbres Mountains in ***Kingston,*** a blink-and-you'll-miss-it community—so check your odometer and don't blink. Kingston, population thirty, is pretty much

Hillsboro General Store

The Mystery of Victorio Peak

Though inaccessible to the public for more than forty years, the lure and legend of Victorio Peak remains strong. Thousands of gold bars are rumored to be stashed in a crevice of the domed mountain, located on the federal government's White Sands Missile Range in Doña Ana County.

Milton "Doc" Noss, a foot doctor and well-known treasure hunter, was killed in 1949, allegedly by a disgruntled business partner, over ownership issues regarding the gold. Noss's widow, Ova "Babe" Noss, along with a crew of treasure hunters, tried unsuccessfully for years to locate the gold—even after she was forced to leave the site when the military boundary was extended in the 1950s. After she died in 1979, her grandson Terry Delonas inherited the family's gold fever. It literally took an act of Congress in 1990 to allow Delonas prolonged access to the range to explore. After years without success, the latest expedition was evicted in the mid-1990s by the military over a dispute regarding fees paid for access. And so the legend lives on, and future treasure-hunting dramas will no doubt play out, as Victorio Peak remains victorious when it comes to giving up its gold.

deserted now, though a tiny museum is housed in the old Percha Valley Bank building and the original schoolhouse is used as the meeting place for the Spit and Whittle Club. Kingston's history mirrors Hillsboro's; it saw more prosperous days during the silver boom of the 1880s, when the population soared to 7,000.

The ivy-covered *Black Range Lodge* stands as testimony to those earlier days. Run by Hollywood escapee and filmmaker/innkeeper Catherine Wanek and her husband, Pete Fust, the lodge is now a bed-and-breakfast with the feel of an Old West boardinghouse. It's one of the few bed-and-breakfasts that welcome pets—a great relief when the kennel fills up at the last minute and Rover needs a weekend getaway just as much as you do.

The innkeepers' background in the entertainment business is evident in the large common area of the lodge's second floor. Those who may need more stimulation will find a piano, a cassette deck, a satellite-television-and-VCR system complete with videotape library, and video games. For those who appreciate the tranquility of the lodge's natural setting, however, hunting for crystals along the rocky trails near the inn is a relaxing pastime—sort of like hunting for seashells on the beach.

The owners' passion for alternative and sustainable housing shows in their luxury "straw-bale" guest house, with fully equipped kitchen, Jacuzzi, and satellite dish. The guest house is uphill from the lodge and thus has breathtaking views of the Black Range.

If you find Kingston, you'll find the Black Range Lodge—trust me; (505) 895–5652; www.blackrangelodge.com. Rates range from $59 to $69 for double occupancy with an extra $15 charge for each additional person in a suite. The guest house is $110 per night for two. Discounts are available for multinight stays.

Doña Ana County

Doña Ana County is home to New Mexico's second-largest city, **Las Cruces** ("The Crosses"), which in turn is home to New Mexico's second-largest college, New Mexico State University. Located in the fertile Mesilla Valley between the Organ Mountains and the Rio Grande, Las Cruces hosts the Whole Enchilada Festival each October, culminating in the cooking of the world's largest enchilada.

Fine art and hospitality meet at **Lundeen's Inn of the Arts,** the most distinctive place to stay in the Las Cruces area, only five minutes from Old Mesilla (see listing below). Run by Linda and Jerry Lundeen, this bed-and-breakfast adjoins Linda's gallery and Jerry's architectural office, but it's hard to tell where one begins and the other ends. Works by Southwestern artists are everywhere, including the guest rooms. And because most of it's for sale, if you enjoy your stay in a particular room, you can arrange to take a piece of it home. If you've always wondered what's entailed in making adobe bricks, Jerry might just give you a lesson, time permitting. Once you find out the process, you'll understand why real adobe homes are so expensive in comparison with stucco-covered-concrete homes passed off as adobe.

newmexicotrivia

Noted astronomer and professor Dr. Clyde Tombaugh, who codiscovered the planet Pluto in 1930, helped found the astronomy department at New Mexico State University in Las Cruces, where he died in 1997, two weeks and four days before his ninety-first birthday.

The inn was formed by joining two historic adobe homes by a great room that has a soaring ceiling. In addition to being the place where breakfast is served, this naturally lighted common area is the focal point for much of the inn's art. Each of the twenty oversize guest rooms is unique in both configuration and decor and is named after an American artist, such as Georgia O'Keeffe or R. C. Gorman. All rooms have queen-size beds and private baths, and some even have fireplaces and limited kitchen facilities. Another one-hundred-year-old adobe on the grounds has been renovated, providing two additional suites, with kitchens and kiva fireplaces, perfect for extended stays; and most recently, a pair of two-bedroom condos has been added.

Arts classes, including silversmithing and pottery making, are offered through the inn, which is located at 618 South Alameda; (505) 526–3326 or (888) 526–3326; www.innofthearts.com. Rates range from $75 to $105; weekly and monthly rates are available.

If you're an urban dweller with kids, a visit to the **New Mexico Farm and Ranch Heritage Museum** in Las Cruces can be especially enjoyable. Located between the lush, irrigated farmlands of the lower Rio Grande Valley and the cattle ranches on the slopes of the dramatic Organ Mountains, the forty-seven-acre museum complex stands as monument to a way of life that is increasingly remote to most Americans. In addition to historical exhibits—such as a pit house from the ancient Mogollon culture of southwestern New Mexico and a replicated grain storage room from Chaco Canyon, as well as horse-drawn plows and early mechanized farm equipment—the center also showcases the computerized, laser-leveling implements of the modern, scientific agricultural era. Outdoor exhibits include an adobe blacksmith shop, a relocated log cabin, and a windmill. Regular demonstrations include blacksmithing, weaving, quilting, and butter churning; however, the milking demonstration in the dairy barn has proved to be the most popular among old and young alike. The museum also sponsors such classes as adobe making, gardening, roping and other cowboy skills, photography, and wool spinning. Besides dairy cows,

Famous New Mexican Entertainers and Artists

Greer Garson, actress	Gene Hackman, actor
William Hanna, cartoonist	Bo Diddley, singer and songwriter
Eliot Porter, nature photographer	Vivian Vance, actress
Kathy Baker, actress	Bill Daily, actor
Demi Moore, actress	Ali McGraw, actress
Burl Ives, musician	R. C. Gorman, Navajo artist
Jim Morrison, lead singer of The Doors	Ottmar Liebert, musician
Georgia O'Keeffe, artist	Shirley MacLaine, actress
Buddy Holly, musician	Marsha Mason, actress
Val Kilmer, actor	Carol Burnett, comedienne
Roger Miller, musician	Peter Hurd, artist

other animals on the grounds include Belgian draft horses, longhorn cattle, Jerusalem donkeys, and churro sheep and goats. The museum hosts La Fiesta de San Ysidro (the patron saint of agriculture) each May; call ahead for details.

The museum is at 4100 Dripping Springs Road (1½ miles east of the NMSU Golf Course; *NOTE:* University Boulevard becomes Dripping Springs Road); (505) 522–4100. It's open 9:00 A.M. to 5:00 P.M. Monday through Saturday and noon to 5:00 P.M. Sunday. Fees are $3.00 for adults, $2.00 for seniors; $1.00 for young people ages six through seventeen, and free for kids age five or younger.

newmexicotrivia

Anthony, New Mexico, is a twin city with Anthony, Texas, between Las Cruces, New Mexico, and El Paso, Texas.

Although a separate community, **Mesilla** (alternately La Mesilla or Old Mesilla) connects to the southwest side of Las Cruces. This rural "part" of Las Cruces played an important role in the history of New Mexico. The Gadsden Purchase—which annexed Mesilla to the United States from Mexico and established the current international borders of New Mexico and Arizona—was signed here in 1854. Mesilla is also the place where Billy the Kid was convicted of murder, sentenced to hang, and jailed for a short time in 1881. The village was even briefly declared the Confederate capital of a territory extending all the way to California. The tree-lined Old Mesilla Plaza is anchored by the San Albino Church and is surrounded by uncluttered shops and restaurants; it's a great place to visit on an autumn Saturday afternoon. Just across Highway 28 from Old Mesilla Plaza on Calle del Parian, you'll find the **Gadsden Museum,** which displays Indian, Civil War, and Old West artifacts.

If you've got a few hours after your visit to the museum and would like to savor the flavors of the countryside, consider heading south from Mesilla on the scenic **Oñate Trail** (Highway 28). Named for Spanish explorer Don Juan de Oñate, often cited as the founder of New Mexico, the roadway traces part of the route that de Oñate took into New Mexico more than 400 years ago. Roughly parallel to both the Rio Grande and Interstate 25, this more leisurely route connects the many rural communities southwest of Las Cruces, which are home to several interesting places to stop and shop.

Six miles south of Mesilla, near the village of San Miguel, you'll arrive at **Stahmann's Farms** (505–526–8974; 800–654–6887). Originally started in the 1930s as an innovative move to supplant the onetime cotton farm with the then-foreign pecan crop, Stahmann's now boasts 180,000 pecan trees on 4,000 acres, making it one of the world's largest pecan groves. Besides the beautiful canopy of trees, which produce up to ten million pounds of pecans annually, Stahmann's has a country store filled with pecan confections, specialty foods, gift baskets, and, luckily, samples of their delectable pecans. Hours are 9:00 A.M. to 6:00 P.M. Monday through Saturday and 11:00 A.M. to 5:00 P.M. Sunday.

About 17 miles farther south at 4201 South Highway 28, you'll come across *La Viña Winery* (505–882–7632), New Mexico's oldest winery. La Viña has a tasting room, which features its cabernets, zinfandels, and chardonnays, as well as a wine and gift shop. In addition, the winery also hosts the state's oldest wine festival in October and a jazz and blues festival in April, as well as a grape-stomping contest in mid-August. The winery is open daily from noon to 5:00 P.M., with tours given daily at 11:30 A.M. Note that there is a small fee for both tastings and tours.

Heading north on Interstate 25 out of Las Cruces, you'll come across *Fort Selden State Monument.* The now-abandoned adobe military fort that contributed to the growth of Las Cruces was one of many forts built in the mid-1800s to protect settlers and travelers from Apache Indian attacks. It was the boyhood home of General Douglas MacArthur from 1884 to 1886, when his father was the post commander; moreover, the acclaimed Buffalo Soldiers, a regiment of black soldiers honored for their success in subduing the Plains Indians, were also stationed here.

A visitor center explains the history of the fort and displays articles of interest found here. Outside, you can walk along the trails that wind about the adobe ruins. Interspersed along the trails are interpretive signs whose replicas of old photos show the fort as it was in the 1800s.

The monument is located 15 miles north of Las Cruces off Interstate 25. Take the Radium Springs exit and head west a couple of miles; (505) 526–8911. It's open daily from 8:30 A.M. to 5:00 P.M. The admission charge is $3.00, but young people age sixteen or younger are admitted free.

Though the place is beyond the scope of this book, off-the-beaten-pathers should keep in mind that the Mexican city of Juárez is only 44 miles from Las Cruces, just across the border from El Paso, Texas. And you don't even need a passport to cross. You'll find great Mexican food, potent margaritas, and bargain shopping galore. (*NOTE:* If you've never visited a Mexican border town before, steel yourself for the incessant panhandling and other solicitation, often from very young children and the omnipresent and often heartbreaking poverty.)

In northwestern Doña Ana County, you'll find the community of *Hatch,* the self-proclaimed "Chile Capital of the World." Its reputation is well earned for producing some of the highest quality, as well as largest quantities, of New Mexico's lucrative chile pepper crop. During Labor Day weekend, the community hosts the *Hatch Chile Festival* (505–267–5050), which includes a chile cook-off and ristra (strings of red chiles) arrangement competition, among other events. You'll find Hatch on Highway 26, 2 miles southwest of Interstate 25 (exit 41).

Where to Stay in Southwestern New Mexico

SOCORRO COUNTY

Casa Blanca Bed and Breakfast Guesthouse,
13 Montoya Street,
San Antonio,
(505) 835–3027

Holiday Inn Express,
1100 California Avenue NE,
Socorro,
(505) 838–0556/
(888) 526–4567

San Miguel Inn,
916 California Avenue NE,
Socorro,
(505) 835–0211/
(800) 548–7938

CATRON COUNTY

Lariat Motel,
Highway 180,
Glenwood,
(505) 539–2361

Whitewater Motel,
Highway 180,
Glenwood,
(505) 539–2581

GRANT COUNTY

Bear Creek Cabins,
north of Silver City in
Pinos Altos,
(505) 388–4501

Bear Mountain Lodge,
Silver City,
(505) 538–2538/
(877) 620–2327

Grey Feathers Lodge,
intersection of Highways 15
and 35,
24 miles north of Silver City,
(505) 536–3206

Palace Hotel,
106 West Broadway,
Silver City,
(505) 388–1811

**Spirit Canyon Lodge
and Cafe,**
684 Highway 35 (SE end of
Lake Roberts),
(505) 536–9459

**Wilderness Lodge and Hot
Springs,**
Jackass Lane,
Gila Hot Springs,
(505) 536–9749

HIDALGO COUNTY

**Best Western "Western
Skies Inn,"**
1303 South Main,
Lordsburg,
(505) 542–8807

Days Inn and Suites,
1100 West Motel Drive,
Lordsburg,
(505) 542–3600

LUNA COUNTY

**Best Western Mimbres
Valley Inn,**
1500 West Pine,
Deming,
(505) 546–4544

Holiday Inn Deming,
Interstate 10 at exit 85,
Deming,
(505) 546–2661/
(888) 546–2661

Grand Motor Inn,
1721 East Spruce Street,
Deming,
(505) 546–2632

SIERRA COUNTY

Black Range Lodge,
Main Street,
Kingston,
(505) 895–5652

**Enchanted Villa
Bed & Breakfast,**
Main Street,
Hillsboro,
(505) 895–5686

**Marshall Hot Springs Spa
and Resort,**
311 Marr Street
(at Pershing),
Truth or Consequences,
(505) 894–9286/
(877) 894–9286

**Charles Motel and
Bath House,**
601 Broadway,
Truth or Consequences,
(505) 894–7154/
(800) 317–4518

Quality Inn at the Butte,
401 Highway 195,
Elephant Butte,
(505) 744–5431

**Riverbend Hot Springs
Resort and Hostel,**
100 Austin Street,
Truth or Consequences,
(505) 894–6183

DOÑA ANA COUNTY

Lundeen Inn of the Arts,
618 South Alameda,
Las Cruces,
(505) 526–3326

Mesón de Mesilla
1803 Avenida de Mesilla,
Mesilla,
(505) 525–9212/
(800) 732–6025

**T. R. H. Smith Mansion
Bed and Breakfast,**
909 Alameda Boulevard,
Las Cruces,
(505) 525–2525/
(800) 526–1914

Happy Trails Ranch,
1857 Paisano Road,
Mesilla,
(505) 527–8471

Where to Eat in Southwestern New Mexico

SOCORRO COUNTY

The Owl Bar & Cafe,
on U.S. Highway 380,
10 miles south of Socorro,
San Antonio,
(505) 835–9946.
Inexpensive to moderate.
Fare: Famous green chile
cheeseburgers and New
Mexican food.

Magdalena Cafe,
on Highway 60, west of
Magdalena,
(505) 854–2696.
Inexpensive to moderate.
Fare: Southwestern cuisine,
burgers, and steaks.

El Sombrero,
210 Mesquite,
Socorro,
(505) 835–3945.
Inexpensive. Fare: New
Mexican.

**Valverde Steakhouse
and Lounge,**
203 Manzanares Avenue
East,
(505) 835–3380.
Inexpensive to moderate.
Fare: Steaks, seafood, etc.

**Martha's Black Dog
Coffeehouse,**
110 West Manzanares,
Socorro,
(505) 838–0311.
Inexpensive. Fare:
Sandwiches, pasta, soup
and salads, including
vegetarian entrees.

CATRON COUNTY

Blue Front Cafe and Bar,
Highway 180,
Glenwood,
(505) 539–2561.
Inexpensive. Fare:
Traditional family dining,
excellent breakfasts; smoked
barbecue on weekends.

GRANT COUNTY

Buckhorn Saloon,
Main Street,
Pinos Altos,
(505) 538–9911.
Inexpensive. Fare: Steaks,
burgers, chicken, seafood,
vegetarian.

Jalisco Cafe,
100 South Bullard Street,
Silver City,
(505) 388–2060.
Inexpensive to moderate.
Fare: Traditional Mexican and
eclectic Southwestern.

Diane's Bakery & Cafe
510 North Bullard Street,
Silver City,
(505) 538–8722.
Inexpensive. Fare: Soups,
salads, sandwiches.

El Paisano,
802 East Fifteenth Street,
Silver City,
(505) 538–5803.
Moderate. Fare: Mexican.

**Grey Feathers Lodge
& Restaurant,**
NM35 at NM15,
Silver City,
(505) 536–3206.
Moderate. Fare: American.

Red Barn,
708 Silver Heights
Boulevard,
Silver City,
(505) 538–5666.
Inexpensive to moderate.
Fare: Steaks and seafood.

HIDALGO COUNTY

Grapevine Cafe,
904 East Motel Drive,
Lordsburg,
(505) 542–8696.
Inexpensive to moderate.
Fare: American.

El Charro,
209 South P Boulevard,
Lordsburg,
(505) 542–3400.
Inexpensive to moderate.
Fare: New Mexican and
American.

Kranberry's Restaurant,
1405 South Main,
Lordsburg,
(505) 542–9400.
Inexpensive to moderate.
Fare: American.

LUNA COUNTY

El Camino Real,
900 West Pine,
Deming,
(505) 546–7421.
Inexpensive to moderate.
Fare: New Mexican and
American.

La Fonda Restaurant,
601 East Pine,
Deming,
(505) 546–0465.
Inexpensive to moderate.
Fare: New Mexican and
American.

Primo's Restaurant,
411 South Gold Avenue,
Deming,
(505) 546–0800.
Inexpensive to moderate.
Fare: Mexican and American.

SIERRA COUNTY

Barbershop Cafe,
Main Street,
Hillsboro,
(505) 895–5283.
Inexpensive. Fare: California
cuisine.

Hot Springs Bakery,
313 Broadway,
Truth or Consequences,
(505) 894–5555.
Inexpensive. Fare:
Sandwiches, pizza.

La Cocina,
280 North Date Street,
Truth or Consequences,
(505) 894–6499.
Inexpensive to moderate.
Fare: New Mexican and
American.

**Los Arcos Steak and
Lobster House,**
1400 North Date Street,
Truth or Consequences,
(505) 894–6200.
Inexpensive to moderate.
Fare: New Mexican and
American.

SELECTED CHAMBERS OF COMMERCE/VISITOR BUREAUS IN SOUTHWESTERN NEW MEXICO

**Deming/Luna County Chamber of
Commerce,**
P.O. Box 8, 800 East Pine,
Deming, 88031;
(505) 546–2674/(800) 848–4955;
Web site: www.cityofdeming.org

Hatch Chamber of Commerce,
P.O. Box 38, Hatch, 87937;
(505) 267–5050

**Las Cruces Convention and Visitors
Bureau,**
211 North Water Street,
Las Cruces, 88001;
(505) 541–2444/(800) 343–7827;
Web site: www.lascrucescvb.org

Lordsburg Chamber of Commerce,
117 East Second Street,
Lordsburg, 88045;
(505) 542–9864;
Web site: www.hidalgocounty.org

Magdalena Chamber of Commerce,
P.O. Box 145, Magdalena, 87825;
(505) 854–2261/(866) 854–3217;
Web site: www.magdalena-nm.com

Reserve Chamber of Commerce,
P.O. Box 415, Reserve, 87830;
(505) 533–6116;
Web site: www.catroncounty.org/chamber

**Silver City/Grant County Chamber of
Commerce,**
201 North Hudson Avenue,
Silver City, 88061;
(505) 538–3785/(800) 548–9378;
Web site: www.silvercity.org/

**Socorro County Chamber of
Commerce,**
P.O. Box 743, Socorro, 87801;
(505) 835–0424;
Web site: www.socorro-nm.com

**Truth or Consequences/Sierra County
Chamber of Commerce,**
P.O. Box 31,
Truth or Consequences, 87901;
(505) 894–3536/(800) 831–9487;
Web site: www.truthorconsequences
nm.net

DOÑA ANA COUNTY

Double Eagle,
On the Plaza,
Old Mesilla,
(505) 523–6700.
Moderate to very expensive.
Fare: Eclectic, featuring
steaks and New Mexican
food.

La Posta,
On the Plaza,
Old Mesilla,
(505) 524–3524.
Inexpensive to moderate.
Fare: New Mexican cuisine.

Chilitos,
2405 South Valley Drive,
Las Cruces,
(505) 526–4184.
Inexpensive. Fare: Mexican
and American.

Andele Restaurant,
2184 Avenida de Messilla,
Mesilla,
(505) 526–9631.
Inexpensive. Fare: A locals'
favorite for Mexican food in a
casual atmosphere.

Northwestern New Mexico

Because of its large population of Native Americans, north-western New Mexico proudly bears the name Indian Country. Part of the Navajo Nation—the largest Indian reservation in the United States—is located in this region, as are the Zuni, Acoma, Ramah Navajo, and Laguna Reservations. The vast juniper-dotted mesas and multihued rock formations will leave you in awe, especially if you're an urban dweller. It's a great place to just wander for a few hours or even a few days.

The three counties composing this region are huge, so notable attractions are often widely scattered in this sparsely populated region. Look closely at the mileage scale on your trusty map, and come along to discover some of the special spots in northwestern New Mexico.

McKinley County

Named after David L. Gallup, a paymaster for the Atlantic and Pacific Railroad, the city of **Gallup** was founded in 1881. Situated near the Arizona border along old Route 66, Gallup thrives in the heart of Indian Country. The Navajo and Zuni Indians swell this small town's population to more than 100,000 on weekends, when they come to town to trade.

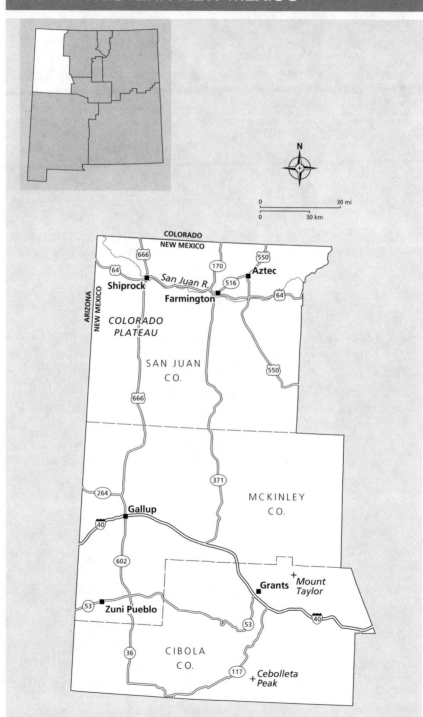

Almost everything in Gallup is located along its main street (alternately Highway 118 and East or West 66 Avenue), a healthy stretch of old *Route 66,* "America's Mother Road," which was stripped of its legendary identity when Interstate 40 homogenized its path in the 1960s. For an overview of Gallup's past, check out the Gallup Historical Society's *Rex Museum* (505–863–1363) at 300 East 66 Avenue. Hours vary seasonally; call ahead. Admission is free.

Gallup's downtown main strip is lined with its own brand of distinctive pawnshops. Whereas in most cities pawnshops are seen as seedy places of last resort for desperate borrowers, in Gallup this image couldn't be farther from reality. In addition to providing ready markets for Indian wares, Gallup's pawnshops act as financial institutions for many Native Americans. An advanced system of barter and credit has evolved over the years.

The pawnshops are veritable museums of Indian jewelry and other artifacts. Display cases and vaults gleam with turquoise and silver. If you want a good deal on authentic Indian arts and crafts, including jewelry, here's the place to buy. Retailers come from all over to Gallup to buy Indian wares, which they then sell elsewhere—at a sizable markup. A favorite of Native Americans and others since 1918, *Richardson's Trading Post* is perhaps the best place

FAVORITE ATTRACTIONS/EVENTS IN NORTHWESTERN NEW MEXICO

El Morro National Monument,
near Ramah
(505) 783–4226

La Ventana Natural Arch,
El Malpais National Monument
(505) 287–7911

Zuni-Acoma Trail,
Cibola and McKinley Counties
No phone

El Rancho Hotel,
Gallup
(505) 863–9311

Mission Church,
Zuni Pueblo
(505) 782–4481

Acoma Pueblo,
Cibola County
(800) 747–0181

Chaco Canyon,
San Juan County
(505) 786–7014

Shiprock,
San Juan County
No phone

Four Corners Monument,
New Mexico, Arizona, Colorado, Utah
No phone

Inter-Tribal Ceremonial,
August, Gallup
(505) 863–3896

Crownpoint Rug Weavers Auction,
third Friday of the month, Crownpoint
(505) 786–7386

to view the trade, as well as to get a great price from a reputable dealer with a wide selection. Located at 222 West 66 Avenue (505–722–4762), Richardson's is open Monday through Saturday from 9:00 A.M. to 6:00 P.M.

East of downtown, the notable *El Rancho Hotel* commands attention from passing motorists. In 1987 the well-known Indian trader Armand Ortega bought the historic property, as it was threatened with demolition. After extensive renovations, the hotel reopened in May 1988.

Originally built in 1937 by the brother of movie mogul D. W. Griffith, El Rancho became known as a Hollywood hideaway in the 1940s and 1950s. Scores of actors were drawn to Gallup by the many films (mostly Westerns) made in the area. Spencer Tracy, Katharine Hepburn, Humphrey Bogart, Rita Hayworth, and Ronald Reagan all stayed at the hotel. Restored to its former rustic glamour, the hotel's two-story lobby is lined with autographed photos of Hollywood's brightest stars of the era who stayed at El Rancho.

El Rancho is located at 1000 East 66 Avenue, (505) 863–9311. Room rates range from $58 for a single in the motel section to $115 for a two-bedroom suite in the original hotel.

Red Rock State Park, minutes from the center of town, is a wonderful place to explore. Red Rock Museum, located in the park, showcases area artifacts from the Ice Age to the present, and rare Indian arts and crafts are also on display. The museum's garden areas identify the plants native to the high mesa region. The park itself, with its exquisite crimson cliffs, is one of New Mexico's top nonforest spots for camping. If you want solitude, however, visit during the week. For good weather without the crowds, plan your stay during early spring or late fall.

Red Rock State Park is off Highway 566 via Highway 118 or Interstate 40, about 10 miles east of Gallup; (505) 722–3839. The museum is open daily from 8:00 A.M. to 6:00 P.M. Memorial Day through Labor Day and Monday through Saturday from 8:00 A.M. to 4:30 P.M. the remainder of the year. Suggested donations are $1.75 for adults and $1.00 for children.

STATE PARKS IN NORTHWESTERN NEW MEXICO
On the Web at: www.emnrd.state.nm.us/nmparks/

Bluewater Lake State Park,
28 miles west of Grants,
(505) 876–2391

Navajo Lake State Park,
25 miles east of Bloomfield,
(505) 632–2278

Talking Turkey about Turquoise

Sue Carlson of Richardson's Trading Company in Gallup, one of the area's oldest and most reputable pawnbrokers, and Native American artisan Jo Ann Valencia of Santa Fe have provided information that helps demystify that most classic of Southwestern jewelry gemstones, turquoise. After a sprinkling of media reports on the proliferation of domestic and Asian-imported knockoffs, some buyers have become more aware of the differing quality, and in some cases, the authenticity, of Southwestern jewelry. There are various types of "turquoise," from the real deal—gem-quality stone—right on down to the most insidious fake: plastic. It's important to work with a reputable dealer, Carlson notes, because some of the fake stuff is pretty difficult to recognize.

Because turquoise is porous, it absorbs body oils and fumes from the air and can change color, usually becoming greener, with years of wearing. Gem-quality turquoise, which ranges in color from pale blue to bright blue, is less porous and therefore less subject to changes in color. Here's the breakdown:*

Natural turquoise: not treated in any way.

Stabilized turquoise: chemically hardened with a polymer of liquid resin or plastic, but its color has not been changed.** Stabilized turquoise is frequently used in Southwestern jewelry because it resists chipping or breaking while it's being worked.

Treated turquoise: altered to produce a change in color of the natural stone, usually detectable by a shiny, unnatural color.

Reconstituted or composite turquoise: turquoise particles and dust, which have been combined with plastic resins and solidly compressed to resemble natural turquoise.

As for the brown or black webbing seen on most turquoise, it's referred to as the "matrix" of a stone and is formed by mineral deposits. Its presence does not necessarily increase or diminish the quality of the stone.

*Information source: *Turquoise—Gem of the Centuries,* by O. T. Branson

**As defined by the federal Indian Arts and Crafts Sales Act of 1978

The park hosts the annual ***Inter-Tribal Ceremonial*** (ITC), held each year since 1922. The ITC includes an all-Indian rodeo, an arts and crafts show, and the ceremonial dances of many tribes throughout the West, from Canada to Mexico. The four-day ITC begins the second Thursday in August and is known as the largest Indian gathering of its kind in the world. The ITC Association can be reached at (505) 863–3896, (888) 685–2564 or www.gallup nm.org/ceremonial.

Between Gallup and the city of Grants along Interstate 40, you'll find the small community of Thoreau located near the Continental Divide, the demarcation separating streams that flow to opposite sides of North America. (Though possibly named after writer Henry David Thoreau, the name of the town is pronounced "through.") South of Thoreau, perched above Bluewater Lake in the foothills of the Zuni Mountains, you'll find some of the most comfortable accommodations in the region at *Zuni Mountain Lodge*. (*NOTE:* Thematically and geographically the lodge fits with McKinley County, even though technically it's just south of the county line in Cibola County.)

Run by innkeepers Dick Morrow and Bob McCuen, Zuni Mountain Lodge offers guests all the natural beauty of a stay in the mountains with all the comforts of home. The lodge's ten large guest rooms, each with its own private bath, are modern and thoughtfully appointed. (There's even a filled candy dish on the dresser!) Two of the guest rooms are located in what's called the "Tree House," a detached building so named because of the piñon trees growing in a corner (and up through the roof!) of each room. In addition, there are communal areas for guests to enjoy, including the Kiva, a comfortably furnished, spacious room complete with cable television and VCR, a video and book library, and various games.

The three-story lodge has views of Bluewater Lake from the glassed-in wraparound veranda on the upper floors, and from certain parts of the nicely landscaped grounds, which include a small orchard and lawn area with a gazebo. Dick and Bob are very knowledgeable about the area's natural environment and history and also welcome the opportunity to direct guests to the scenic hiking and mountain biking trails nearby. As wildlife is abundant, these forest trails are perfect for wilderness enthusiasts and birders alike.

With reservations, and for an additional fee, Zuni Mountain Lodge also provides guided day tours, as well as its popular Western Heritage Tour, a seven-day all-inclusive tour package with day trips to Chaco Canyon, Zuni and Acoma Pueblos, and Arizona's Canyon de Chelly, among other sites.

To get to the lodge, take exit 53 off I–40 at Thoreau; turn south onto Highway 612 and go about 13 miles until you come to a ZML sign at Perch Drive. Take a right, and the lodge is about ¼ mile up the hill at 40 Perch Drive; (505) 862–7616; www.cia-g.com/~zuniml/. Rates range from $60 to $95, which includes a hearty breakfast and, incredibly enough, a delicious dinner to boot.

For those interested in authentic, hand-loomed Navajo rugs, plan your stay at Zuni Mountain Lodge to coincide with an internationally acclaimed local event—the monthly *Crownpoint Rug Weavers Auction,* held the third Friday of every month in the Navajo Nation community of Crownpoint, 25 miles north of Thoreau via Highway 371. Attracting Navajo weavers from around the region and individual and commercial buyers internationally, the auction is more than just a market event—it's also like a small town fair with arts and crafts and

A Glimpse of Northwestern New Mexico: Impressions of Indian Country

Every August, Gallup's Red Rock Park is the site of the Inter-Tribal Ceremonial. Along with Albuquerque's Gathering of Nations, Santa Fe's Indian Market, and the Eight Northern Pueblos Arts and Crafts Show, the ceremonial at Gallup is one of the biggest American Indian events in the United States. Sandwiched between the Navajo and Zuni Reservations, within half a day's drive of eighteen Indian pueblos, it's a veritable Woodstock of brightly painted vans, tepees, fry-bread stands, rodeo riders, women in traditional velvet dresses and turquoise jewelry, and contest dancers costumed in feathers and bells who have come from all over North America to compete for cash prizes. Hypnotic chanting and the irresistible rhythm of giant dance drums give the throng a pulse of its own, creating a cheerful collective spirit that sweeps me away. And the Inter-Tribal Ceremonial is one of the few Indian events in New Mexico where Indians actually outnumber tourists.

But as exciting as ceremonials are, my primary impression of the Indian lands of northwestern New Mexico is solitude. There are the many miles of driving along the base of the Zuni Cliffs, pink by day and glowing magenta at sunset, where I've driven for an hour or more without seeing another car. There are the remote reaches of the Navajo land where horses run wild and people still hold to the ancient tradition of building their hogans far enough apart so that no home can be seen from any other. There are the fortresslike mesas of the Acoma country towering over the vast, black lava flow known as El Malpais, so rugged that it is almost uncrossable on foot or horseback.

I remind myself that these two aspects of Indian Country are actually part of the same phenomenon. It's the isolation of distance that lets the Indian people hold to time-honored traditions, relatively free of intrusions from the American mainstream. And it's the ancient ways of honoring the land that preserve the wide open spaces free from shopping malls, truck stops, and fast-food joints. There's a bit of philosophy to ponder next time you find yourself on an all-day drive across the seemingly empty and endless Indian land of the Four Corners region.

Navajo food vendors. Because you're purchasing direct from the source during the auction, most of the rugs sell for less than comparable ones found in local trading posts. Depending on quality and size, rugs may go for as little as $20 or as much as several thousand dollars. Auctions are held in the local elementary school cafeteria; preview starts at 3:00 P.M., with the auction beginning at 7:00 P.M.; (505) 786–7386; www.crownpointrugauction.com.

About 38 miles south of Gallup you'll come across **_Zuni Pueblo,_** New Mexico's largest Indian pueblo, with a population of about 9,000. Zuni's isolation from New Mexico's Rio Grande–situated pueblos makes its history, culture, and language unique.

The Zuni people have occupied the area of the reservation for more than 1,700 years. Their ancestors played an important role in the early recorded history of the Southwest. In search of the Seven Cities of Cibola—the fabled cities of gold—Spanish explorers first discovered Zuni in 1539. Encouraged by persistent rumors (as well as Indian fabrications to persuade the Spaniards to go elsewhere in search of the gold), more explorers, including Coronado, followed but failed to find riches.

The pueblo has several shops where you can purchase Zuni-made arts including stone- and shell-carved fetishes (birds and other animals used since prehistoric times for luck in hunting and fertility in crops) and the turquoise petit point and needlepoint jewelry for which the pueblo is famous. Zuni is located on Highway 53, via Highway 602, about 38 miles south of Gallup.

The first place to stop during a visit to Zuni is the temporary location of the **A:shiwi A:wan Museum and Heritage Center.** The center's unusual name comes from the name for the Zuni people in their native language. (*NOTE:* Early Spanish explorers in the New Mexico territory gave Spanish names to all of New Mexico's pueblo Indians, which are the common names used today; however, each pueblo has its own unique name in its own language.) While the center's location is deemed temporary, as a larger facility will eventually be built, its present facility and exhibits are certainly impressive. Using an ecomuseum approach—because this approach was determined the most compatible with the Zunis' reverent beliefs toward nature—the center contains historic photographs along with contemporary exhibits to bring alive the history and culture of the Zuni people.

The museum is located adjacent to the Pueblo of Zuni Arts and Crafts Gallery on Highway 53 in Zuni; (505) 782–4403. It's open Monday through Saturday from 9:00 A.M. to 5:00 P.M. Admission is free.

In 1629 the Spanish established **Mission Church of Nuestra Señora de Guadalupe** (also known as Our Lady of Guadalupe and the Old Mission) at Zuni. The church was restored in 1970, and internationally known Zuni artist and muralist Alex Seowtewa began painting his colorful murals on the interior of the church walls. There are now twenty-four murals depicting Zuni kachinas. Seowtewa's work has drawn some famous admirers to Zuni, among them Jackie Onassis and Mother Teresa. In fact, Ms. Onassis had never visited the American Southwest until the mid-1980s, but she is reported to have been affected deeply by its beauty. She was given a personal tour by former secretary of the interior and author Stewart Udall and noted photographer Jerry Jacka. The two were collaborating on a book called *Majestic Journey: Coronado's Inland Empire,* the latest edition of which is dedicated, in memory, to Ms. Onassis. Seowtewa continues work on the murals with the assistance of his son Kenneth and a grant from the National Endowment for the Arts. The church is generally open daily from 9:00 A.M. to 4:00 P.M. during the summer and from 10:00 A.M. to 4:00 P.M. the remainder of the year. Call the tribal offices at (505) 782–4481 for more information or for group tours.

The Inn at Halona offers guests a rare bed-and-breakfast experience, as it's located in the heart of Zuni Pueblo on the south side of the Zuni River at the prehistoric pueblo site of Halona. Operating under special license by the

Tips for Visiting New Mexico's Indian Lands

While visiting New Mexico's pueblo or nonpueblo Indian reservations, keep in mind that they're all sovereign, self-governing nations with their own laws. While almost all pueblos welcome visitors, visitors are expected to observe local rules and etiquette. Here are a few commonsense tips.

If there's a pueblo visitor center, stop there first and register. Many such centers screen films or have museums, which are great ways to orient yourself before visiting pueblo sites. Some pueblos, like Acoma, offer guided tours for a fee.

Photography should always respect people and place. Most pueblos allow photography only by permit, for which a fee must usually be paid. Never photograph dances or ceremonies. These events are traditional, and often religious, ceremonies rather than entertainment. Applause is not appropriate. Never photograph a person or group without asking first. If permission is given, you may be asked to pay a small fee for the privilege.

Sketching or painting on the pueblos may also be restricted. Check with the pueblo governor's office or visitor center.

Observe quiet and orderly conduct when watching pueblo dances and ceremonies. It's good form to stand toward the back of the crowd, so as not to block the ceremony from pueblo residents or participants.

Never enter a pueblo home, kiva, or building without being invited to do so. However, most pueblo churches are open to visitors without special request.

Never take alcohol onto Indian lands.

Do not hike, bike, or four-wheel across open Indian lands without permission. Contact local authorities for permits and information. (See appendix for pueblo listings.).

Zuni Tribe, the Inn at Halona is the only such establishment in the pueblo and possibly in any Indian pueblo. Run by innkeepers Roger Thomas, a native of Chambéry, France, and his wife Elaine Dodson Thomas, the pueblo-style inn was completely remodeled in 1998. Elaine is the granddaughter of Andrew and Effa Vander Wagen, Dutch immigrants and missionaries who first arrived in Zuni in 1897 and later opened a trading post near Halona Plaza, which is currently also run by the Thomases.

The inn boasts eight unique guest rooms on three levels, some with private baths, which are decorated with Zuni and other Southwestern art. Each room contains an ongoing "Room Diary," and guests are encouraged to record their thoughts and impressions during their stay. Several comfortable common areas are available for lounging, including a private flagstone patio, which is lit by lampposts in the evening. Unlike many bed-and-breakfast inns, guests may select their breakfast from a diverse menu, which includes a European-style continental offering, a traditional, full American breakfast, and such chef specialties as *huevos rancheros* or breakfast burritos.

The Inn at Halona is located 3 blocks south of Highway 53, at 23B Pia Mesa Road; (505) 782–4547 or (800) 752–3278; www.halona.com. Rates range from $79 to $99 and may vary depending on the season and length of stay. Group rates are also available.

Though there have been controversial reintroduction efforts of the endangered Mexican wolf, or lobo—limited numbers of which live only in captivity—into the wilderness areas of southeastern Arizona and southwestern New Mexico, most have not survived. The efforts are applauded by environmentalists as loudly as they're cursed by area ranchers. Politics notwithstanding, the best way to begin to experience the untamed majesty of wolves is with a visit to **Wild Spirit Wolf Sanctuary,** formerly known as the Candy Kitchen Rescue Ranch, south of Ramah.

Founded in 1991 by artist Jacque Evans, Wild Spirit Wolf Sanctuary is a nonprofit organization providing sanctuary to abused and abandoned captive-bred wolves and wolf dogs. Its original name came from the fact that the refuge is located at the old headquarters for the Candy Kitchen Ranch, where piñon nut candy was made during the 1920s and 1930s. During Prohibition, it's rumored that liquor was distilled here, with the piñon candy serving as a front for the large amounts of sugar used to make the illegal moonshine. The refuge changed its name in 2004 to better reflect its mission.

Visitors may take advantage of guided tours of the ranch and visit its noble residents, which by necessity are kept in pens; however, to the extent possible, the animals are kept in compatible pairs or small groups. With a focus on

Zuni Pueblo's Shalako

All of New Mexico's Indian pueblos conduct annual ceremonials and feast days—some open to the public and some not—to honor or celebrate certain events or deities. One of the more dramatic is the Shalako Ceremonial at Zuni Pueblo, which is held in late November or early December. As one of the most important events in the Zuni religious calendar, Shalako celebrates the end of the current year and the beginning of the new.

During the ceremony six men impersonate Shalakos, or divine beings, by wearing wood-framed, 10-foot-tall costumes covered with colorfully designed fabrics and topped with masks of Shalakos. The ceremony, which begins with the ritual crossing of the Zuni River, winds through the pueblo's streets as the Shalako performers dance throughout the night and bless the houses that were built during the year. A ritual footrace is conducted the next day, during which participants plant offering sticks in the ground to bring health and fertility to the pueblo.

Because of past instances of disrespect shown by outsiders during Shalako, the event is not necessarily open to the public every year. Call (505) 782–4481 or (505) 782–4403 for current Shalako information. For a dramatic, fictionalized Shalako scene, read Tony Hillerman's *Dance Hall of the Dead,* a murder mystery set on and around the Zuni Reservation.

education, ecology, and the responsible ownership of wolf dogs, the ranch currently cares for seventy-five wolves and wolf dogs, with the hope that rescue organizations will someday no longer be needed.

To get to Wild Spirit, turn south on Highway 125 off Highway 53 (2½ miles west of El Morro National Monument or about 8 miles east of Ramah). Go 8 miles (about halfway, you'll pass through Mountain View); then turn west onto Highway 120 and go 4 miles; (505) 775–3304; www.inetdesign.com/candy kitchen. The ranch is open to the public Thursday through Sunday, with tours given at 11:00 A.M. and 1:00 and 3:00 P.M. Donations are greatly appreciated.

Back in the small community of Ramah, check out the ***Ramah Museum,*** located downtown just off Highway 53. Housed in the Joseph A. B. Bond House, circa 1905, the museum focuses on pioneer Americana and the history of the village, from its earliest days as a Mormon settlement. The museum is open from April through October on Friday and Saturday only, with varying hours; no phone. Donations are welcome and appreciated.

Across Highway 53, you'll find the ***Stagecoach Cafe*** (505–783–4288), just about the only place to eat in the area. Serving New Mexican and American favorites, the Stagecoach is open daily from 11:00 A.M. to 9:00 P.M.

Cibola County

Acoma Pueblo, or "Sky City," as it's sometimes called, is the oldest continuously inhabited community in the United States; archaeologists have traced the pueblo's occupation to 1150. But it wasn't until 1540 that the Spanish explorer Coronado became the first non-Indian to enter Acoma, and outsiders have been fascinated with Sky City ever since.

The pueblo, located on a 367-foot mesa on the Acoma Indian Reservation outside Grants, operates a visitor center that includes a museum and gift shops at the base of the mesa. Guided tours of Acoma—the only way outsiders can view the pueblo—are offered hourly from the visitor center every day, with the exception of private ceremonial periods. Small buses provide transportation to the top of the mesa, and from there an Acoma guide will point out the various elements of the pueblo while filling you in on Acoma's long and colorful history. The mesa-top pueblo provides stunning views of the surrounding area, including the spectacular 400-foot-tall **Enchanted Mesa,** said to be the home of the ancestral Acomas.

The singularly most impressive structure in the pueblo is Mission San Esteban Del Rey, a church completed in 1640 after eleven years of intense labor by Acoma residents. The massive roof beams were carried from the forests of

Ladders at Acoma Pueblo

Enchanted Mesa

Mount Taylor 40 miles away—without ever touching the logs to the ground, according to Acoma legend. The church, whose adobe walls are 7 to 9 feet thick, has no windows, because it was used as a fortress.

Even though the pueblo has no electricity or running water, about twelve families live here; most Acoma Pueblo Indians, however, live in communities nearby. Some of the pueblo residents sell their world-famous, intricately designed pottery during tours, and often you can purchase bread baked in the beehive-shaped *hornos,* or adobe ovens, that dot the pueblo. The tour guide will also point out and explain the use of kivas, or sacred ceremonial chambers; note, though, that entrance to kivas is strictly prohibited for visitors.

To get to the visitor center from Grants, head east on Interstate 40, take exit 96, and follow the signs to the visitor center; (505) 469–1052 or (800) 747–0181. From Albuquerque, head west on Interstate 40 (about 55 miles), take exit 108, and do the same. Tours are held as follows: fall and winter, 8:00 A.M. to 4:00 P.M.; spring, 8:00 A.M. to 6:00 P.M.; and summer, 8:00 A.M. to 7:00 P.M. The visitor center is open daily from 8:00 A.M. to 7:00 P.M. April through October; 8:00 A.M. to 4:30 P.M. the rest of the year. Each year tours cease during Easter weekend (it varies, call ahead), June 24 and 29, July 10–13, July 25, and either the first or second weekend in October (it varies). (*NOTE:* The pueblo may be closed to the public during other times of the year without much advance notice, so call before you venture out.) Tour admission is $10.00 for adults, $9.00 for senior citizens, and $7.00 for children age six or older. Children age five or younger are free. Camera and sketching fees apply, and there are photographic restrictions, including a ban on camcorders and digital cameras. There's no admission fee for the visitor center and museum, however.

The ***Shrine of Los Portales*** lies in a hidden grotto near the old Spanish land-grant village of Syboyeta (sometimes spelled Cebolleta on maps), north of

Laguna Pueblo and east of the city of Grants. A statue of St. Bernadette of Lourdes is the focal point of the beautiful, mysterious shrine.

Brought from Spain, the original statue for the shrine, *Our Lady of Sorrows,* is now protected in the mission church of the same name in Syboyeta. The legend goes that during one of the last Navajo raids in the 1800s, the women and children took refuge in the natural fortress while the men were away. The women vowed that if their husbands and sons returned safely, the women would build a shrine to the Virgin Mary at which to hold an annual mass.

The shallow cave or overhang of the rounded cliff that forms the large semicircular enclave is perfect for meditation or prayer, as evidenced by the many melted candles that can be seen at the shrine. Weatherworn wooden pews face the shrine at an angle. Spring water, considered holy, seeps from the cliff and collects in several small pools. Because of the abundance of moisture, this protected area is unusually green and forms a small oasis that contrasts with the barren land of the surrounding region.

Syboyeta is on Highway 279, off Highway 124, which connects to Interstate 40 near Laguna Pueblo. To get to the shrine, proceed on the main road to Our Lady of Sorrows church at the center of town. Continue winding around the church as the paved road turns to dirt. After ⅒ mile, turn left and continue for 1 mile until you see a very large tree with exposed roots around its base; the approximately 100-yard trail to the shrine begins here. (*NOTE:* If there's been a lot of rain, do not attempt this trek unless you have a four-wheel-drive vehicle.)

Heading west on Interstate 40 you'll soon be in ***Grants,*** the largest town and county seat of Cibola County. Grants's past as a classic Route 66 town is preserved with 1950s-era motels, shops, and cafes along the main strip, now called Santa Fe Avenue. Just off Santa Fe Avenue you'll find the ***New Mexico Museum of Mining*** at 100 Iron Street (505–287–4802 or 800–748–2142)—though it was uranium, not iron, that put Grants on the map. The first floor of the museum traces the history of uranium mining in the area from 1950, the year Paddy Martinez, an Indian laborer and occasional prospector, discovered a mother lode of the dusty yellow rock.

The best part of the museum is the underground portion called Section 26, an eerily accurate reproduction of a working uranium mine. You start by taking an elevator down the mine "shaft." Although you don't travel very far, it feels as though you're hundreds of feet below the earth's surface. The tour uses handheld listening devices that explain the exhibits at scheduled stops. Adding to the realism are artifacts from working mines that fill the space—right down to the tool company "girlie calendar" in the miners' lunchroom.

The museum is open Monday through Saturday from 9:00 A.M. to 5:00 P.M. Admission is $3.00 for adults, $2.00 for seniors and young people ages seven through eighteen, and free for children age six or younger.

Highway 53, which connects Grants with Zuni Pueblo (see McKinley County entry at beginning of this chapter), is the most scenic drive in northwestern New Mexico—and you'll find a few interesting stops along the way.

The recently designated *El Malpais National Monument and Conservation Area* encompasses more than 590 square miles of lava flows and caves, volcanos, sandstone canyons, and forests centered between Highway 53 and Highway 117 south of Grants. Although some of the natural sites are accessible to passenger cars traveling along the two highways, El Malpais (roughly "The Badlands" in Spanish) is heaven to hikers and backpackers.

After several years with only minimal development, the monument and conservation area now have two remote sites where visitors may get information and maps. You'll find a U.S. Park Service visitor center (505–783–4774) about 23 miles south of Grants on Highway 53, as well as a U.S. Bureau of Land Management ranger station (505–287–7911) on Highway 117, 9 miles south of Interstate 40. Both sites are open daily from 8:30 A.M. to 4:30 P.M. In addition, there is the Northwest New Mexico Visitors Center in Grants at 1900 East Santa Fe Avenue (505–876–2783), which offers comprehensive information on the region. The center is open daily from 9:00 A.M. to 5:00 P.M. during daylight saving time; otherwise, it's open from 8:00 A.M. to 5:00 P.M.

Among the sites accessible along Highway 117 are the Sandstone Bluffs Overlook (10 miles from Interstate 40), *La Ventana Natural Arch* (17 miles south of Interstate 40), and *The Narrows* (1 mile farther south), where the highway passes through a narrow corridor created when lava flowed near the base of huge sandstone cliffs. You'll see intriguing lava formations in this area. If you were farsighted enough to pack a picnic, you'll find great spots for lunch at the south end of the Narrows, as well as underneath La Ventana.

One of the more accessible hiking adventures in El Malpais can be had in *Junction Cave* in the *El Calderón Area* of the monument, 20 miles south of Grants on Highway 53. A well-marked trail from the parking area leads to the cave entrance. Though not really a cave, but rather a 3,000-foot-long lava tube, Junction Cave provides hikers with a relatively safe and easy spelunking experience. Plan on bringing good shoes with gripping soles, long pants to protect your legs against the sharp lava if you stumble, and more than one quality flashlight. At times, you may notice bats clinging to the cave's wall; however, don't disturb them, as they're harmless. Another trail from El Calderón parking lot leads you past interesting sinkholes to Bat Cave, which is closed off to humans; however, it's a great area from which to enjoy a dramatic New Mexico sunset and watch the bats emerge at dusk.

Negotiating with private property owners for the sale of parts of El Malpais has been quite a process, and some agreements have yet to be finalized. As a result, two of the more interesting and accessible features of El Malpais are still privately owned, but you can visit them.

The **Candelaria Ice Cave** and **Bandera Crater** are located in a parklike setting covered with ponderosa pine, spruce, and piñon trees. You start your trek at the trading post on the property, which was once a summer resort complete with cabins. After paying the fee, you hike ½ mile alongside lava flows until you reach a wooden stairway. The steps lead to Candelaria Ice Cave (named for the present owners of the property), located in part of a collapsed lava tube where the temperature never rises above thirty-one degrees. Though walking into the cave is prohibited (liability, you know), and this is slightly disappointing, you can get a good view of the greenish ice from the viewing platform.

To see Bandera Crater, brace yourself for a longer and steeper hike—about 1½ miles. The 1,000-foot-deep crater was formed during a volcanic eruption 5,000 years ago. Nature has since transformed the crater into a beautiful spot flecked with hardy ponderosa pines. The breezy coolness of the 8,000-foot altitude makes the ridge of the crater a nice place to relax on a hot summer day.

The entrance to the Candelaria Ice Cave and Bandera Crater is located a little less than 26 miles south of Grants on Highway 53; (505) 783–4303 or (888) 423–2283; www.icecaves.com. Hours are 8:00 A.M. to about an hour before sunset, and admission is $8.00 for adults and teenagers, $6.50 for seniors, and $4.00 for children ages five to twelve, with those age four or younger admitted free. But remember, both the ice cave and the crater are slated to become part of El Malpais and thus will be administered by the National Park Service (though this has been dragging out for more than ten years, so don't hold your breath); accordingly, check at the aforementioned Northwest New Mexico Information Center in Grants before planning a trip.

El Morro National Monument is the nation's oldest national monument. Also known as Inscription Rock, the monument is an oasis in the middle of nowhere; nevertheless, travelers have been stopping here for centuries to drink from the pool of water at the base of the cliff—and to leave behind a little graffiti. A sporadic account of southwestern history from 1605 through the nineteenth century is recorded on what Spanish conquistadores named El Morro, meaning "The Bluff." The inscriptions etched into the vertical stone surface provide a permanent record of the different cultures that influenced the area over the past 400 years. Fifteen years before the Pilgrims landed at Plymouth Rock, the first Spanish inscription was made by explorer Don Juan de Oñate on April 16, 1605, extolling his discovery of the "Sea of the South," now known as the Gulf of California.

Touching the inscriptions or defacing any surface is strictly forbidden. For those who just can't resist the urge to write in stone after viewing El Morro, however, the visitor center provides a rock near the parking area on which travelers may etch a word or two.

Much earlier visitors to El Morro left their own graffiti in the form of petroglyphs, or ancient rock drawings. You'll find ruins of ancient pueblos here as well. Dating from the thirteenth century, these have been traced to certain Anasazi peoples (the ancestors of the Zuni Indians) and can be found, largely unrestored, on the top of El Morro.

You can stay here if you wish, at the monument's nine-site, primitive campground.

El Morro is located just off Highway 53, 43 miles from Grants; (505) 783–4226. Admission is $3.00 per adult, ages seventeen to sixty-one. Youths age sixteen or younger are admitted free; seniors age sixty-two or older are admitted for no additional charge with a lifetime Golden Age Pass, which is available for $10.00. Use of the campground is free, except during summer, when it costs $5.00 per night and is on a first-come, first-served basis; water is available May through October. Daily hours are 9:00 A.M. to 5:00 P.M. for the visitor center; trails close one hour earlier.

For a dose of current culture after your visit to ancient El Morro, head east on Highway 53, 1 mile from the monument turnoff to the **Old School Gallery,** housed in the historic El Morro School building. The gallery contains exceptional work by local artists and also hosts receptions, dances, and various art classes and ongoing events such as drumming, qi gong, yoga, and tai chi. Gallery hours are 11:00 A.M. to 5:00 P.M., Thursday through Sunday; (505) 783–4710; www.elmorroarts.org.

San Juan County

Similar to Gallup's role in McKinley County, Farmington serves as the major trading center in San Juan County for the Navajo Nation just west of the city. Though Farmington is near the center of the vast, dry Four Corners region (more about this later), the city is a virtual oasis and a fisherman's paradise with its three rivers flowing around town—the San Juan, the Animas, and the La Plata. San Juan County is also a great place to get in touch with New Mexico's past by visiting its three significant Anasazi ruins sites.

Chaco Culture National Historical Park (**Chaco Canyon,** for short) contains the finest example of Anasazi pueblo ruins in New Mexico. It may be the single most remote tourist attraction in the state, yet people from all over the world find it every year.

Chaco Canyon emerged as the center of Anasazi life in the early tenth century. (The Navajo word *Anasazi,* meaning "enemies of our ancestors," is the name scientists gave to prehistoric farming peoples of the Four Corners region. They are the ancestors of the present-day Pueblo Indians of New Mexico.) Partly because primitive roads connected Chaco Canyon with outlying Anasazi communities, archaeologists believe Chaco was the "capital" of the Anasazi world. In many ways—in their architecture, community life, and social organization—the Anasazi of Chaco Canyon were far more advanced than any other of the Anasazi peoples of the region.

newmexicotrivia

Contrary to widespread belief, the word Anasazi doesn't mean "the ancient ones," but rather it comes from the Navajo language and means "enemies of our ancestors."

Though Chaco Canyon has been intensely studied for more than a hundred years and scholars theorize about the people who once lived here, many mysteries remain. One of the most intriguing aspects of Chacoan life is the possible connection with the great civilizations of Mexico, such as the ancient Toltecs. Feathers of macaws and other parrots, copper bells, and seashells, all unknown in this area but common in parts of Mexico, have been found in Chaco Canyon. There are also fascinating connections between architecture and astronomy in the remains of the pueblos in the canyon.

The Anasazis' belief that Chaco Canyon was the center of the earth is a powerful one, and the fact that as many as 5,000 people once lived here in a highly civilized society and then mysteriously disappeared is centermost to the lure of the canyon and its ruins. Although rainfall was adequate during the time the Anasazi inhabited Chaco Canyon, persistent droughts are thought to be the reason they finally abandoned the canyon between 1130 and 1180.

To fully experience the park, set aside an entire day for your visit. Otherwise, a stop at the visitor center and a hike around Pueblo Bonito, the largest and most impressive ruin in the canyon, will provide a good overview of the Chaco mystique. Well-marked trails (keyed in a trail guide to selected stops) lead through the maze of chambers.

The park's visitor center has a fine museum and many books on Chaco culture. It's also the only place in the park with water available. The canyon consists of extremely barren, arid land—especially in the summer—so it's smart to bring your own water supply. The small campground ($10 per night) is almost always full; overflow camping is permitted along the roadside for self-contained RVs but not tents.

Although there are two main routes to Chaco Canyon—neither paved—the best approach is to turn off U.S. Highway 550 onto San Juan County Road 7800 at the outpost community of Nageezi, proceed 11 miles to Highway 57, and continue on Highway 57 for 15 miles to the visitor center. These are 26 miles of washboard-type dirt and gravel roads. Though passenger cars are usually adequate, the roads can be impassable during or after substantial rainfall; accordingly, call ahead to check road conditions. Once you get to the federally maintained park, however, the roads are perfectly paved; (505) 786–7014. Admission is $8.00 per vehicle or $4.00 per person for groups and singles. The visitor center is open daily from 8:00 A.M. to 5:00 P.M.

For those who are intrigued by Anasazi ruins but aren't up to a trek to Chaco Canyon, two other sites are closer to Farmington: Aztec Ruins National Monument and Salmon Ruin. Both are easily accessible on paved roads.

The first thing you'll notice about *Aztec Ruins National Monument*—especially if you visited Chaco Canyon first—is the abundance of trees and a nearby river. Despite the name, these ruins had nothing to do with the Aztec Indians of central Mexico. In fact, the Aztecs lived hundreds of years after this Anasazi pueblo was abandoned. Early Anglo settlers named the site Aztec because they mistakenly believed the Mexican Indians had built the pueblos.

The monument's amazing number of ruins concentrated in a small area make things convenient for visitors. The site of these ruins contains the only fully restored great kiva, an especially sacred ceremonial chamber, in North America. A walk through the kiva is definitely the highlight of the visit.

The visitor center of Aztec Ruins is northwest of the city of Aztec (northeast of Farmington), near the junction of U.S. Highway 550 and NM 516; (505) 334–6174. The monument is open daily from 8:00 A.M. to 6:00 P.M. Memorial Day through Labor Day and from 8:00 A.M. to 5:00 P.M. the remainder of the year. Admission is $4.00 per person, with those age fifteen or younger admitted free; Golden Age and Golden Access passes for seniors are accepted.

Salmon Ruin, a Chacoan pueblo village once connected to Chaco Canyon by a prehistoric road, is the other major Anasazi ruin area in San Juan County. Though unique itself and the site of the San Juan Archaeological Research Center and Library, this smaller site, if you're "ruined out," may be the one to skip.

Salmon Ruin is on U.S. Highway 64, 2 miles west of the community of Bloomfield; (505) 632–2013. Hours are from 8:00 A.M. to 5:00 P.M. Monday through Friday and 9:00 A.M. to 5:00 P.M. Saturday and Sunday (winter hours, November through April, on Sunday are noon to 5:00 P.M.), and admission is

$3.00 for adults, $1.00 for children ages six through fifteen, $2.00 for seniors, and free for children age five or younger.

A secret treasure in the mostly featureless landscape of the San Juan Basin, **Angel Peak Recreation Area** is located 12 miles south of Aztec off NM 44. The peak itself is easy to spot from a distance. The rock spire on top of the steep-sided butte resembles a winged angel (if you have a good imagination). The sign marking the road that turns off to the east into the recreation area is not so obvious. Following this wide gravel road for ½ mile will bring you to a scenic vista overlooking Kutz Canyon, a surprise spectacle of red and white painted desert. Continue for another 2 miles and you'll come to a small picnic area and campground from which a trail follows the canyon rim. There is no admission fee. No phone.

newmexicotrivia

Farmington's San Juan County Fair is the oldest continuously operated fair in New Mexico—even older than the New Mexico State Fair held annually in Albuquerque.

Each summer the city of Farmington hosts a historical drama at the **Lions Wilderness Park Amphitheater.** Although times and dates change from year to year, performances usually run from about late June to mid-August. Call the Farmington Convention and Visitors Bureau (505–326–7602 or 800–448–1240) for details.

For an otherworldly experience in northwestern New Mexico, plan a visit to the **Bisti Wilderness,** commonly known as the Bisti Badlands, south of Farmington. The almost 4,000-acre wilderness is a barren landscape of steeply eroded badlands topography, featuring unusual rock spires called "hoodoos." The area's desolate present belies its ancient past as a lush swampland roamed by dinosaurs and other life-forms millions of years ago. Time and the natural elements have etched out a fantasy-world moonscape of strange rock formations and fossils, creating an ever-changing environment.

An easy way to experience the Bisti is to take a leisurely day hike by following the Gateway Wash from the undeveloped parking lot into the heart of the badlands. Because there are no developed trails or signs inhibiting your wilderness experience, take extra care to avoid getting lost. Because this is a primitive wilderness area, there are no services, so plan accordingly and bring lots of drinking water, as this area can get quite hot during summer. The Bisti is a great place not only for hiking but also for photography and primitive camping, especially on full-moon nights.

Besides the natural landscape, you may also find the fossilized remains (isolated teeth and bones) of the various life-forms that once lived here: fish, turtles, lizards, mammals, and dinosaurs. However, federal law prohibits the collection of vertebrate fossils and petrified wood. Any collection interferes with scientific research and eliminates the opportunity for others to view and to photograph these unusual wilderness features. Also, climbing on rock formations is dangerous and prohibited, as it accelerates erosion and destroys the scenic value of the area.

To get to the Bisti Wilderness from Farmington, head south on Highway 371 for about 30 miles and then exit left for 6 miles on a gravel road that will take you past the old Bisti Trading Post to an undeveloped parking area and access to the wilderness. The area can also be approached from Crownpoint, by traveling north on Highway 371 for about 46 miles and following the same gravel road described earlier. Travel on the gravel road is good during dry conditions, but the road can get slippery and rutted during the rainy season, nor-

Traditional Food of New Mexico

Green Chile Stew

Green chile stew is New Mexico's wintertime equivalent to chicken soup for the rest of the country—good for what ails you. Flavorful and satisfying, this dish is made in most homes and available in most restaurants serving New Mexican food. As an alternative, prepare it without meat and add fresh corn—*muy sabroso!*

2 pounds pork or beef, cubed

1 small can tomatoes

3 medium potatoes, peeled and cubed

¼ cup flour

6 cups water

2 tablespoons shortening or corn oil

3 cloves garlic, minced

2 medium onions, chopped

2 cups chopped green chiles (more or less, according to taste)

2 teaspoons salt

1 teaspoon ground cumin

Makes 6–8 servings

1. Dredge the meat in flour. Place the shortening in a heavy skillet and brown meat at medium heat. Place meat in a large stewing pot.
2. Sauté the onions and garlic in the remaining shortening and add to stewing pot.
3. Add all remaining ingredients to stewing pot and simmer at low heat for 1 hour. Serve hot with plenty of warm flour tortillas.

mally in spring and late summer. There's no phone, but for more information, you may contact the Farmington Convention and Visitors Bureau at (505) 326–7602 or (800) 448–1240.

If you've been inspired by the ancient Anasazi cliff dwellings at nearby Mesa Verde National Monument in southwestern Colorado, are in excellent physical condition, and are looking for adventure, then look no further than **Kokopelli's Cave Bed & Breakfast** north of Farmington—the only such establishment I know of that requires guests to sign a waiver of liability for potential accidents.

The brainchild of Farmington geologist Bruce Black, Kokopelli's Cave was blasted out of a 65-million-year-old sandstone formation 280 feet above La Plata River, but unlike the ancient cliff dwellings of the Southwest, this cave is actually 70 feet below the surface of the cliff, accessible by a series of trails, paths, and steps. If you're willing and able to make the climb, you'll be rewarded by views of four states and several mountain ranges. And, despite its remoteness and accessibility challenges, Kokopelli's is pure luxury once you actually make it down into the cave, boasting all the comforts of home plus a cascading "waterfall" shower and a flagstone hot tub.

In lieu of being served breakfast, you'll find the refrigerator and cabinets well stocked with breakfast fixings, including fresh fruit. And remember, pack light, because there are no elevators! Because even getting to the cave's trailhead is complicated, guests are asked to meet their hosts at their home in Farmington to be escorted out to the site. This way you won't get lost, and you'll also get a personal rundown on the systems in the cave, so you'll know how to work them; (505) 325–7855; www.bbonline.com/nm/kokopelli/. Rates are $220 for one or two people; $260 for three or four people, with an additional $50 per individual over four persons, and they may vary seasonally.

The **Hogback Trading Post**, on the edge of the Navajo Reservation, is the place to purchase authentic Navajo arts and crafts in San Juan County. Established in 1871, the Hogback is the oldest trading post—on or off the reservation—serving the Navajos. (The better-known Hubbell Trading Post at Monument Valley wasn't established until 1876.) The Hogback is now run by Tom Wheeler, the great-grandson of the trading post's founder, Joseph Wheeler. The trading post contains almost 10,000 feet of display space on two levels and specializes in fine Navajo-woven rugs. It's located 15 miles west of Farmington on U.S. Highway 64 in the community of Waterflow. The Hogback is open Monday through Saturday, 8:00 A.M. to 5:00 P.M.; (505) 598–5154.

Another interesting trading post nearby is **Big Rock Trading Post**, also in Waterflow, 12 miles west of Farmington on Highway 64. You'll likely first notice Big Rock by seeing its sign on a large, white propane tank out front. Run by father and son Chuck and Charlie Dickens, the Big Rock serves not only as a trading post and a pawnshop (filled with authentic Native American jewelry for sale) but also as something of an Old West cowboy and Indian museum—complete with a saddle collection along with other southwestern artifacts. Big Rock is open Monday through Friday from 8:00 A.M. to 5:30 P.M. and Saturday from 9:00 A.M. to 5:30 P.M.; (505) 598–5184.

One of the most memorable places to visit, purely for its I-stood-on-the-spot value, is the **Four Corners Monument,** a Navajo Nation tribal park, northwest of Farmington. The absolute barrenness of the area is remarkable. But you can stand on the spot—the only such spot in the United States—where you will truly be in four states at once: New Mexico, Arizona, Utah, and Colorado. It's amazing how far people will travel out of their way to visit a spot that would otherwise hold no appeal whatsoever. Still, it is a kick.

To get to Four Corners Monument, take U.S. Highway 64 west of Farmington until it meets with U.S. Highway 160 at Teec Nos Pos. (You're now in Arizona.) Then take U.S. Highway 160 north until it meets with Highway 597. (You're back in New Mexico.) Go left on Highway 597 to the monument. It's always open. Admission is $2.50 per person.

On the way to Four Corners Monument from Farmington—along Highway 64, west of the largest Navajo Nation town of **Shiprock**—you'll pass within viewing distance of one of the most majestic and mysterious rock formations in New Mexico: Shiprock. The 1,700-foot peak gets its name from its shape, which, at a distance, resembles a two-masted ship sailing on a sea of desert. Though Shiprock changes its appearance at different times of the day, it's said that it looks most like a ship during a midsummer sunset, occasionally appearing to shimmer and drift on an imaginary ocean. Navajos refer to the immense formation as *Tse Bi dahi,* which means "The Rock with Wings," and several of their folk myths contain references to it. (Some say that Shiprock switches positions across the horizon as you drive by it.)

Back to civilization, a leisurely walking tour of the Aztec Historic District in downtown Aztec offers a great change of pace. Centering on the **Aztec Museum,** more than seventy-five business and residential buildings, including shops and restaurants, are listed on the National Register of Historic Places. The museum houses a fine collection of early pioneer Americana, plus an old wooden oil drilling rig—a tribute to the lucrative oil-and-gas industry in San Juan County. The museum is at 125 North Main Avenue, (505) 334–9829. Summer hours are 9:00 A.M. to 5:00 P.M. Monday through Saturday; winter hours are 10:00 A.M. to 4:00 P.M. Monday through Saturday. Admission is $2.00 for adults and $1.00 for children age eleven or younger.

Where to Stay in Northwestern New Mexico

MCKINLEY COUNTY

El Rancho Hotel,
1000 East 66 Avenue,
Gallup,
(505) 863–9311

Holiday Inn,
2915 West Highway 66,
Gallup,
(505) 722–2201

The Inn at Halona,
23B Pia Mesa Road,
Zuni Pueblo,
(505) 782–4547/
(800) 752–3278

CIBOLA COUNTY

Zuni Mountain Lodge,
40 Perch Drive,
Thoreau,
(505) 862–7616

Holiday Inn Express,
1496 East Santa Fe Avenue,
Grants,
(505) 285–4676

**Best Western Inn
and Suites,**
1501 East Santa Fe Avenue,
Grants,
(505) 287–7901

SAN JUAN COUNTY

**Farmington Courtyard
by Marriott,**
560 Scott Avenue,
Farmington,
(505) 325–5111

Best Western Inn & Suites,
700 Scott Avenue,
Farmington,
(505) 327–5221/
(800) 600–5221

Holiday Inn of Farmington,
600 East Broadway,
Farmington,
(505) 327–9811

**Silver River Adobe Inn
Bed & Breakfast,**
3151 West Main,
Farmington,
(505) 325–8219/
(800) 382–9251

Stepback Inn,
103 West Aztec Avenue,
Aztec,
(505) 334–1200

Where to Eat in Northwestern New Mexico

MCKINLEY COUNTY

El Rancho,
1003 East Highway 66,
Gallup,
(505) 863–9311.
Inexpensive to moderate.
Fare: Traditional New
Mexican.

Ranch Kitchen,
3001 West Highway 66,
Gallup,
(505) 722–2537.
Inexpensive to moderate.
Fare: Steaks, barbecue.

Roadrunner Cafe,
3014 East Highway 66,
Gallup,
(505) 722–7309.
Inexpensive. Fare: American,
New Mexican.

Earl's Family Restaurant,
1400 East Highway 66,
Gallup,
(505) 863–4201.
Inexpensive to moderate.
Fare: New Mexican and
American.

CIBOLA COUNTY

El Ranchero Cafe,
613 West Highway 66,
Milan,
(505) 876–1032.
Inexpensive to moderate.
Fare: New Mexican.

Monte Carlo Restaurant,
721 West Santa Fe,
Grants,
(505) 287–9250.
Inexpensive to moderate.
Fare: New Mexican.

Uranium Cafe,
519 West Santa Fe Avenue,
Grants,
(505) 287–7540.
Inexpensive. Fare: American.

Mission at Riverwalk,
422 West Santa Fe Avenue,
Grants,
(505) 285–4632.
Moderate. Fare: Mexican.

SAN JUAN COUNTY

**La Fiesta Grande
Restaurant,**
1916 East Main SE,
Farmington,
(505) 326–6476.
Inexpensive to moderate.
Fare: New Mexican.

Los Hermanitos Restaurant,
3501 East Main,
Farmington,
(505) 326–5664.
Inexpensive to moderate.
Fare: New Mexican.

Riverwalk Patio and Grille,
700 Scott Avenue,
Farmington,
(505) 327–5221.
Inexpensive to moderate.
Fare: Eclectic American.

Spare Rib BBQ Company,
1700 East Main Street,
Farmington,
(505) 325–4800.
Inexpensive to moderate.
Fare: Barbecue.

Rocky Mountain Rib Company,
525 East Broadway,
Farmington,
(505) 327–7422.
Inexpensive to moderate.
Fare: Barbecue.

Three Rivers Eatery and Brew House,
101 East Main Street,
Farmington,
(505) 324–2187.
Inexpensive. Fare: Classic pub cuisine in a historic atmosphere.

SELECTED CHAMBERS OF COMMERCE/ VISITOR BUREAUS IN NORTHWESTERN NEW MEXICO

Aztec Chamber of Commerce,
110 North Ash,
Aztec, 87410;
(505) 334–9551/(888) 838–9551;
Web site: www.aztecnm.com

Farmington Convention and Visitors Bureau,
203 West Main, Suite 401,
Farmington, 87401;
(505) 326–7602/(800) 448–1240;
Web site: www.farmingtonnm.org

Gallup Convention & Visitors Bureau,
P.O. Box 600,
Gallup, 87305;
(505) 863–3841/(800) 242–4282;
Web site: www.gallupnm.org

Grants/Cibola County Chamber of Commerce,
P.O. Box 297,
Grants, 87020;
(505) 287–4802/(800) 748–2142;
Web site: www.grants.org

North Central New Mexico

North central New Mexico is a land of Indian pueblos, forested mountains, hidden hot springs, and magnificent rock formations. The region's beauty so inspired artist Georgia O'Keeffe that she made her home here. In contrast, this region also witnessed the production of the world's first atom bomb.

You'll detect a strong tradition of Hispanic culture and pride in north central New Mexico. The first Spanish colony in the territory was established here, and some of the state's oldest Hispanic communities continue to thrive in this region. The Hispanic influence lives on in the old Catholic churches, the centuries-old adobe homes, and the high regard for family and quiet respect for cultural traditions.

As you set out to explore the intrigue of north central New Mexico, keep in mind that once the sun goes down—even during the summer—it's very cool.

Rio Arriba County

Although situated in one of the most economically depressed areas of the state, Rio Arriba County offers the intrepid traveler a host of adventures. As a bridge between the often stark landscape of the Four Corners region to its west and the forested,

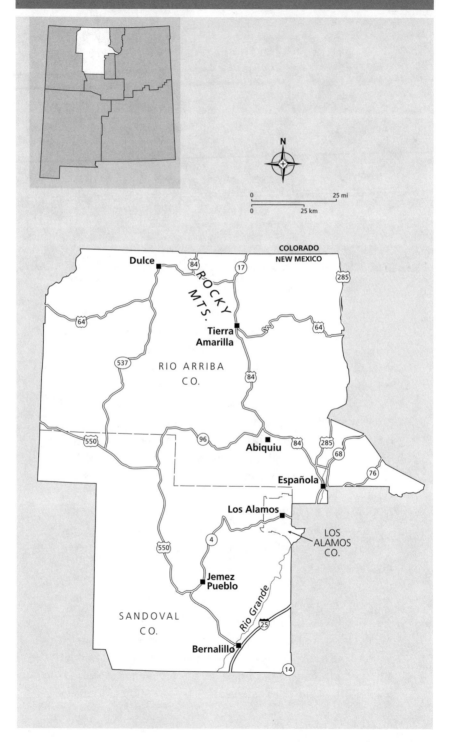

mountainous region to its east, Rio Arriba County is certainly a blending of the two.

In southern Rio Arriba County you'll find the city of **Española** (partly located in Santa Fe County). Lying near the site of the first Spanish settlement in New Mexico, designated San Juan de los Caballeros in 1598 by Spanish explorer Don Juan de Oñate, Española is a good place to fuel up and start exploring the county.

newmexicotrivia

The first Spanish colony in what is now New Mexico was established near San Juan Pueblo, north of present-day Española, in 1598.

Just outside Española lies **Santa Clara Pueblo.** The pueblo itself, like most of New Mexico's Rio Grande–area pueblos, is similar to a small rural town and is centered on a mission church and plaza area. Santa Clara is famous for its solid-black pottery, which is prized by collectors. The neatly maintained pueblo is home to many potters and several small galleries. **Merrock Galeria** on the plaza features the work of Paul Speckled Rock. The multitalented artist channeled his creative energy into other art forms, such as painting, lithography, and sculpture, before venturing into his pueblo's traditional art form in 1983. Although a relative newcomer, Paul has amassed many awards for his works in clay.

FAVORITE ATTRACTIONS/EVENTS IN NORTH CENTRAL NEW MEXICO

Spence Hot Springs,
Jemez Springs
No phone

El Santuario de Chimayó,
Chimayó
(505) 351–4889

Puyé Cliff Dwellings,
Rio Arriba County
(505) 753–7326

Dixon Apple Farm,
Northern Sandoval County
(505) 465–2976

Bandelier National Monument,
Northern Sandoval County
(505) 672–0343

Cumbres & Toltec Scenic Railroad,
Chama
(505) 756–2151

Sandia Man Cave,
near Placitas
No phone

New Mexico Wine Festival,
Labor Day weekend,
Bernalillo
(505) 867–3311

From Española take Highway 30 south (on the west side of the Rio Grande) 1¼ miles. The well-marked pueblo entrance is on the left; (505) 753–7326.

Also on the Santa Clara Reservation but 10 miles west of the pueblo you'll find the *Puyé Cliff Dwellings,* in the Santa Clara Canyon Recreational Area. The drive into the canyon is incredibly scenic as you slowly descend among stands of evergreens into the lush, parklike canyon. Though fishing and camping are allowed, for a fee, the highlight is Puyé, which means "pueblo ruin where the rabbits assemble" in Tewa, the native Santa Clara Indian language.

As a registered National Historic Landmark, the dwellings offer adventure to the Southwestern history buff who likes a good hike. The earlier dwellings here were caves hollowed in the cliffs; later, adobe structures were built along the slopes and top of the mesa. The Anasazi Indians first settled in the Puyé area in the twelfth century and finally abandoned the area around 1580, probably because of continuing drought.

newmexicotrivia

The community of Española is known as the "low-rider capital of New Mexico" because of its preponderance of the specially equipped cars.

You can explore the dwellings on two different walking tours. The cliff trail begins at the visitor center and leads up semisteep trails and ladders, going past many of the ancient dwellings built into the cliffs. Stairways link the two levels of cliff dwellings to the mesa top and its large "Community House." If you prefer a less strenuous course, take the short drive to the mesa-top ruins. Here you can view the 740-room pueblo ruin and its restored ceremonial chamber. Bring a picnic to enjoy the incredible view from this vantage point.

Like exploring many ruins in New Mexico, visiting Puyé can be physically taxing—wear good nonslip shoes or sneakers. Puyé Cliff Dwellings are located off Highway 602 via Highway 30 from Española; (505) 753–7326. Fees are the same for guided or self-guided tours: adults, $5.00; children (ages seven to fourteen) and seniors, $4.00. Open daily during summer, 8:00 A.M. to 7:00 P.M.; call ahead for hours the remainder of the year.

While northern New Mexico claims several very good wineries, *La Chiripada Winery* is particularly worth seeking out. Situated among the apple orchards in the small community of Dixon, La Chiripada's tasting room is housed in a whitewashed adobe surrounded by colorful gardens and vineyards. Besides its selection of wines with their Mimbres Indian design labels, the tasting room also sells contemporary pottery. Brothers Michael and Patrick Johnson planted their ten acres of grapes in 1977 and opened the winery on the banks of the Rio Embudo four years later. La Chiripada (meaning "A Stroke

Traditional Food of New Mexico

Simply Salsa

Why pay for expensive salsas when you can whip up a batch of your own in mere minutes at a fraction of the cost? The following recipe comes from Joseph Aguirre, who wouldn't dream of ever buying the bottled stuff.

1 large can tomatoes (or one pound fresh tomatoes*)

½ onion, quartered

3 fresh jalepeño peppers, quartered (or 3 dried cayenne chiles, broken up)

2 cloves garlic, quartered

½ to 1 teaspoon salt (to taste)

Freshly ground black pepper (to taste)

1 tablespoon fresh cilantro (optional)

Put all ingredients in a blender and pulse until desired consistency, but not too smooth. Serve with tostadas or corn tortilla chips. Makes about 2–3 cups salsa.
*Roasting or grilling the fresh tomatoes first adds a nice smoky flavor.

of Luck") gets half its grapes from its own vineyards and the remainder from other New Mexico growers.

La Chiripada is on Highway 75 in Dixon; (505) 579–4437 or (800) 528–7801; www.lachiripada.com. Tasting-room hours are 10:00 A.M. to 5:00 P.M. Monday through Saturday and noon to 5:00 P.M. Sunday. The winery also has a tasting room off the plaza in Taos that is open from 11:00 A.M. to 6:00 P.M. Monday through Saturday and noon to 6:00 P.M. Sunday; (505) 751–1311.

Embudo Station, a historic, 1880s narrow-gauge railroad station between Santa Fe and Taos, is now a casual restaurant on the banks of the Rio Grande. Embudo Station has an outdoor area for patio dining, as well as a country smokehouse shop featuring trout, cheese, and various meats. The restaurant serves barbecued ribs and brisket, ham, turkey, trout, and catfish. Even if you're not hungry, Embudo Station is a pleasant place to enjoy an appetizer and a beer or a glass of La Chiripada wine while sitting outdoors under the huge cottonwoods. The restaurant now boasts its own microbrewery, serving up various flavored ales, including green chile and red chile. Embudo Station also offers float trips on the Rio Grande. In contrast to the white-water experience farther north near Taos, the water is much calmer on this stretch. In addition, Embudo Station has a guest cabin available for $100 to $150 a night for up to four guests.

The restaurant and float headquarters are located on Highway 68 about 17 miles north of Española; (505) 852–4707. Hours are noon to 9:00 P.M. Tuesday through Sunday, April through October. The restaurant closes November through March. At press time, Embudo Station was for sale by the owners, so make sure to call before you go.

Just inside Rio Arriba County near its border with Santa Fe County, the village of **Chimayó** lies on the **High Road to Taos,** that romantic-sounding name for the scenic though less than direct path connecting Santa Fe to Taos. The old Spanish community of Chimayó is the most interesting stop on the High Road and boasts several "must sees."

The first place to stop is **El Santuario de Chimayó,** known as "Little Lourdes" because of its reputation of miraculous healing and cures similar to those of the famous site in France. Built in 1816, the adobe chapel is widely known as the destination of an annual Holy Week pilgrimage during which thousands walk from all over New Mexico, neighboring states, and even Mexico. Nonetheless, people visit the *santuario* all year long.

The chapel's intricately carved and colorful altar spotlights a 6-foot crucifix, while scores of votive candles maintain a glow nearby. Two side rooms are attached to the chapel. The larger space is devoted to holding the various offerings made over the years, such as small statues, paintings, personal messages of thanks, and photographs. The walls of this room are also lined with the crutches of those who have been cured at Chimayó. The smaller chamber shelters the hole in the floor that contains the sacred, healing dirt (visitors are welcome to take small amounts with them).

Chimayó is accessible from Highway 285 north of Santa Fe via Highway 503 and then Highway 520. The santuario is located on the right, just as you enter the village of Chimayó on Highway 520; (505) 351–4889 (parish office). Services are still held in El Santuario de Chimayó, with an 11:00 A.M. mass on weekdays, noon on Sundays, and it's open to the public daily from 9:00 A.M. to 4:00 P.M. October through April, until 5:00 P.M. May through September.

Less than ½ mile farther on Highway 520, you'll see the **Restaurante Rancho de Chimayó** on your right and the **Hacienda Rancho de Chimayó** (a bed-and-breakfast inn) on your left. If you want a romantic hideaway, stay at the hacienda. If you're hungry, visit the restaurant—and even if you're not hungry, go anyway to enjoy the surroundings.

The restaurant is the former home of Hermenegildo and Trinidad Jaramillo and has been open since 1965. The hundred-year-old adobe provides an intimate dining experience in several small rooms inside and a delightful openness on the terraced patios outside. During spring and summer, colorful flowers and warm temperatures make outside dining the obvious choice. Native New Mexican foods are prepared according to traditional family recipes that stress locally grown products, including the peerless Chimayó red chile. The restaurant has a full bar and carries many Mexican beers, but the house specialty is the potent Chimayó Cocktail. A waitress revealed the recipe as tequila, apple juice, triple sec, creme de cassis, and a dash of lime. The proportions are a secret, but the apple-juice ice cubes and apple-slice garnish make it a perfect before-dinner drink.

The restaurant is open daily from 11:30 A.M. to 9:00 P.M. and for breakfast on weekends from 8:30 to 10:30 A.M., with the exception of Mondays during winter (December through April), when it is closed; (505) 351–4444; www.ran chochimayo.com. (*NOTE:* The restaurant closes for one week during either the first or second week in January; call ahead.)

The family home of Epifanio and Adelaida Jaramillo became Hacienda Rancho de Chimayó in 1984, after the traditional adobe had been renovated into seven guest rooms filled with turn-of-the-twentieth-century antiques. Each room has a private bath and sitting area and opens onto an enclosed courtyard. Every morning, your hosts serve a continental breakfast featuring pastries, fruit, fresh-squeezed orange juice, and coffee or tea. Room rates range from $69 to $105; (505) 351–2222; www.ranchochimayo.com.

Continuing on Highway 520 to its junction with Highway 76, you'll come across **Ortega's Weaving Shop** (505–351–4215) and **Galeria Ortega** (505–351–2288; www.ortegasdechimayo.com). No matter what time of year you visit, these two neighboring stores are the perfect places to do your Christmas shopping. Eight generations of masterful weaving by the Ortega family are evident in the

El Santuario de Chimayó

Cattle Mutilations and UFOs

Reports of mysterious cattle mutilations in northern New Mexico have cropped up every few years since the 1960s, most recently during 1996. The latest report came from two Chimayó ranchers who discovered the mutilated carcass of one of their bulls. As with previous slayings, the bull's heart was removed through a hole cut in its chest, and its sexual organs, intestines, and tongue also were removed. No blood was detected on the wounds, on the carcass, or on the surrounding grass—and there were no tire tracks or unusual markings around the remains.

Although there has never been conclusive evidence, or consensus, regarding the purpose or the cause of the slayings, several theories exist. The FBI says the mutilations are the result of predators and scavengers; New Mexico's livestock board says they're possibly caused by secret Satanic groups, whereas others blame organ-harvesting UFOs, and still others blame chupacabras, or goat-suckers, the mythological creatures of Mexican lore.

The large number of UFO-theory proponents, who say northern New Mexico ranks with Nevada's top-secret Area 51 as one of the country's UFO hot spots, believe that the cattle are taken aboard the alien crafts to be mutilated. The obvious question then becomes, "Why cattle?" UFO theorists believe the answer may lie in the bovine's blood. It's supposedly so similar to that of humans that it is regularly used in medical laboratories to create human blood plasma. It's an indication, theorists say, that the aliens may be studying the cattle to find out more about humans.

fine wool rugs, coats, and other outerwear for sale at the weaving shop. You can even watch weavers hand-loom rugs in a room just off the sales area. In addition, the shop has a great selection of Santa Clara Pueblo pottery and books on the Southwest. It's also the place to stock up on dried Chimayó red chile.

Galeria Ortega markets contemporary New Mexican art forms. Wood carvings are featured, including a variety of *bultos,* or representations of saints crafted out of pine or cottonwood limbs. Made by *santeros,* these carvings are uniquely local in appearance. There's also a fine collection of pottery, hand-painted shirts, and handcrafted Nambé ware (bowls, platters, candleholders, etc., that are made from a secret, shiny alloy—named after Nambé Pueblo).

Ortega's Weaving Shop and Galeria Ortega are both open Monday through Saturday, 8:30 A.M. to 5:30 P.M. during daylight saving time and 9:00 A.M. to 5:00 P.M. the rest of the year; both are open Sunday, 11:00 A.M. to 5:00 P.M. during daylight saving time. They both close on Sunday, however, during standard time.

Continuing along the High Road to Taos, you'll discover a series of pastoral villages dating from the eighteenth century, where time-honored traditions live on. Among them are Cordova, known for its hand-carved figures of saints, and Las Trampas, with its photogenic old mission church. My favorite, **Truchas,** is set against the boundary of the vast, mountainous Pecos Wilderness at an elevation of 8,000 feet. Several of the vintage adobe buildings were constructed in the 1750s. Cattle graze by the side of the road, and many residents live self-sufficiently, making their own clothes, shopping at the village's only store, chopping their own firewood for heat in the winter, and relying on local *curanderas* (healers), who pick curative herbs in the surrounding meadows and forests. Traditional handcrafted items are displayed at Los Siete Craft Store, a cooperative on the way into town where you can often see weavers at work on their looms.

Until recently, the people of Truchas did not welcome outsiders, but that has changed with an influx of artists and craftspeople relocating from Santa Fe. A half-dozen galleries and thirty or more working studios line the road through town, and there's even a bed-and-breakfast—**Rancho Arriba,** a stylish adobe residence built around a Spanish colonial–style courtyard. The interior features viga ceilings, handmade furnishings, and a kiva fireplace. Three guest rooms have shared baths, and one has a private bath. Room rates of $50 to $90 include a full breakfast cooked on a woodstove with eggs from the chickens that live on the premises. P.O. Box 338, Truchas, NM 87578; (505) 689–2374.

The village of **Abiquiu** is known for its most famous resident, artist Georgia O'Keeffe, and for the stunning landscape that inspired her, which she referred to as the Faraway. Although O'Keeffe died in 1986 at the age of ninety-eight, for years people have been coming from all over to look at the massive adobe walls that guard her home. Now, if they plan their trip carefully, they'll actually be able to take a look inside. After years of being off-limits to the public, the **Georgia O'Keeffe Home** is open to visitors, though on a very limited basis. Only scheduled, guided tours are allowed, and you may even need to reserve your space months in advance.

To the extent possible, the house remains as it was left by O'Keeffe in 1984, when she moved from Abiquiu to Santa Fe prior to her death. After much speculation about the future of her home (some of which had the home slated to become a state museum), the Georgia O'Keeffe Foundation was formed to preserve not only the artist's home but her legacy as well. As foundation president Elizabeth Glassman has said, "Few places exist in America where one can see how an artist lived and worked. To experience the space created by O'Keeffe and to see the places she so often painted allow the visitor a glimpse of the artist."

O'Keeffe purchased the property—parts of which date back to the early eighteenth century—from the Catholic church in 1945. After the death of her husband, Alfred Stieglitz, in 1946, O'Keeffe spent the next three years having the house rebuilt and renovated. By 1949 the property was ready, and O'Keeffe took up full-time residence in New Mexico. Many of her best-known works were inspired by the Abiquiu house and its views, including its patio and black door, the cottonwood trees along the Chama River, and the road to Santa Fe. Once you experience the otherworldly beauty of the Abiquiu landscape, you'll see why this area enchanted O'Keeffe and others seeking artistic and spiritual awakenings.

Visitors are received on a by-appointment-only basis in small groups for tours of the property and house. Tours are April through November on Tuesday, Thursday, and Saturday. Requested donation per person is $22. To schedule a tour, call the foundation office at (505) 685–4539. Reservations should be made far in advance for these popular tours.

Just down the hill from O'Keeffe's home, you'll find the **Tin Moon Gallery and Studio.** Opened in 1998 by artist Ans Zoutenbier, the Tin Moon features contemporary art. Permanently on show are Zoutenbier's contemporary tin designs, which step away from traditional New Mexican tinwork even though the same techniques are applied. The gallery also displays the following variety of works: jewelry, paintings, photography, pottery, weavings, and handmade books and notecards. In addition, the Tin Moon provides a place for local as well as national and international artists.

The Tin Moon is located on Highway 84 in Abiquiu across from Bode's General Merchandise; (505) 685–4829. Hours are 10:00 A.M. to 5:00 P.M. Monday through Saturday in summer and Tuesday through Saturday in winter; closed during the month of February.

There's something about the awe-inspiring landscape around Abiquiu that's downright spiritual and seems to attract a global religious presence. Not only will you find the Christ in the Desert Monastery and the Presbyterian-church-owned Ghost Ranch in this area, but it's also home to the hauntingly beautiful **Dar al-Islam Mosque.**

The mosque was built in the early 1980s to serve the spiritual needs of the large Muslim population of the area. The complex, which includes a 17,000-square-foot school and library as well as a beautiful courtyard garden, is open to visitors. After visiting the mosque, continue your visit with a hike around Plaza Blanca, a beautiful white rock canyon on the grounds of Dar al-Islam.

To get to Dar al-Islam, turn right on Highway 155, ½ mile north of Abiquiu. Go about 2¼ miles; the entrance will be on your left. When the road makes a Y, stay left; (505) 685–4515.

Abiquiu has been occupied by American Indians for almost a thousand years, and many of the residents today are descendants of indigenous people. You can see the little-known archaeological site of **Poshuouinge** by hiking a steep, rocky ½-mile trail to a vista point overlooking the ruins. The ancient settlement was among the largest in the region, with 700 ground-floor rooms and two large plazas, with a ceremonial kiva in the larger one. Only stone foundations mark the spot today. The inconspicuous trailhead is 2½ miles south of Abiquiu on the west side of Highway 84.

North of Abiquiu off U.S. Highway 84, you'll find the **Ghost Ranch Conference Center** (505–685–4333 or 877–804–4678; www.ghostranch.org), which contains two fine museums: the **Florence Hawley Ellis Museum of Anthropology** and the **Ruth Hall Museum of Paleontology.** The entire 21,000 acres that constitute what used to be the working Ghost Ranch were donated to the Presbyterian Church (U.S.A.) in 1955. (The ranch got its name from the *brujas,* or witches, that were said to haunt the canyons on the ranch.) The conference center serves as a national adult study center and as a steward of the northern New Mexico environment. The anthropology museum centers on past and present peoples who lived within a 60-mile radius of the ranch over a span of 12,000 years, whereas the paleontology museum's focus is fossils, specifically the study of *Coelophysis,* a type of dinosaur whose mass burial site was discovered here in 1947.

Hours for both museums are Tuesday through Saturday, 9:00 A.M. to noon and 1:00 to 5:00 P.M. From Memorial Day through Labor Day, both museums are also open on Sunday from 1:00 to 5:00 P.M. The museums are closed during December. Suggested donation for both museums is $2.00 for adults and $1.00 for children age twelve or younger and seniors. Also note that there are great hiking opportunities at Ghost Ranch; free trail maps are available at the conference center.

Farther north, about 8 miles north of the turnoff to Abiquiu Lake on Highway 84, you'll see a sign for **Echo Amphitheater.** No, it's not New Mexico's answer to Colorado's famed Red Rocks performance venue, but it looks as though it could be. Rather, Echo Amphitheater is a natural formation carved into a towering sandstone cliff by eons of wind and rain. Its base is accented by boulders that appear frozen in midtumble and by piñon trees and other evergreens. It's a great place to view some of the grandeur of the region—especially the way the light plays off the majestic sandstone cliff around sunset. Camping is allowed for a fee.

The first thing you'll notice after arriving at **Monastery of Christ in the Desert** is the quiet. Getting there is another story. The monastery lies in an isolated but dramatically beautiful canyon along the Chama River, about 27 miles north of Abiquiu, and is surrounded by miles of national forest land. Though the monastery was founded in June 1964 by three monks from New York, the present monastic community began arriving in 1974, seeking the Benedictine life of prayer, reading, studying, and manual labor. If inspiration comes with solitude, then this is the place to get it. Because the monks believe they can best continue the tradition of offering hospitality in the desert by giving their guests an opportunity to share in their way of life, limited accommodations are offered to travelers.

If you're planning an overnight stay, remember that this is not the place to bring a spouse, the kids, or even a friend. It's a place to experience alone. For overnight guests, vegetarian meals are served, and library hours are maintained. The serenity of the Chama Canyon wilderness is perfect for escaping daily stresses, meditating, hiking, and just getting back in touch with yourself.

You don't have to stay overnight to experience Christ in the Desert, though. The impressive, contemporary pueblo revival-style chapel and a gift shop are open to nonovernight visitors, whereas other buildings and the remainder of the grounds are private. The gift shop is filled with books, cards, and other items of a religious nature. (*NOTE:* Wearing short pants is unacceptable, and dogs are not welcome.)

The monastery is located off U.S. Highway 84, some 75 miles northwest of Santa Fe. To get there, turn left (north) about ½ mile past Ghost Ranch Living Museum at Forest Service Road Marker 151. Most of the 13-mile drive is not paved but is usually passable in passenger cars; however, during winter and spring a four-wheel-drive vehicle may be needed. Chapel and gift shop hours are 10:00 A.M. to 5:00 P.M. Monday through Saturday; no phone; fax (419) 831–9113; www.christdesert.com. Though there is no fixed fee to stay in the guest house, a $50 to $75 donation (depending on room type) per person per day is expected to cover monastery expenses. However, the brothers are serious when they

STATE PARKS IN NORTH CENTRAL NEW MEXICO (INCLUDING SANTA FE COUNTY)
On the Web: www.emnrd.state.nm.us/nmparks/

Coyote Creek/Morphy Lake State Park,
near Mora, (505) 387–2328

El Vado Lake Lake State Park,
14 miles southwest of Tierra Amarilla,
(505) 588–7247

Fenton Lake Lake State Park,
33 miles northwest of San Ysidro (near Jemez Springs),
(505) 829–3630

Heron Lake Lake State Park,
11 miles west of Tierra Amarilla,
(505) 588–7470

Hyde Memorial Lake State Park,
12 miles northeast of Santa Fe,
(505) 983–7175

advise you to pay only what you can afford. For a summer or fall stay in the guest house, reservations two or three months in advance may be necessary. Note that several of the buildings, including the chapel, have been undergoing extensive renovations. Check their Web site for the latest updates from the abbot.

Continuing north on U.S. Highway 84 brings you to Tierra Amarilla ("Yellow Earth"), the county seat of Rio Arriba County and the place named for the peculiar dirt found in the area. The adjacent village of Los Ojos offers visitors a glimpse at the rich wool-raising and weaving tradition of the area in the form of the *Tierra Wools* store. The shop showcases hand-spun and -dyed yarn, along with handwoven rugs, pillows, jackets, and other items. You'll usually find artisans at work in the back "loom room"—you're welcome to watch. The walls of the store are lined with thousands of multicolored skeins of yarn and rugs that set off the natural beauty of the timeworn wood-planked floors. The Tierra Wools cooperative is a program of Ganados del Valle ("Livestock Growers of the Valley"), whose goal is to ensure that weaving, wool growing, and sheepherding continue as a way of life in this remote region of New Mexico.

newmexicotrivia

Eighty-five percent of New Mexico is more than 4,000 feet in elevation.

The Tierra Wools shop is on the main street of the tiny community of Los Ojos, just west of U.S. Highway 84, north of Tierra Amarilla; (505) 588–7231 or (888) 709–0979. From June through October, the shop is open Monday through Saturday from 9:00 A.M. to 6:00 P.M. and Sunday from 11:00 A.M. to 4:00 P.M.; the rest of the year it's open Monday through Saturday from 10:00 A.M. to 5:00 P.M.

Your trek up U.S. Highway 84 ends in *Chama,* less than 10 miles from the Colorado border. Chama is a popular spot for sports enthusiasts and thus affords many choices of rustic, low-cost lodging. The area offers big-game hunting, fishing in the Chama River and nearby Heron and El Vado reservoirs, and some of the West's best and most consistent cross-country skiing in winter. The town's also a popular place for the nonsporting set because it's the New Mexican home of the *Cumbres & Toltec Scenic Railroad,* North America's longest and highest narrow-gauge steam railroad. The railroad, which connects Chama with Antonito, Colorado, is on the National Historic Register and is owned by both New Mexico and Colorado.

The railroad offers one-way and round-trip excursions (to a midway point and back from either Chama or Antonito) from late spring through midfall. The train has fully enclosed and semienclosed cars, all of which provide for unobstructed viewing in comfort during your journey through groves of pine and aspen, striking rock formations, and other breathtaking views. Consider a late

Cumbres & Toltec Scenic Railroad

September trip so as to miss the crowds and catch the aspens at their golden best. Also note that all the trips take the better part of a day (10:30 A.M. to 4:30 P.M., 10:00 A.M. to 5:00 P.M., etc.), and although summer is usually warm and pleasant, it's best to be prepared for cooler weather by wearing long pants and bringing a light jacket.

The 64 miles of railroad are the finest remaining example of a vast network that once connected commercial outposts in the Rocky Mountain region. Spiked down in 1880 as the San Juan Extension of the Denver & Rio Grande Railroad, the Cumbres & Toltec was built to serve the rich mining camps in the mountains.

The Chama depot is on Terrace Street downtown; (505) 756–2151 or (888) 286–2737; www.cumbrestoltec.org. Though tickets may be available for purchase at the depot, it's best to make reservations as far in advance as possible. The railroad has several ride options daily except Friday from late May through mid-October. Fares range from $60 for adults and $30 for children age eleven or younger in coach seating, to more than $100 for a seat in a parlor car, which includes lunch.

Heading west out of Chama on U.S. Highway 84 (it will meet U.S. Highway 64 about 15 miles west—continue on U.S. 64, otherwise you'll end up in

Pagosa Springs, Colorado), you'll drive through parts of the vast **Jicarilla Apache Reservation** and into the community of **Dulce,** the headquarters of the Indian reservation. Unlike New Mexico's Pueblo Indians, ancestors of the Jicarilla Apache were nomadic—their lifestyle was determined by the seasons and migration of wildlife. They traveled throughout southern Colorado, northeastern New Mexico, and the panhandles of Texas and Oklahoma. The reservation was established in 1887. The Spanish word *jicarilla* means "wicker basket," after the craft for which the Jicarillas were traditionally best known.

To learn more about the Jicarilla Apache, visit the **Jicarilla Arts and Crafts Museum** (505–759–3242, ext. 274), housed in a modest green building on U.S. Highway 64 (Jicarilla Boulevard) in Dulce. The museum is open daily from 8:00 A.M. to noon and 1:00 to 5:00 P.M.; there's no admission charge. Please note that the museum may be closed during feast days, so it's best to call ahead. The reservation will also issue permits for camping, hunting, and fishing. Call (505) 759–3242 for any information regarding the Jicarilla Apache. For thoroughly modern lodging, the **Best Western Jicarilla Inn** is the place to stay. It's located on U.S. Highway 64; rates range from $65 for a single to $110 for a suite; (505) 759–3663 or (800) 742–1938.

Los Alamos County

A small city on the Pajarito Plateau, **Los Alamos** was once home only to a handful of ranchers and to a school for boys. But world events in the 1940s made Los Alamos forever a household name.

Los Alamos, county seat of New Mexico's smallest county of the same name, has a fascinating history because of the role it played in the top-secret Project Y (a.k.a. the Manhattan Project)—the development of the world's first atom bomb—during World War II. For historical reasons alone, Los Alamos is an interesting place to visit, but the community also happens to be set in one of New Mexico's most beautiful sites—a military requirement, along with its remoteness, to keep the scientists content during the long ordeal.

In some ways Los Alamos has the feel of a company town because Los Alamos National Laboratory, technological successor to the Manhattan Project days, is by far the community's largest employer, providing thousands of jobs. Operated by the University of California for the U.S. Department of Energy, the lab itself contains the most interesting attraction of all in Los Alamos: the **Bradbury Science Museum.**

The extensive museum chronicles the dawning of the atomic age by focusing on achievements in weapons development, alternate energy sources, and biomedical research. Photographs, documents, and newspaper headlines provide a timeline of significant world events covering the early 1930s to the mid-1960s.

Throughout the day, the museum's theater presents a twenty-minute film called *The City That Never Was,* which traces Los Alamos's history with actual period film footage and reenactments of notable events in the city's past.

The exhibits are very well presented, employing lots of interactive video screens to make things a little more accessible and comfortable to nontechies. More than thirty-five hands-on exhibits invite visitor participation: You can align a laser, pinch plasma, and monitor radiation.

The museum is located at Fifteenth and Central in Los Alamos, in the lab's Museum Park complex; (505) 667–4444; www.lanl.gov/museum. It's open Tuesday through Friday from 9:00 A.M. to 5:00 P.M. and Saturday, Sunday, and Monday from 1:00 to 5:00 P.M.

For an alternative viewpoint, make sure to stop by the infamous ***Black Hole,*** a post-nuclear resale shop selling "atomic waste" from the U.S. nuclear weapons program. Run by Ed Grothus, a scientist/philosopher turned entre-preneurial pack rat who quit his job at Los Alamos National Lab more than thirty years ago, the Black Hole is filled with fascinating clutter, including an array of shiny alloy thingamajigs. Ed was recently the subject of an award-winning, humorous documentary by film-maker Ellen Spiro called *Atomic Ed and the Black Hole.* You'll find the Black Hole at 4015 Arkansas Street; (505) 662–5053. It's open Monday through Friday from 10:00 A.M. to 5:00 P.M. and Saturday from 11:00 A.M. to 5:00 P.M.

newmexicotrivia

Beat generation author William Borroughs (*Naked Lunch*) attended the former Los Alamos Ranch School during the 1930s.

While the Bradbury Science Museum is high-tech and scientific, the ***Los Alamos Historical Museum*** is a little more low-key and personal. It traces the area's history beyond its military role, although the war years get big play here also. The small stone-and-log museum—the former infirmary and guest house of the Los Alamos Ranch School—preserves artifacts from Los Alamos's past, including a geology exhibit and household items common during the war years. It also has a well-stocked bookstore.

The Los Alamos Historical Museum is at 1921 Juniper on the grounds of the ***Fuller Lodge Cultural Center;*** (505) 662–6272. Hours are 10:00 A.M. to 4:00 P.M. Monday through Saturday and 1:00 to 4:00 P.M. Sunday; summer hours are 9:30 A.M. to 4:30 P.M. Monday through Saturday and 11:00 A.M. to 5:00 P.M. Sunday. There is no admission charge.

Fuller Lodge provided the first housing for the Manhattan Project scientists, before the establishment was turned into a hotel and restaurant. Today it's the Fuller Lodge Cultural Center, a multipurpose community center that houses the Fuller Lodge Art Center and Gallery. The art center features the works of regional artists in its permanent collection, together with collections on loan from Los Alamos citizens, as well as traveling exhibits. Many items are for sale to the public. The art center also sponsors various classes, lectures, and shows throughout the year.

The art center is on the second floor of the Fuller Lodge Cultural Center (though it has its own entrance), at 2123 Central Avenue; (505) 662–9331; www.artfulnm.org. Gallery hours are 10:00 A.M. to 4:00 P.M. Monday through Saturday.

Sandoval County

Although Sandoval County has led New Mexico in population growth since the mid-1990s, its growth is due to the population explosion of one city—Rio Rancho, a boomtown bedroom community of Albuquerque. Rio Rancho is, however, very atypical of the rest of the county. The remainder of Sandoval County is pleasantly rural, containing rock formations, forests, mountains, and Indian pueblos.

Southern Sandoval County would normally be considered more "central" than "north central" New Mexico, but because this book is divided by county, it'll be classified as the latter. The region, however, will be divided into northern and southern Sandoval County.

Northern Sandoval County

Beyond Cochiti Lake and nearby Cochiti Pueblo, you'll find ***Dixon Apple Farm.*** Visitors are welcome to the quaint orchard at the base of the Canada Valley's crimson cliffs all year, but it's the few weeks in middle to late September and early October that make this place special to those who partake in the annual fall pilgrimage, mostly Albuquerqueans, in search of Dixon's patented and prized Champagne apple. Along with the Champagne, the farm grows and sells Double Red Delicious during opening weekend; a few weeks later Dixon's other patented apple, Sparkling Burgundy, arrives, as does the popular Rome.

Off the salesroom you can watch the apples being washed, sorted, and packed. Only flawless ones make it to the salesroom; the rest are destined to become cider for those who want their apples without the crunch.

A tiny, rapidly flowing brook runs through the farm, adding even more to the valley's allure. A scattering of picnic tables is available for those wanting to linger awhile. Take a wedge of sharp cheddar to have with a crisp Champagne along the brook for your own little bit of heaven.

There's no set date when apple season begins at Dixon—fine apple growing is an art as well as a science, you know—so if you don't want to be left out, start calling (505) 465–2976 in mid-September. During season, hours are 8:00 A.M. to 5:00 P.M. daily.

To get to Dixon's, take the Cochiti Lake exit off Interstate 25, about 28 miles north of Albuquerque. Go left, toward Cochiti Pueblo, about 18½ miles (the last 2 of which are gravel) to get to the orchards.

About 5 miles northwest of Cochiti Pueblo, you'll discover the nation's newest national monument, ***Kasha-Katuwe Tent Rocks National Monument,*** or Tent Rocks for short, which was given monument status by President Clinton in January 2001. The delightfully surreal, conical rock formations that are the focus of the monument are somewhat uniform in shape, ranging in height from about 3 feet to almost 100 feet, and have been alternately described as looming giant tents (a la tepees, thus the name), mushrooms, castles, and inverted ice cream cones. They look like they could be the setting of a fantastical Dr. Seuss story. However, the story of their formation goes something like this: About 6.8 million years ago, volcanic explosions dumped a 1,000-foot layer of pumice, ash, sand, and gravel onto what is now the monument area. Over time, wind and water eroded the deposits to create the massive formations. Though the newly designated monument encompasses more than 4,000 acres, rest assured that a mere 2-mile loop trail will lead you through the heart of the magical rock formations.

To get to Tent Rocks, take the Cochiti Lake exit off Interstate 25, about 28 miles north of Albuquerque. Go left on Highway 22 and follow the signs to Cochiti Pueblo; turn right at the pueblo water tower (painted like a drum) onto Tribal Route 92 (connects to Forest Road 266) and travel 5 miles on a dirt road to the parking area. The monument is open daily from 7:00 A.M. to 6:00 P.M. April 1 through October 31, and from 8:00 A.M. to 5:00 P.M. the remainder of the year. Day passes cost $5.00 for vehicles with fewer than ten passengers and $10.00 for vehicles carrying ten or more; (505) 761–8700 or (800) 252–0191 (*NOTE:* Phone numbers are for the Bureau of Land Management and the Sandoval County Visitors Center, respectively, as the monument infrastructure was not built as of press time.); www.nm.blm.gov. Access to the monument may be closed due to poor road conditions or by order of the governor of nearby Cochiti Pueblo, which jointly manages the area with the BLM, so call ahead.

The Jemez Mountains, particularly the *Jemez Springs* area, are a favorite with hiking, camping, and cross-country-skiing devotees. Named for the many hot springs hidden in the area, the village of Jemez Springs provides the perfect getaway weekend for weary city folks.

Let the *Jemez Mountain Inn* be your base for the weekend. The main part of the inn has been the center of activity in the area for more than a hundred years, serving as the town silver assayer's office and barbershop, among other things. The building assumed its role as the Amber Lodge in 1936 until 1989, when it was transformed into the Jemez Mountain Inn. Each of the six suites is different, and each has a story. There have even been claims that mobsters from the East Coast lay low here in the 1930s.

Like nearly everything else in Jemez Springs, the Jemez Mountain Inn is on the main drag (Highway 4), within walking distance of other places and attractions; (505) 829–3926 or (888) 819-1075; www.jemezmtninn.com. Rates range from $79 to $115, lower during winter. Children are not allowed.

The *Jemez Springs Bath House* has also been around for more than a hundred years, having originally been built by the Jemez Indians to utilize the curative waters that bubble from the ground along the Jemez River. Now owned by the town and leased out, the bathhouse is bare-bones and basic, qualities that add to its peculiar attraction.

Separate women's and men's wings each have four smooth, concrete tubs that are meticulously scrubbed after every use, even though they may not look like it because of the high mineral buildup over time. In addition to mineral soaks, which are said to relax muscles and heal sore joints, the bathhouse offers sweat wraps and massages. The bathhouse also has an outdoor cedar tub for those who don't like to soak alone.

The bathhouse now has an exercise studio and a gift shop, which features a selection of aromatherapy products and natural health and beauty supplies. Baths run from $10 to $20, and massages range from $32 to $78. The outdoor tub goes for $30 per hour. Hours are 9:00 A.M. to 9:00 P.M. in summer and 10:00 A.M. to 6:00 P.M. Monday through Thursday and 10:00 A.M. to 8:00 P.M. Friday through Sunday the remainder of the year. The Jemez Springs Bath House is on Highway 4 in Jemez Springs; (505) 829–3303; www.jemezsprings bathhouse.com.

If you like your soaks au naturel, head to the pools of *Spence Hot Springs*. The pools are the more accessible springs in the mountainous area under USDA Forest Service jurisdiction. The forest service warns, though,

"Don't drink or snort the water up your nose, because some hot springs in the area may contain an amoeba called *Naegleri fowlerii,* which can cause a fatal brain infection called PAM, Primary Amoebic Meningoencephalitis." Though deaths are rare, keep your head above water just in case.

Spence Hot Springs are in the vicinity of mile markers 24 and 25 on Highway 4, 7 miles north of the Jemez Springs Bath House, on the right side of the road. You'll see a crude parking area and a sign that says NO PARKING AFTER 10 P.M. (There used to be a Spence Hot Springs sign, but apparently every time one was put up someone stole it.) Then follow the primitive path a little less than 1 mile up the hill. There are no admission charges or designated hours, but it's a good bet you won't be there after 10:00 P.M.

A Glimpse of North Central New Mexico: Impressions of Los Ojos

Just as the Catskills provide an easy weekend escape for New Yorkers, so do the Jemez Mountains for Albuquerqueans. Blessed with a beautiful, heavily forested setting, and less than an hour's drive from Albuquerque or Santa Fe, the striking red-rock Jemez Mountains and the welcoming community of Jemez Springs are the perfect destination for a spontaneous day trip.

During a recent autumn trip to Spence Hot Springs in "the Jemez," I was again reminded how fortunate I am to live in New Mexico. While soaking in a natural hot tub dug into the side of a mountain and gazing through towering ponderosa pines to distant rock formations, I found myself absentmindedly following a conversation between two fellow soakers, one of whom had a thick southern accent.

"I can't believe y'all got a place like this. I'm from Atlanta and I'm just amazed."

"Welcome to New Mexico," the other bather said dryly.

"I can't believe there aren't any rangers around, or that nobody gets harassed for the nudity and all."

"Look around," the other said, gesturing to the remote location reachable only by a spirited trek. "Who'd bother to police this?"

The Georgian just shook his head. "If this were Georgia, you can bet your lucky stars that clothes would not be an option. In fact," he laughed, "I'd imagine some wealthy Holy Roller would buy the whole dang place and turn it into a church camp. Hell, he'd probably even charge admission."

I just smiled and turned toward a new view, thankful once again for the space and the freedom, and for the comforting *los ojos,* or springs, that New Mexico offers up so graciously.

For a beer and burger after your soak, check out **Los Ojos Restaurant and Saloon,** across Highway 4 from the Jemez Mountain Inn (505– 829–3547). It's been around since 1947. Los Ojos is HOME OF THE FAMOUS JEMEZ BURGER—ONE JELLUVA JAMBURGER, as its sign proclaims. (At the very least, the sign makes it clear how to pronounce Jemez: rhymes with "famous.") You can even play a game of pool while you wait for your jamburger.

Los Ojos serves food from 11:00 A.M. to 9:00 P.M. Sunday through Thursday and until 9:30 P.M. Friday and Saturday. During the winter, shave a half-hour from the evening hours. The saloon is open until 2:00 A.M. daily, with the exception of Sunday, when it closes at midnight.

For those of you who just must include something educational when you travel, don't miss the **Jemez State Monument,** 1 mile north of Jemez Springs on, what else, Highway 4; (505) 829–3530. The monument preserves the ruins of both the old village of Guisewa, built approximately 600 years ago by the ancestors of the nearby Jemez Pueblo Indians, and the mission church of San Jose de los Jemez, built by Spanish colonists in the early 1620s. The visitor center exhibits interpret the area's history from the perspective of the Jemez Indians. The monument is open Wednesday through Monday from 8:30 A.M. to 5:00 P.M. Admission is $3.00 for adults; young people age sixteen or younger are admitted free.

Nearby **Soda Dam** is about ½ mile farther north on Highway 4 from Jemez State Monument. The natural dam on the Jemez River does not create a lake but, rather, channels the river through a short tunnel to provide a small waterfall and pool on the other side—perfect for cooling off in the summer. (*NOTE:* The pool's depth is unpredictable because of rocks often deposited by the river; accordingly, never attempt to dive into the small pool.) During cooler times of the year, when the summer crowds are gone, sightseers and picnickers can walk up the trail that snakes to the top of the rock formation and provides a peek at the river on the other side. Eventually, the USDA Forest Service plans a visitor information center at Soda Dam.

Bandelier National Monument, in northeast Sandoval County, is one of the most spectacular places to hike in New Mexico. It was designated a National Monument in 1916 to protect one of the largest concentrations of archaeological sites in the Southwest. It contains more than 70 miles of trails and 23,000 acres of designated wilderness.

The 50-square-mile monument is named for Adolph Bandelier, a Swiss-American scholar who extensively surveyed the prehistoric ruins in the region and studied the Pueblo Indians around Santa Fe in the 1880s. The most accessible feature of Bandelier National Monument is the ruins in Frijoles ("Beans")

Canyon and the cliff dwellings set in the canyon walls. Most of the ruins belong to the late pre-Spanish period, although a few date back to the twelfth century.

The easiest way to experience Bandelier is first to orient yourself by stopping at the visitor center and viewing the slide program and then to walk the Main Ruins Trail, a 1-mile paved loop that takes about forty-five minutes. If you can stay a little longer, continue up the canyon to the base of the Ceremonial Cave. The cave is accessible only by climbing four steep ladders for a total of 140 feet! This ascent is not for wimps, but if you're unafraid of heights and have nonslip shoes, go for it. Once you're in the chamber, have a friend stand at one end while you stand at the other and then quietly talk into the stone walls—it's like a prehistoric intercom. Pretty cool.

Campsites are available. Backcountry hikes, including overnight trips that require a wilderness permit, are also allowed if you want to spend a significant amount of time exploring Bandelier. Because there are a lot of rules regarding the exploration of Bandelier's backcountry, always check with the visitor center first. Keep in mind that, as with many parts of New Mexico, brief afternoon thunderstorms are common in late summer.

The entrance to Bandelier National Monument is about 13 miles south of Los Alamos off Highway 4; (505) 672–0343. The visitor center is open daily from 8:00 A.M. to 6:00 P.M. during summer and from 8:00 A.M. to 4:30 P.M. in winter. Frijoles Canyon and other selected hiking areas are open dawn to dusk. Admission is $10 per car for a seven-day permit; no admission is charged for those age sixty-two or older or age sixteen or younger. Camping fees are $35 per site per night.

Seven of New Mexico's nineteen Indian pueblos are located in Sandoval County, thereby making Sandoval the county with the most Native American communities in New Mexico. The pueblos in Sandoval County are Cochiti, Jemez, Sandia, San Felipe, Santa Ana, Santo Domingo, and Zia. (Gamblers, take note: Sandia, San Felipe, and Santa Ana Pueblos have casinos.)

The pueblos are each unique, with varying histories, beliefs, ceremonies, and customs. They are actually autonomous "nations" with laws of their own. Many of the pueblos are similar to small, rural towns, and most have a mission church as the most prominent architectural feature, the legacy of Spanish missionaries during the seventeenth and eighteenth centuries.

Although many pueblos welcome or even encourage tourists, it's best to remember that most have been around for centuries and do not exist for tourists. If you're interested in visiting the pueblos, it's a good idea to call ahead and request specific visitor information and policies, which vary greatly. The simplest way to get information is by calling the Indian Pueblo Cultural Center in Albuquerque (see Bernalillo County entry in the Central New Mexico chapter) at (505) 843–7270 or the Eight Northern Indian Pueblos Council at (505) 747–0700. Or, if you have a specific pueblo in mind, contact it directly (see the list on pages 201–02).

Southern Sandoval County

The village of **Corrales** is an old, rural community adjoining Albuquerque's North Valley along the Rio Grande. While some descendants of the area's early Hispanic settlers still farm the area, many newer residents who commute to Albuquerque enjoy the large lots for their extensive gardens, apple orchards, and horses.

Corrales, which hosts a harvest festival each October on the grounds near the historic San Ysidro Church to celebrate its agricultural heritage, has several points of interest for the weekend traveler or urban dweller who wants a change of pace. At the center of the village along the main road, appropriately named Corrales Road, you'll find several distinctive shops, restaurants, and galleries.

Through the years the tranquil, elongated village has seen quaint bed-and-breakfast inns and wineries come and go. Among the newer offerings is the **Corrales Winery,** a few miles north of the village center. Proprietors Keith and Barbara Johnstone, who resurrected existing area vineyards, opened the winery's tasting room to the public in the spring of 2001. Though the winery produces a Cabernet Sauvignon, it specializes in fruity, sweeter wines, such as their Riesling, Muscat, Corrales Sunset, and Viñadora varieties.

The winery is open Wednesday through Sunday from noon to 5:00 P.M., with possible extended hours during summer; call ahead. Corrales Winery is located down a lane at 6275 Corrales Road (there's a sign), 5 miles north of its intersection with Highway 528 (Alameda Boulevard); (505) 898–5165; www .corraleswinery.com.

In the lodging category, even farther north on Corrales Road (about 6¼ miles north of its intersection with Highway 528/Alameda Boulevard), you'll come across the unusual ***Vista Hermosa Llama Farm Bed and Breakfast*** (505–898–0864 or 800–339–4709), adjacent to the Corrales Bosque Nature Preserve. While the lodging is comfortable enough, it's the working farm's menagerie of animals that makes the place unique. In addition to more than fifty llamas, visitors may see potbellied pigs, peacocks, pheasants, a miniature horse, a swamp water buffalo, a dromedary camel, a big red kangaroo, champion Scottish Highland cattle, a miniature donkey, Watusi-Ankoli cattle, and giant shire, Belgian, and Clydesdale draft horses. In addition to individual bed-and-breakfast lodging, the farm specializes in hosting groups for retreats and conferences.

Like Corrales, the town of **Bernalillo** is a bedroom community of Albuquerque with a rural flavor. Bernalillo lies along Interstate 25 north of Albuquerque and is home to one of the finest restaurants in the Albuquerque metro area—**Prairie Star** at the Santa Ana Indian Pueblo. Housed in a large adobe, the restaurant commands the most dramatic view of the Sandia Mountains at sunset, when they turn an intense watermelon red; after dark, the view is replaced by the glittering lights of Albuquerque. Prairie Star's menu, which changes seasonally, is a worthy match for the view. Featuring contemporary Southwestern cuisine with an international flair, the restaurant serves such tempting creations as Bison Quesadillas, Rock Shrimp Chile Relleno, Elk Tenderloin, Drunken Goat Empanada, and Wild Mushroom Bruschetta.

Prairie Star is 2 miles west of I–25 on Highway 550 near Bernalillo; (505) 867–3327. Dinner is served Tuesday through Sunday from 5:30 to 9:00 P.M.

The annual **New Mexico Wine Festival** is held in Bernalillo on Labor Day weekend to celebrate the long wine-making tradition in New Mexico generally and in Bernalillo specifically. Spanish colonists brought grapes along with other reminders of home, and the missionaries of the period began making wine for sacramental and personal uses. Bernalillo became the center of wine production in New Mexico during the eighteenth and nineteenth centuries. The festival includes a juried art show, food booths, entertainment, and, of course, wine tastings from most of New Mexico's wineries. (See the list of wineries on pages 202–03.)

Coronado State Monument, located near Bernalillo, is popular with Albuquerque visitors because of its proximity to the city. The monument commemorates the 1540 expedition of Francisco Vásquez de Coronado in search of the riches of the legendary Seven Cities of Cibola. Coronado and his soldiers camped near the now-deserted Kuaua Pueblo, the site of the monument. The park contains a trail through the pueblo ruins, which include a reconstructed kiva (or ceremonial chamber). The visitor center contains exhibits on the history of the Rio Grande Valley. You can even try on an armored conquistador outfit complete with headgear, just like the kind Coronado wore.

The monument is located 1 mile northwest of Bernalillo on Highway 44; (505) 867–5351. It's open Wednesday through Monday from 8:30 A.M. to 5:00 P.M. Admission is $3.00 for those age seventeen or older.

The small community of **Placitas** lies east of Bernalillo, across Interstate 25 in the foothills of the Sandia Mountains. Placitas was a popular place for communes in the late 1960s and is now a popular place for pricey new homes in the rambling adobe tradition, though old adobes still exist near the community's center. An interesting site near Placitas in the beautifully lush Las Huertas Canyon is **Sandia Man Cave,** where artifacts of Sandia Man (prehistoric people of the area) were excavated by University of New Mexico archaeologists in the late 1930s. Though it's too dark to really see, the cave doesn't go more than about 20 feet before becoming a narrow tunnel that reaches back 300 feet. Attempting to venture far into the cave may be dangerous even with a flashlight; nevertheless, the first few feet give a good sense of what life was like for Sandia Man more than 10,000 years ago. A brief trip to the cave is a perfect urban escape from nearby Albuquerque, providing an awesome short hike to a fascinating spot. Older kids will love this!

The cave is about 4 miles southeast of Placitas on Highway 165 (3 of these miles are gravel through Cibola National Forest). You'll see a sign marking the parking area at the start of the ½-mile trail to the steps at the cave's entrance.

Along the Rio Grande between Albuquerque and Santa Fe, you'll find the small rural community of **Algodones,** a pastoral favorite of those who opt out of the city but need to keep their city jobs. Here you'll discover ***Hacienda Vargas,*** a bed-and-breakfast inn that offers guests the grace and elegance of historical New Mexico. In fact, the site itself has been both a stagecoach stop and an Indian trading post. There's even an adobe chapel nearby.

Each of the seven guest rooms and suites boasts a kiva fireplace, French doors, and a private bathroom. And the entire inn is furnished with New Mexico antiques. You'll find the tranquility you seek in the inn's courtyard and garden areas, which contain barbecue facilities.

Rates range from $89 to $189. To get to Hacienda Vargas from Albuquerque, head north on Interstate 25. About 5 miles past the town of Bernalillo, take the

Sandia Man Cave

Algodones exit and head left to Highway 313 (El Camino Real). Turn left, and the inn is the first house on the right; (505) 867–9115 or (800) 261–0006 (out of state); www.haciendavargas.com.

Where to Stay in North Central New Mexico

RIO ARRIBA COUNTY

Hacienda Rancho de Chimayó,
Highway 520,
Chimayó,
(505) 351–2222/
(888) 270–2320

Abiquiu Inn,
Highway 84, Abiquiu,
(505) 685–4378/
(800) 447–5621

Rancho de San Juan,
Highway 285 at mile marker 340,
Española,
(505) 753–6818

Branding Iron Motel,
1511 West Main Street,
Chama,
(505) 756–2162/
(800) 446–2650

Chama Trails Inn,
2362 Highway 17,
Chama,
(505) 756–2156/
(800) 289–1421

Best Western Jicarilla Inn,
Highway 64,
Dulce,
(505) 759–3663/
(800) 742–1938

LOS ALAMOS COUNTY

Adobe Pines Bed & Breakfast,
2101 Loma Linda Drive,
Los Alamos,
(505) 661–8828

Orange Street B & B,
3496 Orange Street,
Los Alamos,
(505) 662–2651

Hilltop House and L.A. Suites,
400 Trinity at Central,
Los Alamos,
(505) 662–2441/
(800) 462–0936

Los Alamos Inn,
2201 Trinity Drive,
Los Alamos,
(505) 662–7211/
(800) 279–9279

NORTHERN SANDOVAL COUNTY

Jemez Mountain Inn,
Highway 4,
Jemez Springs,
(505) 829–3926

The River Dancer Retreat and Bed and Breakfast,
16445 Scenic Highway 4,
Jemez Springs,
(505) 829–3262/
(800) 809–3262

SOUTHERN SANDOVAL COUNTY

Hacienda Vargas
(bed-and-breakfast),
Highway 313,
Algodones,
(505) 867–9115/
(800) 732–2194

La Hacienda Grande
(bed-and-breakfast),
21 Baros Lane,
Bernalillo,
(505) 867–1887/
(800) 353–1887

Where to Eat in North Central New Mexico

RIO ARRIBA COUNTY

Embudo Station,
Highway 68,
Embudo,
(505) 852–4707.
Moderate. Fare: Eclectic Southwestern.

Restaurante Rancho de Chimayó,
Highway 520,
Chimayó,
(505) 351–4444.
Moderate. Fare: Traditional New Mexican.

Anthony's at the Delta,
228 Oñate,
Española,
(505) 753-4511.
Moderate. Fare: Eclectic, featuring steak, seafood, chicken, and New Mexican dishes.

El Paragua Restaurant,
603 Santa Cruz Road,
Española,
(505) 753–3211.
Inexpensive to moderate.
Fare: New Mexican.

Rancho de San Juan,
Highway 285 at Mile
Marker 340,
Española,
(505) 753–6818.
Very expensive (prix fixe
dinner only). Fare: Eclectic
continental cuisine.

**Branding Iron Restaurant &
Lounge,**
1511 West Main Street,
Chama,
(505) 756–9195.
Inexpensive to moderate.
Fare: New Mexican, sand-
wiches, steaks, seafood.

LOS ALAMOS COUNTY

**De Colores Restaurant
& Lounge,**
820 Trinity,
Los Alamos,
(505) 662–6285.
Inexpensive to moderate.
Fare: New Mexican and
American.

Tarpon Steakhouse,
3801-G Arkansas Street,
Los Alamos,
(505) 662–2324.
Moderate. Fare: Steaks.

China Moon,
121 Central Park Square,
Los Alamos,
(505) 662–2883.
Inexpensive. Fare: Chinese.

Central Avenue Grill,
1789 Central Avenue,
Los Alamos,
(505) 662–2005.
Inexpensive. Fare: Burgers,
sandwiches.

**NORTHERN SANDOVAL
COUNTY**

**Los Ojos Restaurant &
Saloon,**
Highway 4,
Jemez Springs,
(505) 829–3547.
Inexpensive. Fare:
Hamburgers, New Mexican
fare.

**SOUTHERN SANDOVAL
COUNTY**

Prairie Star,
2 miles west of Interstate 25
on Highway 44,
Bernalillo,

(505) 867–3327.
Moderate to expensive.
Fare: Contemporary with
Southwestern flair.

Cafe de Placitas,
664 Highway 165,
Placitas,
(505) 867–1610.
Moderate to expensive.
Fare: Eclectic American.

Casa Vieja,
4541 Corrales Road NW,
Corrales,
(505) 898–7489.
Moderate to expensive.
Fare: Eclectic, upscale
American culinary creations.

Range Cafe,
925 Camino del Pueblo,
Bernalillo,
(505) 867–1700.
Inexpensive to moderate.
Fare: Innovative and eclectic
Southwestern and traditional
New Mexican.

SELECTED CHAMBERS OF COMMERCE/ VISITOR BUREAUS IN NORTH CENTRAL NEW MEXICO

Chama Chamber of Commerce,
P.O. Box 306, Chama, 87520;
(505) 756–2306/(800) 477–0149;
Web site: www.chamavalley.com

**Española Valley Chamber of
Commerce,**
One Calle de las Españolas,
Plaza Mission Convento,
Española, 87532;
(505) 753–2831;
Web site:
www.espanolanmchamber.com

Los Alamos Chamber of Commerce,
109 Central Park Square/
P.O. Box 460,
Los Alamos, 87544;
(505) 662–8105/(800) 444–0707;
Web site: www.losalamoschamber.net

**Sandoval County Region Tourism
Association,**
243 Camino del Pueblo/
P.O. Box 40, Bernalillo, 87004;
(505) 867–8687/(800) 252–0191;
Web site: www.sctourism.com

Santa Fe and Taos Region

The counties that boast the art meccas of Santa Fe and Taos have more to offer the traveler than what's confined inside these cities' boundaries. Oh, but what those city limits enclose! When people daydream about New Mexico, they're most likely to conjure up images of the historic districts of Santa Fe and Taos: the narrow streets, the richly textured curves of adobe walls, the quaint shops, hidden cafes, and ever-present art galleries—all set against glorious tree-covered mountains.

But in this region, beyond the city limits, you'll discover New Mexico's highest mountain and wildest river. You'll also find Indian pueblos, first-class downhill and cross-country skiing, historic museums, a revived ghost town, and a mineral springs resort. But most of all you'll encounter spectacular scenery and awesome adventures no matter what time of year you visit.

Santa Fe County

It's a city, it's a style, it's even a cologne and a cookie (by Pepperidge Farms). It's *Santa Fe,* of course, and it's New Mexico's own. Set against the breathtaking Sangre de Cristo ("Blood of Christ") Mountains, the city of Santa Fe, aptly located

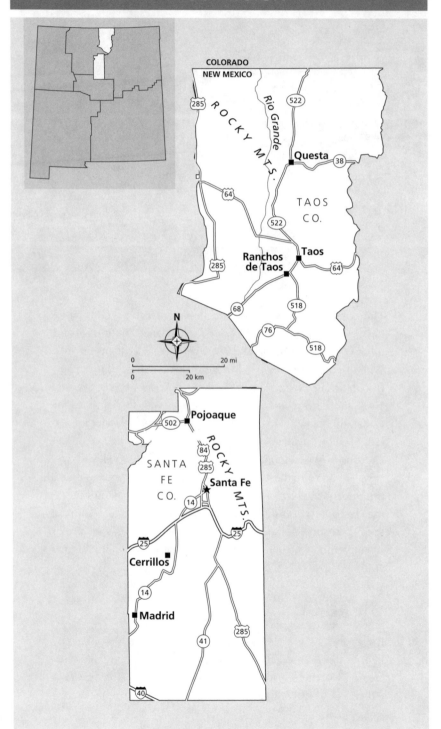

in Santa Fe County, is a city of superlatives built around a historic plaza: It's the nation's oldest capital (founded in 1610); it's also the nation's highest capital (at 7,000 feet); and it boasts the nation's oldest church (San Miguel Chapel) as well as oldest public building (Palace of the Governors, now a museum).

Despite its fame—or, rather, because of it—Santa Fe presents a major dilemma when writing a book such as this. Writing only one chapter in a guide-book—albeit a selective guide—on Santa Fe is a little like being asked to explain nuclear physics in a hundred words or less. It's a little overwhelming. Add to that the rest of Santa Fe County, and it gets more than a little over-whelming. Santa Fe is certainly the most written-about city in New Mexico, and its paths have been so well beaten by visitors from all over the globe that it hardly seems anything new could be written about "The City Different" in a travel book. Acknowledging that fact, this chapter will first advise you on expe-riencing the city's historic/shopping district without directing you to particular spots; it will then cover a few places outside the inner core, before moving on to concentrate on those places in Santa Fe County that are outside the city.

FAVORITE ATTRACTIONS/EVENTS IN SANTA FE AND TAOS

El Rancho de las Golondrinas,
La Cienega
(505) 471–2261

Ten Thousand Waves,
Santa Fe
(505) 992–5025

Shidoni Sculpture Garden and Galleries,
Tesuque
(505) 988–8001

Rio Grande Gorge Bridge,
north of Taos
No phone

D. H. Lawrence Memorial,
Taos County
No phone

Wild Rivers Recreation Area,
Questa
(505) 758–8851

Taos Pueblo,
Taos County
(505) 758–1028

Madrid,
New Mexico
No phone

Taos Talking Picture Festival,
April, Taos
(505) 758–3873/
(800) 732–8267

The Burning of Zozobra,
Fiesta de Santa Fe,
September, Santa Fe
(505) 988–7575

It's hard not to fall in love with Santa Fe. The city oozes quaintness, uniqueness, and all those other "nesses" that have made it New Mexico's most popular visitor destination for decades. If ever there was a New Mexico city perfect for exploring on foot, Santa Fe would be it. Several museums and countless galleries, shops, cafes, and historic sites are within easy walking distance from the Santa Fe Plaza. Surprises lurk around every corner. To advise visitors on what to see here is pointless and would undermine the sense of discovery that Santa Fe is all about. This is not a cop-out on the part of a lazy travel writer. Trust me.

Secrets of the Cathedral

One of Santa Fe's most recognizable landmarks is St. Francis Cathedral, the Gothic-style church with oddly truncated towers that stands at the east end of San Francisco Street. Most visitors, however, don't recognize the cathedral's unique features.

Inside the church, be sure to stop in at the Chapel of La Conquistadora, part of an older church that stood on the site during Spanish colonial times. The 18-inch-tall figure of the Virgin Mary in the chapel was carried to Santa Fe by settlers coming back from eleven years in exile after the Pueblo Revolt of 1680. During Fiestas each year she is carried through the streets in a reenactment of the triumphant return, and local Catholics continue to revere her today, as attested to by the many candles burning on the altar below her. La Conquistadora has a whole wardrobe of her own and is dressed and cared for by a cofradía of women.

Notice the keystone over the arched front doorway of the cathedral. On it are carved the Hebrew letters for YHWH (for Yahweh, a word representing God). While Archbishop Lamy, the city's first non-Hispanic Catholic clergyman, was building the cathedral, he went far over budget and ran out of money before the roof was finished. After much deliberation, the local Jewish community decided to fund the completion of the cathedral roof. In return, they asked that the inscription be carved over the church door as a lasting reminder of the unusual bond between Santa Fe's Catholics and Jews.

The roof was completed, but the Gothic spires Lamy envisioned were not. Recently, downtown real estate developers have offered to finish the spires at their own expense. Far from philanthropic, the move would evade the Latin American tradition that no building in a town can be taller than the cathedral. Fortunately, the offer has always been rejected.

To learn more about the church and its secrets, including its private collection of classical paintings, check out the *Archdiocese of Santa Fe Museum,* hidden away at 223 Cathedral Place; (505) 983–3811. Open Monday through Friday from 8:30 A.M. to 4:30 P.M., it's the least-known of Santa Fe's many museums; even most locals have never visited it.

If you must, go ahead and consult your conventional guidebook on the slickest galleries, the toniest restaurants, and the most chic shops. Then put it away and heed the following advice to "experience" Santa Fe's downtown by yourself or with a friend (avoid going with a group if it's your first visit).

Take off your watch and take a deep breath. Park near the plaza, if you can find a spot. Then skip the plaza (though you'll probably want to check out the jewelry sold by Native Americans under the Palace of the Governors portal). Head out on any one of the streets and wind around until you think you're a little lost. Relax. Drift around, entering whichever places appeal to you. And don't try to see everything; you'll never have time, even if you stay here for days. Duck into a cafe for a cup of coffee or a glass of wine and rest your feet awhile. Check out the museums and historic churches, if you're so inclined. Time seems to stop when you're in Santa Fe, so above all, don't hurry. Just enjoy the sensory pleasures of the city: the smell of burning piñon wafting from the chimneys, the rich textures and curves of adobe and wood, the muted colors of the city set against that intense azure sky. You'll see much more, have more fun, and be less stressed than if you felt you had to see certain places within a specified time frame. Now you're almost ready to venture out a bit.

Before leaving the downtown area, however, head toward the southwest corner of the plaza and stroll down to 211 West San Francisco Street (at Sandoval) to check out the historic **Lensic Theatre Performing Arts Center** (505–988–7050; box office 505–988–1234; www.lensic.com).

The Lensic first opened in 1931 when West San Francisco Street was still a dirt road, and it quickly became known for its elaborate faux Moorish-Spanish Renaissance architecture. In its heyday the Lensic hosted vaudeville shows, screened films, and welcomed such guests as Errol Flynn, Rita Hayworth, Olivia de Havilland, Judy Garland, and Roy Rogers. An $8.2 million renovation completed in 2001 took more than three years but was well worth the wait, as the new Lensic is not only beautiful but state-of-the-art as well: it boasts a revolutionary sound system that simulates various acoustics—one of only two such systems in the United States. The Lensic presents a range of diverse, affordable programming that encompasses theater, dance, music, literary events, and film. There's something happening several times a week year-round.

To get an idea of Santa Fe's upscale appeal, take a stroll down **Canyon Road,** about 8 blocks southeast of the plaza. The most coveted address in town, this 2-mile avenue was once part of an Indian trail to the Pecos pueblos and is now synonymous with art and money, though it's remained slightly "beyond the fray" of rampant tourism so as to retain its inherent charms. You'll find many of the city's finer galleries along this narrow promenade, as well as a distinctive medley of restaurants and shops.

Even if you can't afford to purchase anything, one of the more interesting stops along Canyon Road is ***Morning Star Gallery.*** Though it deals in investment-quality antique American Indian art, Morning Star seems more like a museum that allows visitors to purchase the exhibits. The gallery doesn't limit itself to Indian art from New Mexico, though you'll certainly find plenty of it here. An exquisite Acoma Pueblo pot may go for as much as $4,500, and Navajo blankets from the 1800s reach into the $45,000–$50,000 range. It's incredible to see these items up close and wonder what the potter or weaver would have done with all that money.

Morning Star is located at 513 Canyon Road; (505) 982–8187. It's open Monday through Saturday from 9:00 A.M. to 5:00 P.M.

There's more to Canyon Road than painting and sculpture galleries. One of the most unusual shops, ***Project Tibet*** is tucked away in a cul-de-sac at 403 Canyon Road. Selling everything from prayer flags and incense to Tibetan clothing, it raises funds for the nonprofit group that sponsors Santa Fe's Tibetan refugee community, the first in the United States and still one of the largest. (Tibetans from Santa Fe were once flown to the Andes to work as extras in the film *Seven Years in Tibet*.) That explains the "Free Tibet" bumper stickers you see all over town. Open daily from 9:00 A.M. to 5:00 P.M.; (505) 982–3002.

All along Canyon Road, some of the most intriguing places are hidden behind the buildings that line the road. Keep an eye out for ***Gypsy Alley,*** an inconspicuous compound full of small galleries and studios. You'll usually find food and entertainment there during the self-guided Canyon Road ArtWalks held every Friday afternoon from about 4:30 P.M. on during the summer months.

Following an afternoon of gallery-hopping along Canyon Road, ease into ***El Farol*** for a taste of the unexpected and expect to be entertained. This fine restaurant specializes in tapas (roughly translated as "appetizers"), a serving style native to Spain, where each selection is presented on its own small plate. Choose several to make a meal from the extensive menu. They come hot or cold and run the gamut from meat and chicken to seafood and vegetarian. This is a great way to sample a variety of different foods. El Farol's bar has live entertainment every night, variously featuring jazz, blues, flamenco, and folk sounds.

El Farol is at 808 Canyon Road; (505) 983–9912. It's open daily for lunch, 11:30 A.M. to 4:00 P.M., and for dinner, 5:30 to 10:00 P.M.; bar hours are noon to 2:00 A.M.

For a quick nature escape from gallery-hopping along Canyon Road, head up the road to the ***Randall Davey Audubon Center***. An information wall outside of the center's office indicates the recent sightings of particular birds and other wildlife species on the grounds of this wildlife refuge on the eastern edge of Santa Fe. The main attraction here is El Temporal Nature Trail, which winds among the native piñon-juniper vegetation of the foothills of the Sangre de Cristo Mountains. It's a great spot for a minihike for those who may not be inclined to take advantage of the more challenging and remote hiking trails in the mountains.

To get to the center, head east on Canyon Road and continue east on Upper Canyon Road until it dead-ends at the center; (505) 983–4609. A self-pay box accepts $1.00 admission to the hiking trail. Gates are open daily, 9:00 A.M. to 5:00 P.M.

The Audubon Center adjoins other recently created natural areas that make the mouth of Santa Fe Canyon a nature lovers' paradise. Across from the center, the 188-acre

newmexicotrivia

Fiesta de Santa Fe in September is the oldest continuously celebrated public event in the United States.

Santa Fe Canyon Preserve was set aside by the Nature Conservancy to protect wildlife habitat; formerly owned by the local water company, parts of the preserve had been off-limits to the public for almost seventy years before it was opened to visitors in 2002. No dogs. Near the preserve's entrance is one of several trailheads for the new *Dale Ball Trail System.* The 22-mile network of trails among the piñon-covered hills on the city's outskirts takes hikers and mountain bikers to hidden canyons and ridgelines with scenic vistas—and also practically through the backyards of some of Santa Fe's most expensive homes.

Another scenic, noncommercial spot in Santa Fe is the hill on which rests the *Cross of the Martyrs.* A brief but spirited hike takes you up a trail to the hilltop containing the statuesque white cross commemorating the crucifixion of Jesus Christ and other religious martyrs. Though there are other trails atop, the primary point of interest here is the picturesque and improbably intimate view of Santa Fe and the surrounding area—yet merely blocks from downtown. The hillside's trailhead is at Paseo del Paralta and Hillside Avenue (1 block north of East Marcy); no phone; no fee.

In contrast to the museums in downtown Santa Fe, the museums off Camino Lejo in southeast Santa Fe have an open, contemporary feel. Alongside the *Wheelwright Museum of the American Indian* and the *Museum of Indian Arts and Culture,* you'll find the more unusual *Museum of International Folk Art.* Set aside a few hours to soak up the eclectic exhibits of various folk arts from more than a hundred countries.

As the largest museum of its kind in the world, the facility's highlight is the Girard Collection, the lifetime collection of the famous architect Alexander Girard and his wife. The brightly colored displays reflect diverse cultures' special talents at channeling their creativity into toys, textiles, costumes, masks, and more. There are no labels in the Girard Collection wing to interfere with the aesthetics of the exhibits. There is, however, a printed guide whose entries correspond to the numbered exhibits so that you can make your excursion as "left brain" as you want.

The Folk Art Museum is at 706 Camino Lejo; (505) 476–1200; www.moifa .org. Admission is $7.00 for adults, and young people sixteen or younger are admitted free. (*NOTE:* A four-day pass for the five Santa Fe state museums— Palace of the Governors, Museum of Fine Arts, Museum of Spanish Colonial Arts, Museum of Indian Arts and Culture, and the Folk Art Museum—is available for $15.00.) The museum is open Tuesday through Sunday from 10:00 A.M. to 5:00 P.M.

After decades of disappointed tourists wandering the streets of Santa Fe, wondering where they could see the paintings of New Mexico's most famous artist, the long-awaited **Georgia O'Keeffe Museum** opened in Santa Fe during the summer of 1997. Dedicated to preserving and presenting the lifework of one of America's most remarkable artists, the museum houses a permanent collection of O'Keeffe's art unequaled by any museum in the world. The museum features more than eighty of O'Keeffe's works, including some of the more famous—large-scale flowers and bleached desert bones—as well as abstracts, nudes, landscapes, cityscapes, and still lifes.

Tucked away behind the Eldorado Hotel (the biggest building in downtown Santa Fe), the Georgia O'Keeffe Museum is located a few blocks from the plaza at 217 Johnson Street; (505) 946–1000; www.okeeffemuseum.org. Admission is $8.00 for adults, and youths age sixteen or younger are admitted free. Admission is $4.00 for New Mexico residents with ID, and seniors are admitted for $7.00 on Thursday. On Friday from 5:00 to 8:00 P.M. the museum is free to all. The museum is open daily from 10:00 A.M. to 5:00 P.M. (until 8:00 P.M. on Friday), with the exception of Wednesday, when hours from July through October are noon to 5:00 P.M. and when it is closed from November through June.

When it comes to lodging, Santa Fe's outstanding choices include historic downtown hotels, quaint bed-and-breakfasts, and modern resorts. But the one to check out when you're interested in checking in for a while is the **Bishop's Lodge,** just five minutes north of the city in the tranquil Tesuque Valley.

In the 1800s this 1,000-acre ranch was the personal retreat of Father Jean Baptiste Lamy, who became the archbishop of Santa Fe. Father Lamy's story lives on in Willa Cather's book *Death Comes for the Archbishop,* and his chapel still stands just as he left it, as a focal point on the ranch. The historical aspect of the lodge blends well with the modern accommodations and comforts. Its guest rooms are done in classic, Southwestern/Santa Fe style, many with fire-places and balconies or terraces. As a full-service resort, the lodge allows you to opt out of going into the city for fun every day. There's much to do on the grounds of the lodge itself, and sports enthusiasts will find tennis courts, a skeet- and trap-shooting range, a swimming pool, and horses for riding. In addition, the Bishop's Lodge also boasts a first-class restaurant featuring contemporary American cuisine with just a hint of the Southwest.

The Bishop's Lodge is located off Bishop's Lodge Road; (505) 983–6377 or (800) 732–2240; www.bishopslodge.com. Rates, without meals, range from $129 to $499, depending on the season and type of room or suite. The presidential suite is available for $1,500 per night. A modified American plan, which includes breakfast and dinner, is also available from Memorial Day weekend through August.

An aside is appropriate here: Avoid the city of Santa Fe during summer if you can. Though many businesses depend on this "tourist season," Santa Feans will heartily thank me if any of you heed this advice. And you too will be grateful after you've explored this captivating city without so many people. Avoiding Santa Fe in the summer is, however, impossible if you're a devout opera fan who's always dreamed of attending the world-famous **Santa Fe Opera;** (505) 986–5900 or (800) 280–4654; www.santa feopera.org. You guessed it; the opera season runs from the end of June (with an often outrageously flamboyant Gala Opening) through August, ending with the opera's "Grande Finale Fiesta." Keep in mind, though, that it's not unheard of for tickets for specific performances to sell out months in advance. (*NOTE:* Inexpensive standing-room-only tickets are often surprisingly easy to come by the day of each performance; call for ticket prices and details.) And although there can be crowds in Santa Fe around the Christmas holidays as well, that's just such a magical time to be in Santa Fe that it's hard to tell someone to avoid December too.

The community of **Tesuque,** named for nearby Tesuque Pueblo, is about 8 miles north of Santa Fe via Highway 590 (or U.S. Highway 84/285 and then Highway 591). This quiet little community has become quite pricey real estate over the years as Santa Feans and others have come to appreciate the simple tree-covered beauty of this slow-paced valley. Lately, the famous have joined the rich in discovering the appeal of Tesuque. Whether as residents or long-term visitors, the likes of Elizabeth Taylor, Candice Bergen, Robert Redford, Ali

newmexicotrivia

Each August, Santa Fe hosts Indian Market, the world's largest Indian art market, which brings together 1,200 tribal artisans from across the United States, Canada, and Mexico.

MacGraw, and Martina Navratilova have been spotted in town, especially at the Tesuque Village Market.

If you're into fine art with a penchant for sculpture, Shidoni is the place for you. This intriguing spot is actually three spots: Shidoni Contemporary Gallery, Shidoni Bronze Gallery, and Shidoni Sculpture Garden. Shidoni (the word for a Navajo greeting to a friend) is not only a place for art lovers to visit but also an important resource for artists. Established as a foundry in 1971 by sculptor Tommy Hicks, Shidoni has evolved into an internationally known fine-art casting facility. Bronze pourings are held every Saturday from noon to 4:30 P.M., and the public is welcome to watch as 2,000-degree molten bronze is poured into the ceramic shell molds, one of several steps in the casting process.

The sculpture garden is a favorite of many visitors to Shidoni. You're immediately struck that this place is special when you pull into the parking area and are greeted by colorful shapes springing from the earth. As you gaze beyond, you'll notice that there are many more intriguing and sometimes outlandish works of art positioned among old apple trees in a spacious grassy area. A crisp, sunny fall day is perfect for examining the garden.

The Burning of Zozobra

The burning of Zozobra, a 40-foot effigy of Old Man Gloom, marks the beginning of Fiesta de Santa Fe each September, the Thursday after Labor Day. The event invites comparisons with New Year's Eve and Mardi Gras.

Early in the evening locals, thrill seekers, and tourists alike stake out spots in Fort Marcy Park, a couple of blocks from Santa Fe's downtown plaza, awaiting the main event. The symbolic burning is a magical catharsis, ridding gloom and misfortune, in preparation for the weekend-long celebration.

After dusk the action heats up. Led by the traditional Firedancer, other dancers perform around the base of the intricately engineered Zozobra, who begins taunting the crowd with moaning and groaning as he arrogantly awaits his fate. (The moans are provided by an amplified human voice cleverly in sync with the puppet's mouth movements.) As the crowd claps and chants, "Burn him, burn him," Zozobra moans louder. The crowd's enthusiasm builds to a frenzied crescendo as the shouting continues. Finally, the Firedancer torches Zozobra and simultaneously sets off hundreds of colorful fireworks into the clear, dark Santa Fe sky.

Zozobra continues to moan until he's completely engulfed in flames. The crowd of thousands, now thoroughly primed, cheers and begins the trek back to the plaza for music, merrymaking, and dancing in the streets—now that all the gloom has been dispelled.

Shidoni is 5 miles north of Santa Fe, just south of Tesuque on Bishop's Lodge Road; (505) 988–8001; www.shidoni.com. The galleries and garden are open Monday through Saturday from 9:00 A.M. to 5:00 P.M.

If you're hungry after your visit to Shidoni, grab a bite at the ***Tesuque Village Market*** (505–988–8848) on Highway 591 in Tesuque. This laid-back restaurant, deli, and wineshop serves up great soups and sandwiches and wine by the glass; the market is also known for its selection of scrumptious desserts. It's also a great place for breakfast and a leisurely weekend brunch. Patio seating too is available. The market, a welcome change from some of the stuffier places in the city, is open daily from 7:00 A.M. to 9:00 P.M.

While you're in the area, stop at Camel Rock along U.S. Highway 84/285 on Tesuque Pueblo. The site offers a great place to get your picture taken with this striking and appropriately named rock formation.

Its name may sound like a family water park, but leave the kids at home when you visit ***Ten Thousand Waves,*** a truly magnificent Japanese-style spa tucked into the foothills of the Sangre de Cristo Mountains, just east of Santa Fe.

From the parking lot, a series of wooden steps takes you high up through the landscape to the main entrance and into the lobby/registration area, where you'll be greeted with the soft sound of water falling in a Zen fountain. Though the spa offers herbal wraps, massages, salt glows, and aromatherapy among other treatments, the main focus is on the exquisite wooden hot tubs, with their crystal-clear, absolutely clean water. (State-of-the-art purification systems, combined with ultraviolet light, hydrogen peroxide, and ozone, assure this; and though some of the cold plunges are purified with bromine, chlorine is not used in any tub or plunge.) If a private tub is not available (which will probably be the case if you didn't make reservations, which are practically required), opt for the communal tub, which is outdoors on a large wooden deck flocked by fragrant piñon and juniper trees. A cold plunge is nearby, as is an authentic wooden sauna. Ten Thousand Waves is Santa Fe at its holistic, spiritual, sensually indulgent best. If you're not uptight about nudity (bathing suits are optional, but rarely seen) and really want to release stress, this is the place to go to let it go.

Being pampered is part of the deal: Your bathing experience includes kimonos, towels, sandals, soap, shampoo, cedar skin lotion, hair dryers, and lockers. Communal baths are $13.50 per person for unlimited time. TTW's private tubs vary in style—one includes a waterfall, rock deck, and steam room; others include saunas and decks—and range from $23 per person per hour to $27 per person per hour. TTW now has eight luxury guest suites, ranging from $190 to $260 per night. Call for pricing information for other services.

Ten Thousand Waves is open Wednesday through Monday, and though hours of operation vary for different tubs and seasons, it's basically open from late morning until 9:30 P.M., later during summer and on Friday and Saturday; on Tuesday, it's open from late afternoon through normal closing time. You'll find this Far Eastern–Southwestern paradise 3½ miles east of Santa Fe on Artist Road (which becomes Hyde Park Road), the route to the Santa Fe Ski Area. (By the way, if you haven't already guessed, this is the perfect place to wind down after a spirited day of skiing!) Contact (505) 992–5025; www.tenthousand waves.com.

Northwest of Santa Fe you'll discover the *San Ildefonso Pueblo.* Set in the Rio Grande Valley and flanked by vast stands of cottonwood, the pueblo is a beautifully maintained village laid out in the traditional manner with mission church and plaza. The Jemez Mountains in the distance complete the scene. Similar to Santa Clara Pueblo, San Ildefonso is famous for its matte black-on-black pottery, though other types are also created here. One of New Mexico's most famous Native American artists, the late Maria "Poveka" Martinez, was from San Ildefonso and revived this traditional art form. A museum on the pueblo is dedicated to her.

newmexicotrivia

Renowned San Ildefonso potter Maria Martinez is credited with the twentieth-century revival of Pueblo pottery. The pottery of the late Ms. Martinez is among the most valued by collectors.

Though San Ildefonso welcomes visitors Monday through Saturday from 8:00 A.M. to 4:00 P.M., you must first register with the visitor center; call ahead for specific dates of events. There's a $3.00 admission fee per carload, and camera and sketching fees also apply. San Ildefonso is 22 miles northwest of Santa Fe: 16 miles north on U.S. Highway 84/285 and then 6 miles west on Highway 502; (505) 455–3549. Winter hours are subject to change; call ahead.

South of Santa Fe, near the community of La Cienega, you'll find *El Rancho de las Golondrinas* ("The Ranch of the Swallows"). This isolated, 200-acre living-history museum is part of one of the most historic ranches in the Southwest. The ranch (of the same name) was founded in the early 1700s as a stopping place on El Camino Real, "The Royal Road" connecting Mexico City to Santa Fe. The museum has as its main focus eighteenth-century life on a working Spanish colonial ranch. Every effort has been made to re-create the ranch as it was during that period: Crops are grown, orchards and vineyards are tended to, and sheep, goats, turkeys, geese, and ducks mill about. Though there's a small "traditional" indoor museum on the grounds, the joy of a visit to Las Golondrinas is walking among all the outbuildings and gardens.

Las Golondrinas really comes alive during its spring and fall festivals, especially the latter. Each October you can step back in time to all the sights and smells of an authentic fall harvest from the past. You'll witness costumed interpreters first carding, spinning, and dyeing wool and then weaving it into rugs. You can also see sugarcane becoming molasses with the help of a burro-driven press. Then there are blacksmiths and wheelwrights at work and a wonderful water-driven mill spinning among the golden poplars. And gourds, sunflowers, and red chiles lie drying in the sun, while juice is crushed from freshly picked apples (samples available). The stillness and anticipation of an autumn day in the country creep into your soul and take hold at Las Golondrinas and are well worth the trek.

newmexicotrivia

New Mexico boasts the oldest road in the United States, El Camino Real ("The Royal Road"), which roughly follows Interstate 25 from Anthony to Santa Fe. Historically, it connected Mexico City with Santa Fe during the early days of Spanish exploration and occupation.

El Rancho de las Golondrinas is located 15 miles south of Santa Fe. Take the exit off Interstate 25 (exit 276 coming from Santa Fe and exit 276B coming from Albuquerque) and follow the signs; (505) 471–2261; www.golondrinas.org. The museum is open June through September, Wednesday through Sunday, 10:00 A.M. to 4:00 P.M. Admission is $5.00 for adults, $4.00 for seniors and youths

Traditional Food of New Mexico

Holy Guacamole!

Because avocados are native to the tropics, guacamole is not a traditional New Mexican preparation. Nevertheless, it's a favorite adapted Southwestern side, so here is one version.

2 large, ripe avacados, peeled and pitted

1 teaspoon red chile powder

1 tablespoon lemon juice

1 small clove garlic, minced

1 tomato, minced (optional)

1–2 green onions, minced (optional)

1 teaspoon salt

Mash avocados with a fork and mix with remaining ingredients. Serve with *tostadas* or corn tortilla chips. Makes 4 servings.

ages thirteen to seventeen, and $2.00 for children ages five to twelve. Spring Festival takes place the first full weekend in June, and Fall Festival is held the first full weekend in October. Festival hours are 10:00 A.M. to 4:00 P.M. Festival admission is $7.00 for adults, $5.00 for seniors and youths ages thirteen to eighteen, and $3.00 for children ages five to twelve. Call for information regarding Las Golodrinas's Wine Festival (the first full weekend in July) and Civil War Weekend (May).

Though the **Turquoise Trail** starts just outside Albuquerque in Tijeras, the bulk of it is in Santa Fe County, tracing the route of Highway 14, commonly known as North 14. The trail, designated a Scenic and Historic Area, connects the semighost towns of Golden, Madrid, and Cerrillos (among others) along this leisurely behind-the-mountain path linking Albuquerque to Santa Fe.

The trail probably got its name from Mount Chalchihuitl, near Cerrillos, which contained a vast lode of the blue-green gemstones and was the only place in New Mexico where turquoise was mined. The towns along the Turquoise Trail (sometimes known as the Ghost Town Trail) have a boom-and-bust mining legacy similar to that of towns in the southern part of the state. Mined in this area, in addition to turquoise, were coal, lead, copper, silver, and gold.

Though each of the spots along the Turquoise Trail has its own charms and history, the revived ghost town of **Madrid** (pronounced MAD-rid, unlike its namesake in Spain) is perhaps the most fun. Originally an old coal-mining town, Madrid all but died after the last mine shut down in the 1950s, when the demand for coal declined, thus leaving scores of similar, wooden company houses along this strip of North 14.

During the past twenty or so years, Madrid has been rediscovered by artistic types and former hippies drawn to its funky charm. The successful revival of this onetime ghost town was even the subject of a *60 Minutes* spot in 1982. A South American import clothing store and a New Age crystal emporium join ranks with other small shops and restaurants. The commercial establishments share Madrid with the deserted and occupied houses that dot the main drag. More so than many places in New Mexico, Madrid *evolves,* so expect to find something different each time you visit. Then, too, the weather is not the only thing that can get quite hot during the summer in Madrid—the outdoor Madrid jazz and blues concerts have become quite a popular weekend outing for folks from Albuquerque and Santa Fe.

Check out the **Mine Shaft Tavern** (505–473–0743) as a great example of a real mining-town bar. It's rustic, wooden, and dark and contains a large stone fireplace and a dartboard. Hundreds of dollar bills sporting handwritten notes from visitors from all over the world are plastered on the wall above the bar.

Live entertainment is also part of the Mine Shaft experience. In addition to drinks, the tavern serves up generous burgers and steaks, including buffalo steak when available, as well as sandwiches and several New Mexican dishes. The Tavern Burger is a good bet—a half-pound of ground beef laced and topped with bleu cheese: delicious. The sign above the door says it all: WELCOME TO MADRID—MADRID HAS NO TOWN DRUNK, WE ALL TAKE TURNS.

Adjacent to the tavern you'll find the **Old Coal Mine Museum,** which contains the **Engine House Theater.** On weekends and holidays from Memorial Day through mid-October, the theater presents hilarious melodrama productions. Booing, hissing, and throwing marshmallows (available at the door for a small fee) are encouraged. Shows change each season. Call (505) 438-3780 for current show times, admission charges, and reservations.

Midway between Madrid and Santa Fe on a side road off Highway 14, the village of **Cerrillos** feels as if it's stuck in a past time. Lack of water has prevented it from growing much since the nineteenth century, when many of its adobe houses were built. The ghosts of signs painted on its few commercial buildings add to the Old West ambience but were actually added for the shooting of the 1988 movie Young Guns.

Well hidden up an unpaved road north of the village is Santa Fe County's newest—and least known—park, the **Cerrillos Hills Historic Park.** Until it was opened to the public in May 2003, signs used to strongly discourage people from entering the maze of barren gray hills concealed from view by piñon-clad ridges and deep arroyos. Many small hand-dug pit mines were in danger of collapsing and burying hikers. The mines were made by Pueblo Indians as much as a thousand years ago in search of turquoise, which they held sacred. Turquoise from the Cerrillos Hills was traded and used in jewelry throughout the Southwest. Other mines in the area produced lead, used as a glaze by Pueblo potters between 1300 and 1700. Besides the mines, other evidence of ancient visitors includes pottery shards, stone rings, and petroglyphs. Mines close to hiking trails have now been stabilized to prevent accidents. Aside from a small parking lot, rest rooms, and trailheads, there have been no improvements to the 1,116-acre park so far. Look for an information kiosk in the village of Los Cerrillos. Contact: (505) 992-9866; www.cerrilloshills.org.

Taos County

Taos has long been a gathering place for creative people. Its reputation for seducing artists and nurturing their works began before the end of the nineteenth century and continues to this day. The legacy of the Taos Society of Artists and all those who followed lives on in Taos's many fine galleries—more per capita, in fact, than in any other city in the United States. The striking Taos Pueblo and acclaimed Taos Ski Valley have also brought this lovely little town worldwide attention.

Though there's more to Taos County than Taos itself, the city that grew around its now-famous plaza is a good place to start. As with Santa Fe, exploring Taos's downtown museums, galleries, and shops is best done on foot. Taos is actually composed of three communities, all with *Taos* in their names: There's Taos the town, Ranchos de Taos, and Taos Pueblo. First, Taos proper.

The Kit Carson Historic Museums consist of three different museums that collectively bring Taos's illustrious past to life—the Kit Carson Home, Martinez Hacienda, and Ernest L. Blumenschein Home. Admission to each museum is

A Glimpse of Santa Fe and Taos: Impressions of Tourists

Unlike most parts of New Mexico, Santa Fe and Taos are world-famous. Most out-of-state visitors know both cities as cultural centers where generations of artists and authors have come in search of inspiration, picturesque adobe-style towns just about as far removed from mainstream America as you can get without a passport. But for many New Mexicans, Santa Fe means state politics, out-of-state wealth, spirituality, and holistic healing. (New Mexico's loose medical practice regulations, designed to accommodate traditional curanderas and Indian shamans, allowed the first acupuncturists in the United States to practice there starting in the 1970s, laying the foundation for well-respected schools that teach a full range of alternative health approaches, from Chinese medicine to crystals and aromatherapy.) Santa Feans are accustomed to seeing Sikhs and Tibetans on the street but are astonished by the sight of somebody wearing a necktie. Taos is in many ways Santa Fe's smaller sibling, without the politicians and bureaucrats, and it is the only place in northern New Mexico that gets as many tourists in winter as summer. In Santa Fe and Taos alike, tourism is the mainstay of the local economy.

As a Santa Fean for twenty years, I can tell you that most locals love out-of-state visitors. Every once in a while, people in Santa Fe or Taos may roll their eyes and say something disparaging about tourists. Sure, in summer it's almost impossible to find a parking space downtown, and we frequently find ourselves stuck in traffic behind tourists driving very slowly because they're lost, but that's a small price to pay. Thanks to tourism, we have great museums, galleries, and stage performances, not to mention more outstanding restaurants than we can count. Like other upscale resort areas such as Carmel, Cape Cod, or Key West, we have the pleasure of seeing out-of-towners at their happiest, during the weekend or two out of the year when they don't have to go to work. And let's face it: who wants to live in a place that other people wouldn't want to visit?

$5.00 for adults, $4.00 for seniors, and $2.50 for children, with a maximum charge of $6.00 for a family. Discounts apply if you want to visit more than one; you can purchase the multiple ticket at any of the museums.

True to the northern New Mexico tradition of "wonderful things lie hidden behind adobe walls," the **Kit Carson Home** lies behind a plain, storefrontlike facade. But history comes alive behind these adobe walls. Although Christopher "Kit" Carson was born in Kentucky in 1809, the legendary mountain man and scout made his home in Taos. He came to Taos in 1826 to become a trapper because the village was known as the center of the fur trade, owing to the abundance of beaver in the nearby mountain streams. In 1843 Carson bought this twelve-room adobe home as a wedding gift for his bride, Josefa Jaramillo. The home's rooms divide the museum into various exhibits. All periods of Taos's colorful history are depicted, in addition to a special display on Carson himself. Even Kit Carson's cradle is on display in the museum—and his grave is in nearby Kit Carson Park.

The Kit Carson Home is ½ block east of Taos Plaza on Kit Carson Road; (505) 758–0505. Hours are from 9:00 A.M. to 5:00 P.M. daily.

For a view of Spanish colonial life in Taos, the **Martinez Hacienda** has no rivals. This fully restored compound sits defiantly on the banks of the Rio Pueblo just outside Taos as it did nearly 200 years ago. The sprawling, twenty-one-room home of Don Antonio Severino Martinez encloses two *placitas* (courtyard-type areas), has no exterior windows, and looks like a fort. In reality, it did serve as a fortress against the Apache and Comanche raids of the times.

Today the hacienda provides a glimpse back at the many components that made up the self-contained compound. A blacksmith shop, a tack room, a granary, and a weaving room have all been restored, as have living quarters with period furnishings. It's located 2 miles southeast of Taos Plaza on Highway 240; (505) 758–0505. Hours are from 9:00 A.M. to 5:00 P.M. daily.

The **Blumenschein Home,** the third component of the Kit Carson Historic Museums, is an art museum with the feel of a traditional museum in a home-like setting. The furnishings of the Blumenschein family of artists—Ernest; his wife, Mary; and their daughter, Helen—together with their paintings and those of other prominent Taos artists take visitors back to the glory days of art and culture in Taos.

Ernest Blumenschein was the cofounder of the now-legendary Taos Society of Artists. The story of how Blumenschein ended up in Taos—and thus put Taos on the art map—is well known. Blumenschein had originally heard about Taos from a fellow artist while studying in Paris in 1895. Later, during a trip from Denver to Mexico that Blumenschein took with artist Bert Phillips, a wheel on their wagon broke north of Taos. After repairing the wheel in Taos, the artists became captivated by the valley, its inhabitants, and its brilliant light. They decided to stay and urged other artists to come to Taos as well. In 1912 Blumenschein, together with five other artists, founded the Taos Society of Artists, whose purpose was to enable its members as a group to exhibit their art in galleries throughout the country. In 1919, after spending many summers in Taos, Blumenschein and his young family moved from New York to Taos and purchased the home that was to become part of the Kit Carson Historic Museums.

The Blumenschein House is on Ledoux Street, 2 blocks west of Taos Plaza; (505) 758–0505. Hours are from 9:00 A.M. to 5:00 P.M. daily.

Farther west on Ledoux Street you'll find New Mexico's second-oldest museum, the **Harwood Foundation Museum,** which was founded in 1923 and has been operated by the University of New Mexico since 1935. The art museum contains paintings, drawings, prints, sculpture, and photographs by Taos artists from 1898 to the present. The Taos Society of Artists is well represented in this permanent collection. There's also an assortment of nineteenth-century *retablos* (religious paintings on wood) that were given to the foundation by arts patron and writer Mabel Dodge Luhan. Special exhibitions of Taos artists and works from the University of New Mexico's collections are also displayed during the year.

The Harwood Foundation Museum is at 238 Ledoux Street; (505) 758–9826. Summer hours are Tuesday through Saturday from 10:00 A.M. to 5:00 P.M. and Sunday from noon to 5:00 P.M.; call ahead for winter hours, which vary. Admission is $5.00 for adults and seniors, and children age eleven or younger are admitted free. New Mexico residents are admitted free on Sunday.

Like Santa Fe, Taos offers an abundance of distinctive lodging. The **Taos Inn** is the oldest hotel in town and the only one on the National and State Registers of historic places. If you don't want to worry about getting around in your car, the Taos Inn is the best base from which to explore the downtown plaza area, including the shops, galleries, and cafes in the **Bent Street District,** which includes the **Governor Bent House and Museum,** across the street. The inn, restored in 1982, has uniquely outfitted each of its thirty-six guest rooms with pueblo-style furnishings, including hand-loomed Indian bed-spreads; all have adobe kiva fireplaces.

Doc Martin's, the inn's restaurant, is named after Taos's first doctor, who lived and practiced in part of what now accommodates the inn and restaurant. It specializes in innovative fish and pasta dishes and has been honored by *Wine Spectator* for having one of the most outstanding restaurant wine lists in the world. The inn's Adobe Bar is a comfortable, popular gathering place for the arts crowd; local musicians often provide entertainment as well. The bar's seating area flows into the lobby so that patrons can enjoy the atmosphere there as well.

Reservations are often hard to come by, so book early. Daily room rates range from $60 to $225, depending on type of room and season. The Taos Inn is at 125 Paseo del Pueblo Norte; (505) 758–2233 or (888) 518–8267; www.taos inn.com.

Not far from the plaza, but sufficiently hidden, is a wonderful inn with a fascinating past. The ***Bed & Breakfast at the Mabel Dodge Luhan House*** offers guest rooms in the original home as well as in a separate addition. But as the original estate of the Taos writer, designer, and champion of the Southwestern creative arts movement, it's also worth exploring on its own. The existing 200-year-old structure was expanded to its present size of twenty-two rooms in 1922 by Antonio Luhan, Mabel's husband. Spanish colonial and pueblo styles shine throughout.

Stories persist that the home is haunted by either the ghost of Mabel herself or that of a young Taos Pueblo girl. Apparitions aside, if these old adobe walls could talk, present-day visitors would gladly listen: Mabel entertained such guests as D. H. Lawrence, Willa Cather, Aldous Huxley, Georgia O'Keeffe, and Carl Jung here.

A whole different set of characters frequented the estate in the late 1960s and early 1970s, after actor Dennis Hopper purchased it when filming *Easy Rider* near Taos. Peter and Jane Fonda, Jack Nicholson, and Elizabeth Taylor were among Hopper's guests. (Some visitors would no doubt rather hear the walls talk about that period!)

The inn carries on in Mabel's tradition of hosting the creative crowd—many famous contemporary writers and artists enjoy the serenity and sense of history found here. Guests are served a breakfast buffet either in the spacious dining room or outside on the patio among the huge cottonwood, beech, and elm trees. Wine and cheese are often served in the afternoons.

Rates range from $95 to $180, with the two-bedroom gatehouse going for $220 for four ($20 extra for each additional guest). The bed-and-breakfast is located on Morada Street north of Kit Carson Road; (505) 751–9686 or (800) 846–2235; www.mabeldodgeluhan.com.

Adjoining Taos on the south is the village of **Ranchos de Taos,** home of the **San Francisco de Asis Church,** built in 1850. No photographs are allowed of the mission church's interior, but you can click to your heart's desire outside. Photographers and painters have been capturing the image on film and canvas for more than a century, and, oddly enough, it's the backside that most intrigues them. The unusual cruciform shape of the church, together with the soft contours of buttresses that support the adobe walls, is impressive enough, but the added element of the changing shadows combines to make the sight truly inspiring.

The mysterious The **Shadow of the Cross** painting, by Henri Ault, is on display in the rectory hall across from the church. The mystery of the portrait—which is of Christ on the shore of the Sea of Galilee—occurs when it is viewed in the dark: After about ten minutes the portrait becomes luminescent, outlining the figure while clouds over the left shoulder of Jesus form a shadow of a cross.

The painting was completed in 1896, years before the discovery of radium. Moreover, no luminous paint has so far been developed that will not darken and oxidize within a relatively short time. Ault claimed he didn't know why the painting changed in the dark. He even thought he was going crazy when he first went into his studio at night and discovered the luminosity.

The painting was first exhibited at the St. Louis World's Fair in 1904 and, after more than fifty years of exhibition in galleries throughout North America and Europe, is now at its permanent home. Every half-hour from 9:00 A.M. to 3:30 P.M., except from noon to 1:00 P.M. (Monday through Saturday), the church allows viewing of the spectacle by turning out the lights for visitors. There is no admission charge.

An adjacent gift shop sells religious articles, books, and cards Monday through Saturday from 9:00 A.M. to 5:00 P.M. during summer, 10:00 A.M. to 4:00 P.M. during winter. The plaza/parking area is lined with shops and galleries. The church is located just off Highway 68 in Ranchos de Taos; (505) 758–2754. It's open to visitors daily, except Sunday, from 9:00 A.M. to 4:00 P.M.

Falling somewhere between a bed-and-breakfast inn and a classic hotel is the latest incarnation of the newly renovated **San Geronimo Lodge,** a historic ten-room adobe lodge with breathtaking views of Taos Mountain. Not only has it quickly earned a reputation as a relaxing getaway, but it has also become a popular business-retreat destination and romantic setting for weddings. The lodge originally opened in 1925 and was a gathering place for Taos's art and society crowd. In 1994, sisters Allison and Shaunessy Everett purchased the closed lodge and embarked on a painstaking process of authentically restoring the inn to its original state. The dramatic pine vigas (log ceiling beams), kiva fireplaces, and hardwood floors were all refinished by hand. Each of the guest

San Geronimo Lodge

rooms features handcrafted furniture and a completely renovated private bath. All the ambience and comforts inside notwithstanding, you won't want to stay in your room for long. Not only do you have great views of the mountains from the inn's rambling verandas and balconies, you can also enjoy the sweeping grounds that surround the lodge, which include colorful gardens, patios, an open-air hot tub, and a full-size swimming pool. The Everett sisters make fresh preserves for their guests from the cherry, apricot, apple, and pear trees that line the banks of the Acequia Madre ("Mother Ditch") meandering through the grounds.

The lodge is located adjacent to Kit Carson National Forest at 1101 Witt Road; (505) 751–3776 or (800) 894–4119; www.sangeronimolodge.com. Rates range from $95 to $150, double occupancy, and include a full country-style breakfast.

Two miles north of Taos you'll find **Taos Pueblo,** New Mexico's best-known Indian pueblo. Besides its spectacular mountainside setting, Taos Pueblo gets this distinction because of its picturesque, multistory, apartment-like architecture, which sets it apart from other pueblos. Taos Pueblo has been continuously inhabited for centuries, and the Taos Indians have lived at or near the present site for almost 1,000 years.

A walking tour is available to get a feel for the pueblo, its history, and its people. Aside from the obvious addition of tourists and the various Indian-owned shops catering to them, the pueblo looks much the way it did hundreds of years ago. The rapidly flowing, crystal-clear Rio Pueblo de Taos adds to the tranquility of the setting and is still the only source of drinking water for Taos Pueblo residents.

Though certain ceremonial dances and feast days are open to the public, here, as in most pueblos, some sacred activities are restricted to tribal members only. Therefore, if you don't want to inadvertently arrive at a closed pueblo during your visit, it's a good idea to call ahead.

Taos Pueblo is normally open to the public daily from 8:00 A.M. to 5:00 P.M. during the summer and from 8:00 A.M. to 4:00 P.M. during winter; however, the pueblo usually closes to the public for ten weeks during the late winter or early spring, so plan accordingly. The following fees apply: admission, $10.00 for adults ($8.00 per person for groups of five or more), $8.00 for seniors, $5.00 for young people ages thirteen to seventeen and college students with ID, and free for children age twelve or younger; still cameras, $5.00; movie or video cameras, $5.00. Taos Pueblo is 2 miles north of Taos off Highway 68; (505) 758–1028; www.taospueblo.com.

Taos Indian Horse Ranch, an Indian-owned venture near the pueblo, is popular with horse-loving visitors. The ranch, with 80,000 acres of riding trails, provides various rides and excursions. In winter, traditional sleigh rides are given over breathtaking terrain and come complete with Indian storytellers, music, campfires, and marshmallow roasts.

Most of the trail guides are Taos Pueblo Indians who are master riders. The ranch features horses selected for their ability to ride responsively to the novice rider. The place has been owned and operated by Cesario Stormstar Gomez and his family for more than twenty years.

Tour prices range from $40 to $110 per person. Private sleigh-ride packages are available upon request; prices vary. Because all tours are by appointment only, call (505) 758–3212 or (800) 659–3210 for reservations, as well as to get directions.

Taos County's other pueblo, ***Picuris Pueblo,*** is not so well known to tourists and is thus more representative of most New Mexico pueblos. Some feel it offers visitors a more authentic New Mexico Indian experience than the very visible Taos Pueblo.

Because Picuris Pueblo is located in a hidden valley, it was the last of New Mexico's pueblos to be discovered by Spanish explorers. Despite its relative isolation, Picuris is quite receptive to visitors. The ***Picuris Pueblo Museum*** displays pottery, beadwork, and weavings. The Hidden Valley Shop and Restaurant are also on the pueblo. Every August 10 the pueblo celebrates St. Lorenzo Feast Day, which is open to the public.

There is no fee to visit the pueblo or the museum. There are, however, modest fees for self-guided tours, as well as for fishing or camping permits. In addition, there are fees for cameras and sketching. The pueblo is generally open to visitors from 8:00 A.M. to 5:00 P.M. daily. To get to Picuris Pueblo, take Highway 75 east for 13 miles off Highway 68; (505) 587–2519.

The **Millicent Rogers Museum** is one of the finest and most specialized museums in the area. The private, nonprofit institution celebrates the art and culture of the Native American and Hispanic peoples of the Southwest. Built around the extensive collection of the late Millicent Rogers, the museum is a living memorial to this woman who took it upon herself to collect and preserve what she recognized as the rapidly vanishing arts of the area's people during the late 1940s and early 1950s.

In addition to a representative collection of Native American and Hispanic arts, the museum boasts the most important public holding of the lifework of San Ildefonso Pueblo's most famous potter, Maria Martinez, and her talented family.

The museum is 4 miles north of Taos, just off Highway 522; (505) 758–2462. The museum is open daily from 10:00 A.M. to 5:00 P.M. except during the winter, when it's closed on Monday. Admission is $6.00 for adults, $5.00 for students and seniors, and $2.00 for youths ages six to fifteen, with a maximum family rate of $12.00. Group rates are available with twenty-four-hour notice.

After absorbing some of the area's culture at the Millicent Rogers Museum, head over to the **Rio Grande Gorge Bridge** for a spectacular though slightly unnerving experience. There's a parking area on each side of the bridge. From either one you can walk across the bridge—a narrow sidewalk runs alongside the highway—which spans the 1,200-foot-wide gorge. Midway across, a small lookout platform on each side allows you to peer down 600 feet into the gorge

The Taos Hum

On a list of things the Taos Chamber of Commerce would want you to know, its community's infamous hum may not make the cut. Or, on second thought, maybe it would. The thing is, not everyone is convinced the Taos Hum even exists, and if it does, no one really knows what it is. According to the "Taos Hum Homepage" (www.eskimo.com/~billb/hum), the Taos Hum is a low-pitched, reverberating sound heard in many places worldwide, especially in the United States—most notably in Taos—the United Kingdom, and northern Europe.

It's usually heard only in quiet environments and is often described as sounding like a distant diesel engine. Because it has proven undetectable by microphones or VLF antennae, its source and nature remain a mystery. Taos area residents are divided on the issue, with most claiming not to have heard the hum that bears their community's name.

to the wild Rio Grande. Yes, there is a railing. There's even a movement afoot to allow bungee-jumping from the bridge, which proponents feel would draw adventurers nationwide. However, the plan would need legislative approval, so until then, daredevils may only dream about taking the plunge.

The bridge is on U.S. Highway 64, about 11 miles west of the 64/522 junction just north of Taos. No hours, no phone, no admission fee, no rest rooms.

Small organic farms are increasingly popular as tourist attractions, as they give the opportunity to become attuned to a local area's wisdom of using basic, natural means of enriching life. **_Bluebird Herb Farm_** in Taos is certainly evidence of this. Guided tours of the farm's seven display gardens (culinary, medicinal, tea, insect repellent, potpourri, birds and bees, and children's) are available, with tea and a variety of herbal and vegetable-based snacks provided after the tour. Visitors are also welcome to spend time among the gardens, sketching, taking photos, or merely relaxing. Herb and gardening talks as well as workshops on herb-related cooking, crafts, and wild plants are given on a monthly basis. Herbal body care products, teas, and farm-made cooking products are available for sale in the farm's gift shop.

The farm is located 4 miles south of Taos Plaza at 71 Cuchilla Road; (505) 751–1490; www.bluebirdherbfarm.com. Call ahead for reservations for guided tours or for workshop information. The farm is open Tuesday through Friday from May through October from 9:00 A.M. to 1:00 P.M., and selected weekends throughout the year when events or classes are held. Tours are available Wednesday through Friday from 11:00 A.M. to 1:00 P.M.; herb shop hours are Monday through Thursday from 9:00 A.M. to 1:00 P.M. Reservations are required two weeks in advance for guided tours; $8.00 for adults, $4.00 for youth ages twelve to eighteen, free for children age eleven or younger; special arrangements can be made for larger groups and families.

Just north of Taos in a remote mountain area near San Cristobal, persons with a literary bent seek out the **_D. H. Lawrence Memorial,_** which contains the remains of the celebrated English writer. Lawrence, whose novels include _Sons and Lovers_ and _Lady Chatterley's Lover,_ died in Paris in 1930, but in 1937 his widow, Frieda, brought his cremated ashes to New Mexico.

Though the Lawrences lived in northern New Mexico only eleven months, it certainly made an impact on them. Lawrence wrote: "I think New Mexico was the greatest experience from the outside world that I ever had. It certainly changed me forever. . . . What splendour!"

Visitors trek up the sloped walk, bordered by remarkably tall spruce trees, to the memorial site. The small, white building houses an altarlike stone marker that contains Lawrence's ashes. It's interesting to read the comments left by visitors in a guest book inside the memorial, because they often express very personal opinions about Lawrence and his writing—both positive and negative. Just outside the front door is Frieda's grave site. She gave the ranch to the University of New Mexico in 1956, specifying that her husband's memorial be perpetually maintained and kept open to the public.

When climbing the slope, don't look behind you until you reach the door to the memorial. Then turn and be greeted by the spectacular view: Pine and spruce forest in the foreground gives way to a vast expanse of mesa-desert-gorge beyond, north of the Taos Valley.

D. H. Lawrence Memorial

To experience the memorial, head north of Taos on Highway 522 for about 12 miles. A directional sign and historical marker at San Cristobal mark the turnoff. The ranch and memorial are about 7 miles off the highway at the end of a dirt road that climbs into the mountains; there is no phone (though there is a caretaker who lives near the parking area). There is no fee to visit the memorial (though most of the ranch property is off-limits to visitors), and it's open daily during daylight hours.

Fort Burgwin, an 1850s fort south of Taos that protected past residents from Apache and Comanche raids, was rescued from ruin and restored by Southern Methodist University and opened as an external campus of the school in 1974. Though the Fort Burgwin Research Center may be just school to students fortunate enough to study here, to the rest of us Fort Burgwin really comes to life during summer. From June through mid-August, Fort Burgwin hosts several public events, including evening lectures, art exhibits, and music, theater, and dance performances. Call (505) 758–8322 for performance dates and times.

The ***Red River State Trout Hatchery,*** near the community of Questa, is one of those rare functional places that double as tourist attractions. New Mexico is fortunate to have many hatcheries, thus ensuring a steady supply of fish to stock the state's many streams, rivers, and lakes.

Located within the Carson National Forest, the hatchery offers a delightful setting. It was originally built in 1941 and then totally reconstructed during

1985–1986. Pick up a brochure in the unstaffed visitor center to follow the self-guided tour of the hatchery facilities. You'll see huge rainbow trout at the display ponds, as well as fish in various stages of growth, from their beginning as eggs to their development into fully mature trout. The hatchery, New Mexico's largest, produces 300,000 pounds of trout annually.

Picnic tables dot the scenic 2-mile drive on Highway 515, which connects the hatchery to Highway 522, 2½ miles south of Questa; (505) 586–0222. Visitors are welcome from 8:00 A.M. to 5:00 P.M. daily. There's no admission charge.

After you've heard the fish story—the story of fish—at the hatchery, continue on to **Questa** and fill up on the fine fare at **El Seville Restaurant,** a local landmark for more than twenty-five years. Though the menu is varied and extensive, the authentic New Mexican combo plates are the best bet. El Seville offers freshly prepared tortilla chips—some of the best I've had—with its New Mexican entrees. Two combo dinners, including the chips and homemade sopaipillas, can be had for under $20. Get a window table for stunning mountain views. El Seville is not fancy, but owner Virgil Martinez Sr. knows how to consistently satisfy his loyal customers.

El Seville is at the junction of Highway 522 and Highway 38 in Questa; (505) 586–0300. It's open from 7:00 A.M. to 8:00 P.M. daily.

Taos County also offers an array of choices for the outdoor adventurer. From world-class skiing at Taos Ski Valley to white-water river rafting in the Rio Grande Gorge and everything in between, Taos's incredible scenery provides an inspiring setting during every season.

Taos Ski Valley is simply New Mexico's finest ski resort. Built in the European tradition and nurtured by the late Ernie Blake, the father of New Mexico skiing, Taos Ski Valley delivers an extraordinary ski experience. Skiing magazine says, "The secret of Taos is in the mixture. Take European style, southwestern flavor, perfect snow and exquisite mountains and stir. . . . Taos Ski Valley is a resort to fall in love with, whatever your ability." And the London Times says, "Without any argument the best ski resort in the world. Small, intimate and endlessly challenging, Taos simply has no equal." Enough said. Taos Ski Valley is just minutes away from Taos on Highway 150 via Highway 522; (505) 776–2291. See page 204 for ski area information.

Though there's certainly no shortage of lodging near Taos Ski Valley, the **Cottonwood Inn Bed and Breakfast** has emerged as one of the nicest places to stay en route to the ski valley. Originally built in the 1940s, the Cottonwood came into its own as the residence of the flamboyant late artist Wolfgang Pogzeba, who expanded the original structure to accommodate his visiting art patrons. Pogzeba's layout provided each of the seven guest rooms with an extraordinary view and architectural touches while preserving the pueblo-revival style of the original structure. Current owners Bill and Kit Owen—an avid fly fisherman and an accomplished downhill skier, respectively—renovated the home into its current incarnation as one of the most intimate yet secluded bed-and-breakfasts in the Taos area. Each of the guest rooms is unique in style and decor and has a private bath, original art, and locally hand-crafted furnishings, and most rooms have a fireplace. Several of the bathrooms have whirlpool baths, and one room even boasts a full-size spa and separate steam shower. The common areas of the inn display an impressive collection of Taos art and regional artifacts. The grounds of the inn encompass a grove of cottonwoods, thus the name, and extensive herb and colorful perennial gardens. The inn recently added a new outdoor hot tub.

The Cottonwood is located just off Highway 150 (Ski Valley Road) near the junction with Highway 230; (505) 776–5826 or (800) 324–7120. Rates range from $95 to $195 (higher during the Christmas break).

Though the protected stretch of wild and scenic Rio Grande extends 48 miles, the visitor center and **Wild Rivers Recreation Area** of this region are located north of Questa. This segment of the Rio Grande was officially protected when Congress passed the Wild and Scenic Rivers Act in 1968. It's quite deserted country, but when the weather is fair, canoeists and kayakers flock here.

The 18,000-acre recreation area, close to the center of the stretch, contains six maintained hiking trails and eight campsites on the rim and in the canyon.

Forest Magic Preserved with "Zero Impact" Ethics

Despite its image as a desert, New Mexico is blessed with 20 million acres of forested land, almost half of which makes up the state's five national forests. Scattered throughout its high-desert landscape, these mountainous areas are not only wildlife habitat but also green oases where human visitors can escape the summer heat and find physical, mental, and spiritual retreat among the fragrant conifers and web of life that these national treasures contain.

New Mexico forests include Gila National Forest (southwestern mountains), Cibola National Forest (central and western mountains), Santa Fe National Forest (north central mountains), Carson National Forest (Taos and northernmost mountains), and Lincoln National Forest (southeastern mountains). In addition, within these national forests and elsewhere in the state are twenty-one protected wilderness areas, where no human activity is allowed except hiking, backpacking, and camping. To keep these backcountry areas in their wild and pristine state, it's necessary to practice zero-impact ethics by remembering two basic USDA Forest Service commandments: Make it hard for others to notice you, and leave no record of your visit.

Guided hikes and regular campfire presentations are offered during summer. There are picnic facilities if you just want to peer into the vast starkness of the gorge—and you might just see a soaring bald eagle.

To get to the visitor center (505–770–1600), head 3 miles north of Questa on Highway 522 and then go west on Highway 538 for 8 miles. You'll see signs. Visitor center hours are from 9:00 A.M. to 5:00 P.M., Memorial Day weekend through Labor Day weekend; however, the Wild Rivers Recreation Area is open year-round for camping, hiking, fishing, and sight-seeing. Various fees apply.

For the less active outdoor enthusiast—or for active ones just wanting a break and some breathtaking scenery—there's the **Enchanted Circle** drive. The Enchanted Circle is the name for the communities and countryside surrounding Wheeler Peak, New Mexico's highest spot, at 13,161 feet. The loop, which involves several highways, connects the towns of Taos, Arroyo Hondo, Questa, and Red River in Taos County with Angel Fire and Eagle Nest in Colfax County (see pages 105 and 149). Although the views of many areas in the Enchanted Circle are spectacular all year, they really shine during autumn— most specifically during late September and early October, when the aspens give their all before colder weather forces them to drop their amber leaves.

The most scenic stretch can be accessed by taking U.S. Highway 64 in Taos northeast to Eagle Nest and then Highway 38 north to Red River. At a leisurely pace, the drive should take less than two hours.

Red River is an unabashedly successful tourist town charmed with a beautiful storybook setting. Like so many western resort areas (Aspen and Telluride come to mind), Red River started out as a mining town in the 1800s but was savvy enough to capitalize on its mountains and snow when the mines played out. Winter visitors enjoy the family-oriented Red River Ski Area, and year-round visitors enjoy the shopping, food, and scenery. Red River has its own funky appeal, blending a European-chalet style with a big dose of the Old West. Red River is on Highway 38, between Questa and Eagle Nest.

The tiny southeastern Taos County town of Ojo Caliente ("Hot Spring") possesses a marvelous secret bubbling up from the earth. And **Ojo Caliente Mineral Springs,** one of North America's oldest health resorts, is here to take advantage of it. This is not your plush Scottsdale- or Palm Springs-type resort. Far from it. But then again, neither are the prices. The facilities and accommodations at Ojo Caliente are rather plain and limited, but this is the place in northern New Mexico to visit if you want to relax—totally.

Separate women's and men's bathhouses are equipped with pools and tubs for soaking in the natural therapeutic mineral waters that have been attracting folks to this area for probably 2,000 years, starting with the ancestors of New Mexico's Pueblo Indians. The Spanish explorer Cabeza de Vaca described his journey to Ojo Caliente this way:

> *The greatest treasure that I found*
> *these strange people to possess are*
> *some hot springs which burst out*
> *at the foot of a mountain that gives*
> *evidence of being an active vol-*
> *cano. So powerful are the chemi-*
> *cals contained in this water that*
> *the inhabitants have a belief that*
> *they were given to them by their*
> *gods. These springs I have named*
> *Ojo Caliente.*

Lithia spring pump at
Ojo Caliente

Hotel and cabin accommodations are available, and the on-site Mineral Springs Restaurant specializes in healthful meals featuring fish, chicken, and vegetarian fare as well as New Mexican foods. But the mineral waters are the focus at the resort: iron and arsenic for soaking; iron, arsenic, lithia, and soda for drinking. (*NOTE:* The arsenic mineral water has only a trace of arsenic and is said to benefit persons with arthritis, rheumatism, and stomach ulcers as well as to promote relief of burns and eczema.) Various massages, herbal wraps, facials, and rubs are also available.

The resort is ¼ mile west of the town of Ojo Caliente on Highway 285; (505) 583–2233 or (800) 222–9162; www.ojocalientespa.com. Hours are from 8:00 A.M. to 10:00 P.M. daily. Accommodations range from $65 to $100, which includes use of hot springs; soaks, including wraps, are variably priced. Call for details.

Where to Stay in the Santa Fe and Taos Region

SANTA FE COUNTY

Bishop's Lodge,
Tesuque Valley,
off Bishop's Lodge Road,
Tesuque Valley,
(505) 983–6377

Ten Thousand Waves,
Hyde Park Road,
Santa Fe,
(505) 992–5025

La Fonda,
100 East San Francisco,
Santa Fe,
(505) 982–5511/
(800) 523–5002

Inn at Loretto,
211 Old Santa Fe Trail,
Santa Fe,
(505) 988–5531/
(800) 727–5531

Inn of the Anasazi,
113 Washington Avenue,
Santa Fe,
(505) 988–3030

La Posada de Santa Fe,
330 East Palace Avenue,
Santa Fe,
(505) 986–0000

Inn of the Turquoise Bear
(bed-and-breakfast),
342 East Buena Vista Street,
Santa Fe,
(505) 983–0798/
(800) 396–4104

TAOS COUNTY

Taos Inn,
125 Paseo del Pueblo Norte,
Taos,
(505) 758–2233

Bed & Breakfast at the Mabel Dodge Luhan House,
Morada Street,
north of Kit Carson Road,
Taos,
(505) 751–9686

San Geronimo Lodge,
1101 Witt Road,
Taos,
(505) 751–3776/
(800) 894–4119

New Buffalo Bed and Breakfast,
Retreat Center,
1 mile west of Highway 522,
Arroyo Hondo,
(505) 776–2015

Cottonwood Inn Bed and Breakfast,
off Highway 150 (Ski Valley Road), near junction with Highway 230,
Taos Ski Valley,
(505) 776–5826/
(800) 324–7120

Where to Eat in the Santa Fe and Taos Region

SANTA FE COUNTY

Café Paris,
31 Burro Alley
(near the Lensic Theatre),
Santa Fe,
(505) 986–9162.
Moderate to expensive.
Fare: French bistro menu with an emphasis on fresh quality ingredients.

Chow's,
720 St. Michael's Drive,
Sante Fe,
(505) 471–7120.
Moderate. Fare:
Contemporary Chinese.

Dave's Not Here,
1115 Hickox Street,
Santa Fe,
(505) 983–7060.
Inexpensive. Fare: New Mexican.

El Farol,
808 Canyon Road,
Santa Fe,
(505) 983–9912.
Inexpensive to moderate.
Fare: Tapas and other Spanish dishes.

Gabriel's,
U.S. Highway 285 (fifteen minutes north of Santa Fe, 2 miles north of Camel Rock Casino),
(505) 455–7000.
Moderate to expensive.
Fare: Innovative New Mexican.

Harry's Roadhouse,
96 Old Las Vegas Highway,
Santa Fe,
(505) 989–4629.
Inexpensive to moderate.
Fare: Homestyle American, New Mexican, daily gourmet specials.

Los Mayas,
409 West Water Street,
Santa Fe,
(505) 986–9930.
Moderate. Fare: Sophisticated Mexican cuisine.

SELECTED CHAMBERS OF COMMERCE/ VISITOR BUREAUS IN SANTA FE AND TAOS, REGION

Santa Fe Convention & Visitors Bureau,
P.O. Box 909,
Santa Fe, 87504;
(505) 955–6200 or (800) 777–2489;
Web site: www.santafe.org

Taos County Chamber of Commerce,
P.O. Drawer I,
Taos, 87571;
(505) 758–3873 or (800) 732–8267;
Web site: www.taoschamber.com

Maria's New Mexico Kitchen,
555 West Cordova Road,
Santa Fe,
(505) 983–7929.
Inexpensive to moderate.
Fare: New Mexican; famous margaritas.

Mine Shaft Tavern,
Highway 14 (Main Street),
Madrid,
(505) 473–0743.
Inexpensive. Fare: Burgers and New Mexican.

Rio Chama Steakhouse,
414 Old Santa Fe Trail,
Santa Fe,
(505) 955–0765.
Expensive. Fare: Steaks, seafood.

TAOS COUNTY

El Seville Restaurant,
at the junction of Highways 522 and 38,
Questa,
(505) 586–0300.
Inexpensive to moderate.
Fare: Traditional New Mexican.

Doc Martin's,
125 Paseo del Pueblo Norte,
Taos,
(505) 758–1977.
Moderate to expensive.
Fare: Innovative Southwestern.

Apple Tree,
123 Bent Street,
Taos,
(505) 758–1900.
Moderate to expensive.
Fare: Casual fine dining featuring nouvelle New Mexican, fresh fish, and vegetarian entrees.

Lambert's of Taos,
309 Paseo del Pueblo Sur,
Taos,
(505) 758–1009.
Moderate to expensive.
Fare: Contemporary American.

Michael's Kitchen,
304 Paseo del Pueblo Norte,
Taos,
(505) 758–4178.
Inexpensive to moderate.
Fare: New Mexican and American (a favorite with locals).

Los Vaqueros Dining Room
(at Sagebrush Inn),
1508 Paseo del Pueblo Sur,
Taos,
(505) 758–2254/
(800) 428–3626.
Fare: Prime rib, steaks, seafood, New Mexican cuisine.

Central New Mexico

Compared with the other five regions in the state, central New Mexico is small in area but big on influence. Boasting the state's only true urban area (but also very rural sectors), central New Mexico combines facets of all the other regions in the state because it borders them all. That there's much to experience in this region is partly why the largest chunk of the state's population calls central New Mexico home.

Bernalillo County

Because the Albuquerque metropolitan area contains approximately one-third of New Mexico's residents, it tends to dominate Bernalillo County. And, as the state's largest city, *Albuquerque* has its share of attractions to please a variety of interests.

Albuquerque was founded in 1706 by Don Francisco Cuervo y Valdes in honor of the Duke of Alburquerque, Viceroy of New Spain. The first "r" was later dropped, but Albuquerque is still known as the Duke City. The place Valdes actually designated "San Francisco de Alburquerque" is *Old Town,* just west of downtown.

In addition to its status as a historic zone of Albuquerque, anchored by the picturesque San Felipe de Neri Chapel, Old

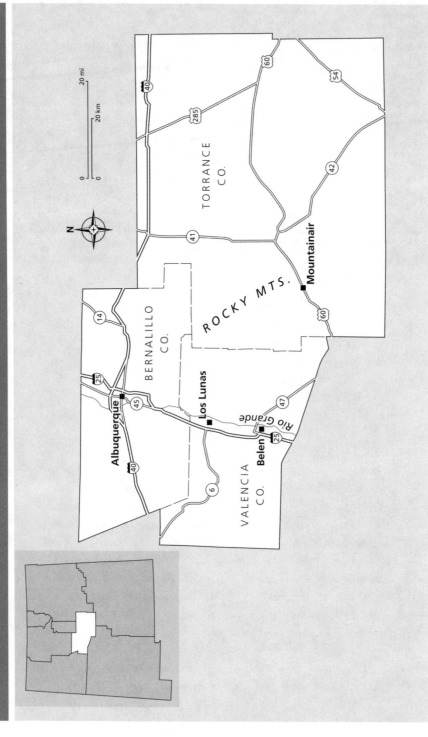

Town is home for many families whose ancestors settled the area. On the surface, the shops around Old Town's plaza seem to cater only to tourists, but the fun part of exploring Old Town is venturing off the plaza into the side streets. There you'll find an array of fun-to-explore shops, galleries, and restaurants. If your friends want to shop but you're in the mood for something noncommercial and contemplative, make arrangements to meet them in an hour at the plaza's gazebo, and then walk on over to the *Capilla de Nuestra Señora de Guadalupe* (Our Lady of Guadalupe Chapel). Despite its obvious Catholic character, this tiny chapel has a decidedly nonreligious, yet very spiritual, feel. Coupled with its beautifully landscaped courtyard, the chapel is a welcome break from the sometimes overwhelming presence of tourists. You'll find no pews inside, but rather two small rooms. The first contains a shrine to the chapel's namesake, complete with candles burning in brightly colored holders, but it's the second room that evokes more philosophical musings. Thought-provoking verses that are not obviously biblical are carved into wooden panels on the walls. No matter what your spiritual leanings are, it's a very welcoming place. You'll find the chapel at the end of Patio Escondido, off San Felipe Avenue. Old Town's plaza is the site of the annual Christmas Eve Luminaria Tour. Here, tens of thousands of luminarias (single candles set in a bed of sand at the bottom of small paper bags) create a golden glow on this special night at the place where Albuquerque began.

Parking is free around the plaza, if you can find a spot, but off the plaza are several parking lots that offer parking for a fee. Old Town is located near

FAVORITE ATTRACTIONS/EVENTS IN CENTRAL NEW MEXICO

University of New Mexico campus,
Albuquerque
(505) 277–1918

Sandia Peak Tramway,
Albuquerque
(505) 856–7325

Petroglyph National Monument,
Albuquerque
(505) 839–0205

Rio Grande Nature Center,
Albuquerque
(505) 344–7240

**Rio Grande Botanic Center/
Albuquerque Aquarium,**
Albuquerque
(505) 764–6200

Gathering of Nations Powwow,
April, Albuquerque
(505) 836–2810

**Albuquerque International
Balloon Fiesta,**
October, Albuquerque
(888) 422–7277

the intersection of Central Avenue and Rio Grande Boulevard. Most retail establishments are open seven days a week and maintain regular business hours whereas others stay open later. As with many destinations in New Mexico, Old Town is most crowded during "tourist season," which basically means summer. If your schedule is flexible, fall and winter (after Christmas) are the most pleasant times to visit.

If you're interested in buying Native American Indian jewelry and crafts, there are, in addition to the shops around Old Town's plaza, two stores nearby that offer discount pricing on jewelry, pottery, kachina dolls, drums, and other authentic crafts. *Gus's Trading Company* is across the street from Old Town's plaza, at 2026 Central SW (505–843–6381), and *Palms Trading Company* is also close, at 1504 Lomas NW (505–247–8504).

Casas de Sueños ("Houses of Dreams"), a bed-and-breakfast inn, opened near Old Town in 1990. The inn, which has several garden areas and courtyards, is within walking distance to many Old Town and downtown attractions, such as the New Mexico Museum of Natural History, the Albuquerque Museum (which connects to the Old Town shopping district via its sculpture garden), and the Rio Grande Zoo. The futuristic entry building, designed by noted Albuquerque architect Bart Prince, contrasts with the traditional old adobe structures that compose the inn. Accommodations range from one- and two-bedroom suites to private casitas, many with kitchens and fireplaces.

Casas de Sueños is at 310 Rio Grande SW; (505) 247–4560; www.casas desuenos.com. Rates range from $85 to $125.

In late 1996 the *Rio Grande Botanic Garden* and the *Albuquerque Aquarium* joined the *Rio Grande Zoo* to form the *Albuquerque Biological Park,* BioPark for short. "Tingley Beach," a favorite urban fishing spot, is currently undergoing a much anticipated, one-year renovation project. When it reopens in March 2005 as the Tingley Aquatic Park, it will boast many new improvements, including a narrow-gauge railroad linking the north and south facilities of the Biological Park. When complete, the BioPark will be the first in the nation to have facilities that are physically connected and under consolidated management. The one-hundred-acre site extends north from the zoo along more than 3 miles of the Rio Grande Bosque, which, like the Sandia Mountain foothills, is the closest thing to wilderness within the city. Planning and construction of the BioPark has been under way for years, but the wait was worth it. The clean lines and modern architecture of the botanic garden's conservatory blend well with the more traditional features of the park's other structures. From the peaceful entry complex to the Spanish-Moorish Court, the botanic garden exudes the best of Southwestern garden influences. A newly opened children's fantasy garden offers a "through the looking glass" magnified look at the world of plants and gardening.

The theme of the 45,000-square-foot aquarium complex, which includes a gift shop and restaurant, is to interpret the story of a drop of water as it enters the upper Rio Grande high in the San Juan Mountains of southern Colorado and flows through the canyons, deserts, and valleys of New Mexico, Mexico, and Texas, through the subtropical forests of the lower Rio Grande Valley, and finally into the Gulf of Mexico. A 285,000-gallon shark tank with floor-to-ceiling viewing contains various species of Gulf sharks as well as giant groupers, moray eels, manta rays, and skates, in addition to schooling fish and

Albuquerque's Central Avenue

If the Rio Grande is the lifeblood of Albuquerque, then Central Avenue is the city's soul. While the river may divide the city geographically into east and west, Central Avenue divides the city in another way. Far from its simple north-south division, the leisurely long avenue—Albuquerque's vestige of historic Route 66—also divides the city psychically. Either residents fear "Central" because their image of the area is outdated or limited, or they're quite fond of the reemerging historic strip and the urban delights it now offers.

For years after Interstate 40 started diverting travelers from the old route in the mid-1960s, much of it fell out of favor and into decay. While there remain several sections of Central that many a suburbanite might consider unsavory, the revitalizations and innovations occurring on the more prominent stretches since the mid-1990s have been especially heartening, considering its illustrious past. For pedestrian quests in search of culinary, shopping, and entertainment adventures, you won't find a better urban venue in the state.

In addition to the renovations made to Central along its border with the University of New Mexico (University Avenue through Girard) and its passage through Downtown (Second through Eighth Streets), the Nob Hill area (Girard to east of Carlisle) has emerged as the preeminent see-and-be-seen district, boasting some of the city's best restaurants and most interesting shops. And, for a tranquil change of pace, the wonderfully landscaped and architecturally significant UNM campus is just minutes away by foot.

various invertebrates. Though there are several great aquariums in the United States (California's Monterey Bay Aquarium comes to mind), it is quite a trip to see one of this scale in the high desert of the Southwest.

Because the BioPark is evolving, please call (505) 764–6200 for up-to-date visitor information, or check their Web site, www.cabq.gov/biopark. To get to the botanic garden/aquarium complex, take Central Avenue west from Old Town about ½ mile to Tingley Drive. You'll see it on your right. Admission to either the zoo or the botanic park and aquarium complex is $7.00 for adults and $3.00 for seniors and children ages six to twelve. Combined admission to all three is $10.00 for adults, and $5.00 for seniors and children. Open daily from 9:00 A.M. to 5:00 P.M., until 6:00 P.M. on Saturday and Sunday in the summer months.

The *Indian Pueblo Cultural Center* near Old Town is the place to go to experience the art, history, and culture of New Mexico's nineteen pueblos (and one, Hopi Pueblo, in Arizona)—before venturing out to explore any of them. The center is owned and operated by the Pueblo Tribes of New Mexico and houses a fine museum and a restaurant that features New Mexican and Pueblo Indian dishes. The museum is divided into three main sections: the prehistoric, the historic, and the contemporary. The new Pueblo House Children's Museum offers hands-on contact with ancient artifacts and modern craft works, aimed at grade school (K–5) children. Open Tuesday, Thursday, and half-day Wednesday, as well as by group appointment.

The center also contains gift shops and art galleries that offer authentic Indian pottery, sculpture, paintings, rugs, sand paintings, kachina dolls, and jewelry. Traditional Indian dance performances, alternated among the pueblos, are held on weekends in summer at 11:00 A.M. and 2:00 P.M.

The Indian Pueblo Cultural Center is at 2401 Twelfth Street NW, just north of Interstate 40; (505) 843–7270. Admission to the museum is $4.00 for adults, $3.00 for seniors, and $1.00 for students. Museum and gift shops are open daily from 9:00 A.M. to 5:30 P.M., and the restaurant is open daily from 8:30 A.M. to 4:30 P.M.

The opening of the new *National Hispanic Cultural Center of New Mexico* in the fall of 2000 was a long-awaited dream come true for many in New Mexico's Hispanic community. The world-class facility, which is located on a sixteen-acre site along the banks of the Rio Grande in the Albuquerque South Valley community of *Barelas,* was conceived to preserve, interpret, and showcase Hispanic arts and culture. Born out of the vision of a handful of artists and community members seventeen years earlier, the center is a complex of buildings around a large central plaza and includes several impressive gallery spaces and performing arts venues, among other educational and cultural offerings. A large *torreon,* or tower, serves as the entry point and information center.

The historic community of Barelas was originally settled for its proximity to a natural ford in the Rio Grande and the Camino Real, the Spanish colonial-era Royal Road connecting Mexico City with Santa Fe. Later, the railroad yards made Barelas a vibrant and economically important neighborhood in Albuquerque. However, as one of the opening art exhibits, "A Pictorial History of Barelas," explains, although the traditional Hispanic neighborhood that surrounds the center was once part of Albuquerque's vibrant core, it fell out of favor as Albuquerque grew and the

newmexicotrivia

Though there is now more speculation about his alleged guilt, convicted cold-war spy Julius Rosenberg was officially arrested at a residence on High Street near Copper in downtown Albuquerque.

greater downtown area declined. Now, along with recent streetscape improvements to the South Fourth Street corridor, the center is the chief catalyst for a renaissance of the Barelas community, just as the adjacent downtown district also continues its own revitalization.

The cultural center's restaurant, La Fonda del Bosque, serves traditional dishes Tuesday through Sunday from 7:30 A.M. to 3:30 P.M. The center is also developing a teaching kitchen that will offer a program of traditional Spanish colonial cooking classes. Call for current status.

The center is located at 1701 Fourth Street SW (at Avenida César Chávez, also known as Bridge Street); (505) 246–2261; www.nhccnm.org. It's open Tuesday through Sunday from 10:00 A.M. to 5:00 P.M.; admission is $3.00 for adults, $2.00 for seniors, and free for children under age sixteen.

Like many cities' downtown areas in the past two decades, Albuquerque's downtown area is experiencing a renaissance of sorts as citizens once again take pride in their city's center. A spot worth a look during your tour of downtown is the ***KiMo Theatre,*** built in 1927 in the pueblo-deco style and later restored by the city. The theater hosts a wide range of performances, especially alternative and cultural performances, which are often more suitable to the ambience of the venue. The KiMo Theatre is at 423 Central NW; (505) 768–3522, box office (505) 768–3544; www.cabq.gov/kimo/schedule.html.

Listed on the National Register of Historic Places, ***La Posada de Albuquerque*** was built in 1939 by Conrad Hilton, his first hotel in his home state. (He was a native of San Antonio, New Mexico.) Among the hotel's claims to fame is its designation as the first air-conditioned building in New Mexico and as the honeymoon hotel for Mr. Hilton and his bride, Zsa Zsa Gabor.

KiMo Theatre

Remodeled to its former glory in 1984, with an extensive upgrade in 2001, La Posada includes a spacious lobby bar and a first-class restaurant, Conrad's Downtown. The chic bistro, done in black and white, features a taste of Old Mexico with a Spanish flair. La Posada is at 125 Second Street NW; (505) 242–9090 or (800) 777–5732; www.laposada-abq.com. Room rates range from $80 to $280 (most are in the $100 range).

A great place to break for lunch downtown is **M. & J. Sanitary Tortilla Factory.** Located on the fringe of the downtown core, M. & J.'s offers up traditional New Mexican fare at reasonable prices. Its red chile and green chile are among the city's most flavorful and hottest—the reason the restaurant provides a pitcher of ice water at each table.

Posted on the walls above the booths are letters, cards, and even messages scrawled on napkins from satisfied diners from all over the globe. They all sing the praises of the fiery food and friendly people. You don't stay in the business for thirty years in the supercompetitive Albuquerque restaurant market unless you keep 'em coming back, something M. & J.'s owners, Bea and Jake Montoya, have always known. The wait staff keeps the complimentary homemade chips and salsa coming before and during the meal, and despite the filling nature of the cuisine, everything's heart-healthy here: The restaurant uses only cholesterol-free oil.

M. & J.'s is at 403 Second Street SW; (505) 242–4890. It's open Monday through Saturday from 9:00 A.M. to 4:00 P.M.

College campuses and the areas surrounding them are usually some of the most interesting places in a city, and the **University of New Mexico** in

Albuquerque is no different. As the largest university in the state, UNM is located along Central Avenue (old Route 66) east of downtown. A stroll around UNM's campus reveals perhaps the finest examples of pueblo revival-style architecture. These buildings were designed by New Mexico's most famous architect, the late John Gaw Meem of Santa Fe, who served as consulting architect for UNM from 1933 to 1959. Zimmermann Library, Scholes Hall, and Alumni Chapel are three of the Meem firm's most striking designs on campus and are worth a look and a few photographs. The beautifully landscaped duck-pond area in the campus's center, adjacent to Zimmermann Library, is an idyllic spot for a country picnic in the middle of the city. The UNM Visitors Center is in an old adobe tucked away on the corner of Redondo Drive at 1700 Las Lomas Boulevard; (505) 277–1989; open Monday through Friday from 8:00 A.M. to 5:00 P.M.

Tamarind Institute, housed in a nondescript building across Central Avenue from the university, is much more than a division of UNM. It's a unique educational facility dedicated to the fine art of collaborative lithography. And it gives the best tour in Albuquerque. The good news is that the tour is free. The bad news is that it happens only once a month—usually the first Friday of each month at 1:30 P.M. (may vary in summer). Reservations are strongly recommended.

If you didn't know a thing about collaborative lithography before your visit to Tamarind, you'll be an expert after the two-hour tour, which includes viewing an Emmy-nominated documentary produced by the institute, a briefing by the director, and a staff-guided tour of the facility.

Tamarind began in 1960 in Los Angeles as the Tamarind Lithography Workshop. Its purpose was to rescue collaborative lithography from becoming a lost art in the United States by training a pool of master printers to work with artists. After ten years in Los Angeles, Tamarind, supported by substantial Ford Foundation grants, moved to Albuquerque in 1970 to become self-sustaining and continue the goals established in California.

If your visit doesn't coincide with a tour, you can still view some of the finished works—a small gallery at the institute displays selected lithographs. Some are available for purchase, and once you understand the lengthy collaborative lithography process, you'll understand the prices.

Tamarind Institute is at 108 Cornell Avenue SE; (505) 277–3901. Gallery hours are 9:00 A.M. to 5:00 P.M. Tuesday through Friday.

To catch the flavor of campus life, stop in at the ***Frontier Restaurant,*** across the street from the main entrance to UNM. This sprawling eatery, which fills an entire city block, serves up budget-priced *huevos rancheros,* green chile stew, and homemade cinnamon rolls the diameter of a dinner plate all day, accompanied by the tapping of laptop keyboards, the murmur of intellectual discourse, and the din of video games. Contact: 2400 Central Avenue; (505) 266–0550; www.frontierrestaurant.com.

The *Nob Hill–Highland District,* just east of UNM along Central Avenue near Carlisle Boulevard, re-creates that old Route 66 ambience. This recently revived, and continually evolving, section of Albuquerque showcases antiques shops, vintage-clothing stores, other shops, theaters, and cafes, all interspersed among more practical businesses to create an eclectic mix perfect for a Saturday afternoon stroll. Among the places not to miss are Buster's Route 66 Diner, Absolutely Neon Studios, Nob Hill Artists' Co-op, and PeaceCraft, a non-profit shop featuring handmade goods from developing nations.

Although individual antiques stores abound in and around the Nob Hill District (mostly along Central and Morningside Avenues), the largest selection of antiques and collector items under one roof is at *Classic Century Square.* This old department-store building houses three levels of antiques, collectibles, furniture, glassware, books, jewelry, and other items in more than 125 wall-less shops. There's an exceptionally large collection of vintage dolls in one section of the complex. You could spend a whole afternoon browsing and still not see everything.

Traditional Food of New Mexico

Calabacitas

Calabacitas, a New Mexican-style squash concoction, is a favorite local dish.

2 cups whole kernel corn

4 tablespoons corn oil

¼ teaspoon black pepper

½ chopped onion

2 cups chopped green chiles (more
or less, according to taste)

½ cup water

¾ cup grated Monterey Jack cheese

1 clove garlic, minced

1 teaspoon salt

4 medium yellow and/or zucchini squashes, sliced

Combine all ingredients, except cheese, in a large saucepan. Cook at medium heat until squash is tender, approximately 20 minutes. Garnish with cheese before serving. Makes 4–6 servings.

Classic Century Square is at 4616 Central Avenue SE, just west of San Mateo Boulevard; (505) 255–1850. It's open Monday through Saturday from 10:00 A.M. to 6:00 P.M. and Sunday from noon to 5:00 P.M.

Albuquerque's rural North Valley, situated near the Rio Grande, contains some of the area's most fertile land, planted with apple orchards, alfalfa fields, extensive gardens—and grapes for wine at **Anderson Valley Vineyards.** The award-winning winery, near the vineyards, offers wine tastings and tours, in addition to a gift shop selling wine- and gourmet-related items. An outdoor patio overlooking alfalfa fields is a great spot to enjoy a picnic with friends— accompanied by a bottle of Anderson Valley wine, of course.

Anderson Valley was started in 1984 by the late Maxie Anderson and his wife. Maxie was a famous hot-air-balloon pilot who set world records with a transcontinental balloon flight (along with his son, Kris) and a transatlantic flight (with Ben Abruzzo). His family continues the wine-making tradition he began.

Tours are held on the hour from 1:00 to 4:00 P.M. daily in summer and sporadically the rest of the year. Anderson Valley's tasting room is at 4920 Rio Grande Boulevard NW; (505) 344–7266. As with the tours, the tasting room's hours change seasonally, so call ahead.

Hot-air ballooning is extremely popular in New Mexico because of the state's predictably pleasant fall weather and clear skies. To celebrate this colorful sport, New Mexico's largest city hosts the **Albuquerque International Balloon Fiesta** each October.

Balloonists and spectators come from all over the world to take part in the nine-day event, which draws more than 100,000 spectators. The mass ascensions on the four weekend mornings during the fiesta are worth an early rising (while it's still dark out) for the trek to Balloon Fiesta Park, located on Alameda Boulevard off Interstate 25. Up to 600 balloons take off to thousands of "oohs and ahs," while amateur and professional photogra-

newmexicotrivia

Legendary '60s rocker Jim Morrison, lead singer of the Doors, was born in Albuquerque.

phers click away at what has surpassed Pasadena's Tournament of Roses Parade as the most photographed annual event in the world.

In addition to the mass ascensions, the yearly Balloon Glow has become quite a popular event. After sunset, hundreds of inflated hot-air balloons fire up in synchronized patterns to create huge spheres of colorful, glowing light. If you make it to Albuquerque for the fiesta, don't miss the Balloon Glow. Another fun ballooning event during the fiesta is the Special Shapes Rodeo, limited to those balloons tailored a bit differently from the usual inverted teardrop configuration. You'll see Mickey Mouse, the Planter's Peanut Man, a Pepsi can, a cow jumping over a moon, and scores more of the huge floating representations of familiar items.

The fiesta begins the first weekend of each October. For more information, call (505) 821–1000/(888) 422–7277; www.balloonfiesta.com.

Though not as well known as the Albuquerque International Balloon Fiesta, the **Gathering of Nations Powwow,** held annually the last weekend of April (Thursday through Saturday), is also a significant event for Albuquerque. Billed as the largest Native American powwow, or social get-together, in North America, the cultural gathering attracts more than 3,000 dancers and singers— representing more than 700 indigenous tribes from Canada and the United States—who participate socially and competitively. In addition to various forms of entertainment, such as ceremonial dances, drumming, singing, and other musical performances, the event includes Native American foods and shopping at the Indian Traders Market, as well as the annual crowning of Miss Indian World. And though the event is staged primarily for Native Americans, every-one is welcome at the family-oriented event, as evidenced by the tens of thou-sands of nonnatives who attend each year.

The gathering is held at the UNM Arena (commonly called "The Pit"), about a mile south of the University of New Mexico campus; entrance fees vary; (505) 836–2810; www.gatheringofnations.com.

New Mexico is a nature lover's paradise, and Albuquerque fits right in. The **Rio Grande Nature Center** in Albuquerque's North Valley lies, as its name implies, along the Rio Grande and is a wonderful place for leisurely walks or brisk hikes. The outside part of the center consists of 270 acres of riverside for-est and meadows that include stands of hundred-year-old cottonwoods, among other trees, and a three-acre pond. The *bosque,* as wooded areas are called in the Southwest, is threaded with 2 miles of trails whose unobtrusive signs iden-tify the various forms of plant life.

The inside part of the center contains self-guided exhibits that provide insight into the natural, historical, and social implications of the Rio Grande. In the library area, there's also a glassed-in viewing room from which you can observe the wildlife at the pond without being noticed. A sign hanging here, THIS WEEK'S VISITORS, lists the species of birds and other animals that have been spotted recently.

Nature walks and children's hikes are scheduled, and you can borrow a pair of binoculars if you have a photo ID. Although the center makes for an enjoyable outing throughout the year, weekdays during fall and winter are especially tranquil. It's not—as a sign at the center's entrance prominently points out—a place to have a picnic, ride your bike or horse, run or jog, or walk your dog.

The Rio Grande Nature Center State Park is at 2901 Candelaria NW (where Candelaria dead-ends); (505) 344–7240. The visitor center is open daily from 10:00 A.M. to 5:00 P.M., and the grounds are open from 8:00 A.M. to 5:00 P.M. (And they mean it: Cars left in the parking lot after 5:00 P.M. will be locked in.) Admission is $1.00 for adults, 50 cents for children, and 25 cents for children in school groups.

The west side of Albuquerque is often referred to as the West Mesa because, well, it is a mesa. It rises out of Albuquerque's valley to form a wonderfully flat horizon (except for a few dormant volcanos, for visual interest) perfect for the setting sun to sink into. It's on the West Mesa that you'll find **Petroglyph National Monument.** At a distance, the park is a barren, unimpressive pile of rocks on a hill. But look a little closer and

newmexicotrivia

Approximately one-third of New Mexico's population of 1.8 million reside in the Albuquerque metropolitan area.

you'll see why the place got its name: The rocks are "decorated" with ancient Indian petroglyphs, or images carved in rock. Markers along the trails indicate and interpret the drawings. The monument is a fun place to spend a couple of hours on a sunny, brisk winter day. It may be too hot, though, because of the lack of shade, for some folks during the peak of summer.

To get to the petroglyphs, take Interstate 40 west and exit north onto Unser Boulevard. Proceed 3 miles to the park visitor center; (505) 899–0205; www.nps.gov/petr/. It's open daily from 8:00 A.M. to 5:00 P.M. There are no admission fees in most of the park; however, the parking fee at the Boca Negra Unit is $1.00 per car weekdays, $2.00 on weekends.

Although most of the unique places lie near the older parts of town—Old Town, downtown, the university area, the North Valley—there's much to see in the "newer" parts of Albuquerque. The Heights, specifically the Far Northeast Heights, are blessed with the Sandia Mountains, which form a lovely backdrop for the city while bordering its east side. The Spaniards named the mountains Sandia, which means "watermelon," because of the red color they turn when hit by the setting sun.

To explore the Sandias from Albuquerque, consider a hike on **La Luz Trail.** In Spanish, the name of this scenic 8-mile trail means "the light." The trail, known as the site of La Luz Trail Run held each August, begins at the Juan Tabo recreation area and follows the western slope of the Sandias. The well-marked trail averages a 12 percent grade over the 3,700-foot rise; thus, the three- to five-hour (or more!) hike is quite a workout.

Bring along plenty of water, snacks, and matches, as well as a flashlight and bad-weather gear. It gets quite brisk at the higher elevations, even during the summer months, so dress appropriately. Because of temperature extremes, winter is not the best time to tackle La Luz. Being prepared and using common sense cannot be stressed enough, as evidenced by the media attention given to the several hikers per year who fall or become stranded. For this reason, be sure to tell someone where you are going when you hike La Luz. The ever-changing views and scenery along this trail are amazingly beautiful. For a less strenuous hike, take the tram (see below) to the top and hike down. If you're careful to time the last leg of your descent at sunset, you'll see why the trail is called La Luz—incredible!

From Interstate 25 in north Albuquerque, exit at Tramway Boulevard and go 4 miles east to the Juan Tabo turnoff. Follow the road to the trailhead.

The foothills of the Sandias provide a wonderful vantage point from which to view the spectacular sunsets for which New Mexico is famous. And a comfortable spot for the nightly show is the restaurant and lounge nestled in the foothills at the base of the ***Sandia Peak Tramway,*** the world's longest aerial tramway, which will smoothly transport you to the top of 10,400-foot Sandia Peak in about fifteen minutes. At the top of the tram you'll find another restaurant, ***High Finance,*** which has an eagle's-eye view of Albuquerque. In addition to serving fine food, High Finance is also a great place for skiers to take a break at the top of the lifts on the other side of the mountain at Sandia Peak Ski Area.

Tram rides are popular at all times of the year, but be aware that winter temperatures can be more than thirty degrees colder at the top, which doesn't make for very comfortable sight-seeing. Still, you can always hang out at High Finance and have a cup of coffee or a glass of wine. And if you're lucky, you might see a brave hang-glider pilot take the plunge—harnessed in his or her glider, we hope—toward the Rio Grande valley 1 mile below.

The Tramway (505–856–7325; www.sandiapeak.com) is at 38 Tramway Road off Tramway Boulevard. Though there's no set schedule, the tram departs about every twenty to thirty minutes from 9:00 A.M. to 9:00 P.M. daily Memorial Day through Labor Day and during Balloon Fiesta, and from 9:00 A.M. to 8:00 P.M. daily (on Wednesday, tram departures begin at noon) the rest of the years. Round-trip tickets are $15 for adults, $12 for seniors, and $10 for children. Each tram departure is announced in the adjacent restaurant, so you can wait for your "flight" in the bar if you like.

The top and the other side of the Sandias are also worth exploring. It's amazing that although most Albuquerque residents see the Sandias every day, many of them still don't realize that they can drive to the very top—***Sandia Crest,*** at 10,678 feet—in less than an hour via Interstate 40 and the Sandia Crest Highway (Highway 536), which has been designated a National Scenic Byway; it's also the highest scenic drive in the Southwest. At the top, you'll find things a lot different than they were back "on the ground." Here, it's a lot cooler, which is refreshing during summer; even so, you might want to bring a sweater or light jacket.

A Glimpse of Central New Mexico: Impressions of the *Bosque,* the Mountains, and the Volcanoes

By using Albuquerque merely as a gateway to New Mexico's more far-flung nature adventures, visitors often ignore what many Albuquerqueans also take for granted: its vast wonderland of hiking opportunities, literally minutes from any neighborhood in town. The three most impressive are the *bosque,* the foothills, and the volcanoes. And the best part is that they're free to enjoy anytime and they're usually quite deserted, despite their proximity.

The *bosque,* or wooded area that stretches along the Rio Grande throughout central New Mexico, has always been a beautiful place through which to hike or bike. But it's the arrival of the city's long-awaited botanic center and aquarium (see page 126) that has brought the neighboring *bosque* new respect and visibility. Accessible from a small parking area along Central Avenue, the Rio Grande State Park allows access to the *bosque* via a system of trails through cottonwood groves along the river. It's a great place for morning and evening walks, especially during spring and fall, because of the activity among the native birds that nest, and migratory birds that rest, in the sanctuary of the *bosque.*

The foothills of the Sandia Mountains, which form Albuquerque's eastern border, provide another welcome nature escape. In addition to the celebrated La Luz Trail (see page 135), there are many other well-marked trails, such as the Piedra Lisa Trail, which begins east of Tramway Boulevard. Trail maps are available from the USDA Forest Service at 333 Broadway SE in Albuquerque; (505) 842–3292. And as you might imagine, the sunsets are always quite spectacular from the foothills.

Albuquerque's West Mesa, with its five dormant volcanic peaks and its shrubby high-desert vegetation, provides an austere contrast to the *bosque* and the foothills. And, as you might also expect, the views of the Sandia and Manzano Mountains are quite spectacular and unobstructed, due to the mesa's elevation above the city.

To get to the volcanoes, head west on Interstate 40 for about 9 miles, take Paseo del Volcan exit, and head north for a couple of miles until you find primitive parking areas and trailheads.

The views from the crest are incredible. It's hard to imagine that the "small town" over the edge is bustling Albuquerque. The city becomes a distant, twinkling fairyland after sunset. From the observation deck at the summit, you can see more than 15,000 square miles of central New Mexico. You're not totally isolated, however: The **Sandia Crest House**—a combination gift shop, restaurant, and all-around base for hiking and cross-country skiing in winter—is perched at the top; (505) 243–0605.

Once you've conquered the crest, check out **Tinkertown Museum** on your way back down the mountain. The museum is subtitled "Wood-Carved Miniature Village and Glass Bottle House" and is a place not to be missed. Even for people who don't think they like this sort of thing, I repeat, it's a place not to be missed!

Billed as "a collection of collections," Tinkertown explores a world gone by as well as a slightly skewed one that never existed. You'll get a month's worth of smiles after an hour of following the arrows directing you through the displays of miniature exhibits, including a general store and three-ring circus. Some displays involve mechanical action that brings the figures to life. You'll see ghost-town relics from New Mexico's Billy the Kid Country, as well as "The Wishing Buddha," accompanied by a sign that reads WISH FOR PEACE ON EARTH, NOT JUST A PIECE OF THE ACTION The self-guided tour takes you through a structure built out of glass bottles as the sounds of old-time frontier music further remove you from time and place.

Tinkertown is the result of more than forty years of tinkering by owner-creator-curator-artist Ross Ward. And just when you're wondering when he found the time to do all this, you'll see his motto posted on the wall: I DID ALL THIS WHILE YOU WERE WATCHING TV!

Tinkertown is about 1¼ miles up Highway 536 off Highway 14; (505) 281–5233; www.tinkertown.com. It's open daily 9:00 A.M. to 6:00 P.M. from April through October. Admission is $3.00 for adults, $2.50 for seniors, and $1.00 for youths ages four to fifteen, while children age three or younger get a free peek at Ward's world.

One beautifully constructed and maintained bed-and-breakfast inn perched in the Sandias is **Elaine's.** Elaine Nelson O'Neil built this lodgepole pine home for herself more than twenty years ago and turned the top two floors of it into a bed-and-breakfast in 1988. There are five guest rooms, and the common area of the no-smoking-permitted inn has a vaulted ceiling, a huge stone fireplace, and an upright piano, all with a fantastic alpine view through floor-to-ceiling windows.

Rates run from $89 to $139 per night. To get to Elaine's, take the Tijeras/Cedar Crest (Highway 14) exit and, as you drive under Interstate 40, check your odometer; then go slightly over 4 miles north on Highway 14. Turn left at the Turquoise Trail Campground (approximately 1 mile past Bella Vista Restaurant). Go straight on the dirt road approximately ½ mile. Turn left at the T. As you enter the gate marked "Snowline Estates," you'll see Elaine's on your right at the top of the hill. Follow the road up the hill and around the corner; (505) 281–2467 or (800) 821–3092; www.elainesbnb.com.

For many years the *National Atomic Museum* was located on Kirtland Air Force Base, a key distribution and collection point for America's nuclear weapons. Due to heightened security following the 9/11 terrorist attacks, Kirtland is now off-limits to the general public. The museum was closed for several months and has now relocated in temporary quarters at 1905 Mountain Road Northwest until 2006, when it's slated to move into a larger building now under construction at the Albuquerque Balloon Park. Even devout pacifists can enjoy this fascinating display, which objectively portrays New Mexico's nuclear heritage: the development of the first atom bombs during the 1940s in Los Alamos (see Los Alamos County entry in North Central New Mexico chapter) and, subsequently, the first atomic blast at the Trinity Site (see Socorro County entry in the chapter on Southwestern New Mexico). The museum takes you through these historical developments and displays nuclear artifacts. New exhibits on nuclear science and medicine reflect the museum's change of focus away from military applications. Showings of two documentaries, *10 Seconds That Shook the World* and the newer *Commitment to Peace,* alternate throughout the day. Open daily from 9:00 A.M. to 5:00 P.M.; (505) 284–3243; www.atom icmuseum.com. Admission is $4.00 for adults and $3.00 for seniors and young people ages seven to eighteen; children age six or younger and active-duty military personnel and their dependents are admitted free.

In extreme western Bernalillo County near the Cibola County line, you'll find truly remote yet thoroughly modern lodging at the *Apache Canyon Ranch Bed and Breakfast Inn.* Ava and Theron Bowers converted their 3,600-square-foot home into a bed-and-breakfast in 1996 to share their home, along with the austere beauty of the landscape and endless mountain and mesa views, with their guests. Grazing cattle and wild horses are the Bowers' nearest neighbors, and in the late evening, while enjoying the cool high desert air on the patio, guests will likely be serenaded by distant coyotes. The ranch borders both To'hajiilee Navajo lands and the Laguna Indian Reservation.

Ava has combined the art and antiques from Native American, Hispanic, and her own African-American culture to create a welcoming, unique decor. The largest of the inn's five guest rooms is the Sky City Suite, which includes a fireplace, a king-size bed, and a whirlpool bath. Rates range from $90 to $265. To get to Apache Canyon Ranch, head west from Albuquerque on

STATE PARKS IN CENTRAL NEW MEXICO
On the Web at: www.emnrd.state.nm.us/nmparks/

Coronado State Monument,
in Bernalillo (north of Albuquerque),
(505) 867–5351

Manzano Mountains State Park,
13 miles northwest of Mountainair
(southeast of Albuquerque),
April 15 to October 31,
(505) 847–2820
November 1 to March 31,
(505) 344–7240

Rio Grande Nature Center State Park,
in Albuquerque,
(505) 344–7240

Interstate 40 (about thirty minutes) to the To'hajiilee exit; then head north for about 3 miles; (505) 836–7220 or (800) 808–8310; www.apachecanyon.com.

Valencia County

South of Albuquerque along Interstate 25 you'll find the rural communities of Valencia County: Belen, Los Lunas, Bosque Farms, Jarales, and Tomé, among others. Many of the residents of this area enjoy the rural solitude of life along the Rio Grande while benefiting from the big-city advantages of Albuquerque, only a half-hour's commute to the north.

Settled by the Spanish in 1741, *Belen* became a major New Mexico railroad center in the 1880s. Though the railroad remains important to Belen, the heyday of passenger trains carrying travelers out west is long gone. But the Valencia County Historical Society's *Harvey House Museum* remembers. Located in the former Belen Harvey House, the small museum takes up just a part of the historic dining stop, whereas the rest of the restored mission-style building is occupied by the Belen Harvey House Civic Center.

In addition to displaying a variety of antique items donated by or on loan from area citizens, the museum pays homage to Fred Harvey and the days when his Harvey House restaurants were scattered along the railway throughout the West. Impeccable service, fine food, and the young, gracious Harvey Girls (waitresses) helped tame the wild frontier from the turn of the twentieth century until World War II, when other forms of travel took hold. One room in the museum is outfitted with furnishings typical of Harvey Girls' boarding rooms, which usually were upstairs from the dining area.

Though most of these oases of civility no longer exist, the citizens of Belen fought to save their Harvey House in the early 1980s when it faced demolition. The railroad sold the structure to the city of Belen, and residents rallied to preserve the legacy of Fred Harvey in their town.

The museum is at 104 North First Street in Belen; (505) 861–0581. It's open Tuesday through Saturday from 12:30 to 3:30 P.M.

For a look at farm life and items from yesteryear, a visit to the ***P & M Chavez Farm Museum*** in nearby Jarales is a smart move. Run by Pablo and Manuela Chavez in and around their farmhouse since 1986, the museum is a wonderful mishmash of antiques and other items ranging from a late 1880s, horse-drawn hearse to a collection of 1960s Barbie dolls.

When the Chavezes were stationed in California in 1942, a fortune-teller predicted that Manuela would someday have a museum of her own. The prophecy has been fulfilled in the museum, which contains artifacts collected by the Chavezes for nearly fifty years. The museum occupies several rooms in the Chavezes' house, separate from living areas, plus detached buildings, barns, and outside areas. A fine collection of antique cars—including a 1925 Studebaker, a 1959 Edsel, and a 1929 Model A Ford—and of farm implements is a highlight of the barn and outdoor exhibits. Manuela will gladly detail the background of some of the more notable displays. But don't make the mistake of asking if an item is for sale. "Nothing is for sale; this is a museum," she'll answer proudly.

From Highway 309 (Reinken Avenue) in Belen, take Highway 109 south for 3½ miles to Jarales. The museum will be on your right; (505) 864–8354. It's open Monday through Saturday from 9:00 A.M. to 11:00 A.M. and 1:00 to 5:00 P.M,. Sunday from 1:00 to 5:00 P.M. Call ahead to verify hours, which are subject to change. Guided tours of the museum are $5.00 for adults, $4.00 for seniors, $3.00 for children ages five to seventeen, and free for kids age four or younger. Group discounts are available; call ahead.

Though the Luna-Otero Mansion was once the headquarters of a livestock and land dynasty, since 1977 the stately home has been serving up appetizing entrees as the ***Luna Mansion*** restaurant. A National Historic Landmark, this is a restaurant with a story.

Domingo de Luna and Don Pedro Otero both came to New Mexico from Spain on land grants near the end of the seventeenth century. After nearly 200 years of amassing fortunes in land, livestock, and political influence,

newmexicotrivia

"Christmas" is not only a holiday in New Mexico, but it's also the proper response to a local waiter if you want your New Mexican entree topped with both green and red chiles.

Luna Mansion

descendants of the two men's families were united by marriage in the late 1800s to create what is known as the Luna-Otero Dynasty.

The Luna-Otero Mansion was built by the Santa Fe Railroad in 1881 in exchange for right-of-way privileges through the Luna property (which meant the existing Luna home had to go). The Southern colonial architectural design of the mansion is said to have been inspired by trips through the South by the Luna family. Though the design certainly seems out of place in New Mexico, the building material is not. You guessed it—it's constructed out of adobe.

Perhaps ironically, the restaurant serves up just about everything except New Mexican food—steaks, chicken, prime rib, pasta, and seafood dishes dominate the menu. The closest thing to New Mexican is the Red Chile Linguini.

The Luna Mansion is at the junction of Highways 6 and 314 in Los Lunas; (505) 865–7333. It is open Wednesday through Sunday from 5:00 to 9:00 P.M. but is open until 9:30 on Friday and Saturday.

Torrance County

Torrance County attaches to Bernalillo County's southeast side and is therefore a quick drive from Albuquerque. Many city residents enjoy a Sunday afternoon drive on the backside of the Sandia and Manzano Mountains on Highway 337 (old South 14) and Highway 55. The atmosphere is decidedly rural and dotted with small towns along the route—Chilili (Bernalillo County), Tajique, Torreon, Manzano.

One particular bypass along the way is the ***Tajique-Torreon Loop,*** an incredibly scenic unpaved 17-mile stretch of road that indirectly connects the two towns. In Tajique, head east on Forest Road 55 (the road directing you to Fourth of July Campground off Highway 55). Unless you're in a four-wheel-drive vehicle, don't attempt to go past the Fourth of July Campground at the 7-mile mark—the road is clearly marked "primitive" at this point. The Manzano Mountain Wilderness, which is what the loop takes you through, is one of the few places in New Mexico where oak, maple, and aspen trees are interspersed with the usual mountain evergreens. It's a beautiful autumn drive. And if you're into camping or just want to have a picnic, the Fourth of July Campground (commonly known as ***Fourth of July Canyon***) at the midway point is a great spot.

Old Catholic churches are the historic highlights of the towns along Highway 55 and attest to the rich Spanish traditional values of the villages. If you plan your visit during harvesttime, check out the area apple orchards. (Manzano means "apple tree" in Spanish, you know.) In recent years, the creative set has discovered some of the communities. You'll find artists, weavers, potters, and wood-carvers if you take the time to explore the area.

The ruins of impressive seventeenth-century mission churches and earlier pueblos are the focal points of the three units of ***Salinas Pueblo Missions National Monument.*** The areas included in the monument are in a basin that once held a huge lake. Because a salt marsh was left when the lake started to

From Mountainair to the White House

Mountainair's all-time most prominent citizen, the late Clem "Pop" Shaffer earned an international reputation as a folk artist. Shaffer started as the town blacksmith, but when his shop burned to the ground, he decided to build a hotel and restaurant on the site instead. As this edition goes to press, the ***Shaffer Hotel*** is under new ownership and is closed for renovations, but you can still admire the unique handcrafted ornamentation, such as the colorful roof trim, the American Indian motifs visible through the front windows, and the bright stones embedded in the outside walls to form animal-shaped mosaics. The newly renovated building is scheduled to reopen in summer 2004. Call (505) 847-2888 for an update

After Shaffer finished building the hotel, his wife ran it while he turned his talents to wood carving. His fanciful animals fashioned from tree roots became so well known that the state of New Mexico gave one as an official gift to each newly elected U.S. president. Many of his carvings are still stored in his studio at ***Rancho Bonito*** outside of town. The ranch and studio are also presently closed to the public, though guided tours are occasionally held. Inquire at the Mountainair Chamber of Commerce, (505) 847-2795.

dry out, the Spanish explorers, upon seeing the area, named it Salinas for the salt flats. (And long before the Spanish arrived, the Indians living here used the salt as trade currency.) In the early 1600s, friars built missions at many of the pueblos in the basin. But drought, famine, and Apache raids caused both the Spaniards and the Pueblo Indians to abandon the sites by the 1670s. Over the years, the pueblos and missions were vandalized and started to collapse. These ruins are now protected by the monument.

Although the ruins don't respect county lines, the monument headquarters are conveniently located between the units in Torrance County. The visitor center is located on U.S. Highway 60 in the community of Mountainair; (505) 847–2585. When in Mountainair, check out the historic Shaffer Hotel for lunch; (505) 847–2888. Also, if you're visiting in August, check out the community's Sunflower Festival held the last weekend of that month. Call the Mountainair Chamber of Commerce (505) 847–2795) for details.

Each unit of the Salinas Pueblo Missions moument has a visitor center, picnic tables, and rest rooms, but camping is not allowed. They're all open daily from 9:00 A.M. to 6:00 P.M. during summer and 9:00 A.M. to 5:00 P.M. the rest of the year. There's no admission charge.

The most beautiful of the ruins are in the ***Quarai*** unit of the monument and are located on a well-marked road 1 mile west of the village of Punta de Agua on Highway 55. The 5-foot-thick red sandstone walls reach heights of 40 feet. Twenty-six miles south of Mountainair on Highway 55, you'll find the ***Gran Quivira*** unit. Though these are the most extensive of the ruins in the monument, because they are composed of gray limestone, they are not quite as striking as those at Quarai. The ruins at the ***Abó*** unit are similar to those at Quarai in that they are made out of red sandstone. The Abó unit is 9 miles west of Mountainair on U.S. Highway 60.

Where to Stay in Central New Mexico

BERNALILLO COUNTY

La Posada de
Albuquerque,
125 Second Street NW,
Albuquerque,
(505) 242–9090/
(800) 777–5732

**Apache Canyon Ranch
Bed and Breakfast Inn,**
To'hajiilee,
(505) 836–7220

Casas de Sueños
(bed-and-breakfast),
310 Rio Grande SW,
Albuquerque,
(505) 247–4560

Elaine's
(bed-and-breakfast),
Sandia Mountains,
(505) 281–2467

Hyatt Regency
(downtown),
330 Tijeras NW,
Albuquerque,
(505) 842–1234

Sheraton Old Town,
800 Rio Grande
Boulevard NW,
Albuquerque,
(505) 843–6300

Rio Grande Inn,
1015 Rio Grande Boulevard
NW (Old Town area),
Albuquerque,
(505) 843–9500/
(800) 959–4726

**The Mauger Estate
Bed and Breakfast Inn,**
701 Roma Avenue NW,
Albuquerque,
(505) 242–8755/
(800) 719–9189

VALENCIA COUNTY

Super 8 Motel,
428 South Main,
Belen,
(505) 864–8188

Comfort Inn,
1711 Main Street SW,
Los Lunas,
(505) 865–5100

Days Inn West,
1919 Main Street,
Los Lunas,
(505) 865–5995

TORRANCE COUNTY

Days Inn,
just off Interstate 40,
Moriarty,
(505) 832–4451

Lariat Lodge,
just off Interstate 40,
Moriarty,
(505) 832–4351

Ponderosa Motel,
just off Interstate 40,
Moriarty,
(505) 832–4404

Super 8 Motel,
just off Interstate 40,
Moriarty,
(505) 832–6730

Where to Eat in Central New Mexico

BERNALILLO COUNTY

M. & J. Sanitary Tortilla Factory,
403 Second Street SW,
Albuquerque,
(505) 242–4890.
Inexpensive. Fare: Traditional
New Mexican.

El Patio de Albuquerque,
142 Harvard SE
(university area),
Albuquerque,
(505) 268–4245.
Inexpensive to moderate.
Fare: Traditional New
Mexican with some heart-
healthy choices.

Geezamboni's,
3851 Rio Grande NW
(North Valley),
Albuquerque,
(505) 345–3354.
Inexpensive to moderate.
Fare: Large menu, featuring
great sandwiches, burgers,
barbecue (great patio).

Frontier Restaurant,
2400 Central Avenue,
Albuquerque,
(505) 266–0550.
Inexpensive. Fare:
New Mexican, American.

Kai's Chinese Restaurant,
138 Harvard SE
(university area),
Albuquerque,
(505) 266–8388.
Inexpensive to moderate.
Fare: The best Chinese food
in New Mexico, specializing
in Szechwan and Mandarin
cuisines.

Los Cuates,
4901 Lomas Boulevard NE,
Albuquerque,
(505) 255–5079.
Inexpensive to moderate.
Fare: Authentic New Mexican
(great salsa and margaritas).

Monte Vista Fire Station,
3201 Central NE
(Nob Hill–Highland area),
Albuquerque,
(505) 255–2424.
Moderate to very expensive.
Fare: Upscale, creative
New American cuisine,
emphasizing Southwestern
ingredients.

Seasons,
2031 Mountain Road NW
(Old Town area),
Albuquerque,
(505) 766–5100.
Moderate to expensive. Fare:
Upscale eclectic American
grille (a way-cool rooftop
patio bar).

Chez Axel,
6209 Montgomery NE (at
San Pedro),
Albuquerque,
(505) 881–8104.
Moderate to expensive. Fare:
Authentic cuisine of
Provence, France.

Terra Bistro,
1119 Alameda Boulevard
NW (at Rio Grande
Boulevard),
Albuquerque,
(505) 792–1700.
Moderate to expensive. Fare:
New American cuisine in a
casual bistro style.

Yanni's Mediterranean Bar and Grill,
3109 Central NE
(Nob Hill–Highland area),
Albuquerque,
(505) 268–9250.
Moderate to expensive. Fare:
Upscale but casual Greek;
some Italian dishes.

VALENCIA COUNTY

Luna Mansion,
Junction of Highways 6/304,
Los Lunas,
(505) 865–7333.
Moderate to expensive. Fare:
Innovative Southwestern.

Teofilos,
Main near Highway 304,
Los Lunas,
(505) 865–5511.
Inexpensive to moderate.
Fare: New Mexican.

Henrietta's,
740 Main Street,
Los Lunas,
(505) 865–5284.
Inexpensive. Fare: American,
New Mexican diner.

Pete's Cafe,
105 First Street,
Belen,
(505) 864–4811.
Inexpensive to moderate.
Fare: New Mexican.

TORRANCE COUNTY

El Comedor de Anayas,
Old Route 66,
Moriarty,
(505) 832–4391.
Inexpensive to moderate.
Fare: New Mexican and
American.

Rip Griffin's Restaurant,
Old Route 66,
Moriarty,
(505) 832–4421.
Inexpensive to moderate.
Fare: American.

SELECTED CHAMBERS OF COMMERCE/ VISITOR BUREAUS IN CENTRAL NEW MEXICO

Albuquerque Convention & Visitors Bureau,
20 First Plaza, Suite 601,
P.O. Box 26866,
Albuquerque, 87125–6866;
(505) 842–9918/(800) 284–2282;
Web site: www.abqcvb.org

Belen Chamber of Commerce,
712 Dailies Avenue,
Box 6, Belen, 87002;
(505) 864–8091;
Web site: www.belennm.com

Los Lunas Chamber of Commerce,
3447 Lambros, P.O. Box 13,
Los Lunas, 87031;
(505) 865–1581;
Web site: www.ci.los-lunas.nm.us/

Moriarty Chamber of Commerce,
P.O. Box 96,
Moriarty, 87035;
(505) 832–4087;
Web site: www.moriartychamber.com

Mountainair Chamber of Commerce,
P.O. Box 595,
Mountainair, 87036;
(505) 847–2795;
Web site: www.mountainairchamber.org

Northeastern New Mexico

The scenery of New Mexico's northeastern quadrant is quite different from that most associated with the state. Grasslands upon rolling hills and plains dominate the landscape, giving it a softer quality in comparison with the state's expansive desert regions. Some of New Mexico's oldest and largest ranches share this area with modern ski resorts.

The historic *Santa Fe Trail* snakes through northeastern New Mexico and figures prominently in the region's geography and history. The 900-mile trail connecting Old Franklin, Missouri, to Santa Fe was the lifeline linking the New Mexico Territory to the eastern United States from 1821 to the coming of the railroad to New Mexico in 1879. Not only did the trail bring much-needed goods and prosperity; it also brought a new people, language, skills, and customs—for better or worse, the Anglo had come to New Mexico.

A decisive battle of the Civil War was also fought in this region on March 28, 1862, at the summit of Glorieta Pass, between Santa Fe and Pecos. In the Battle of Glorieta Pass, Union troops defeated the Confederates, thus destroying Southern hopes for taking over New Mexico.

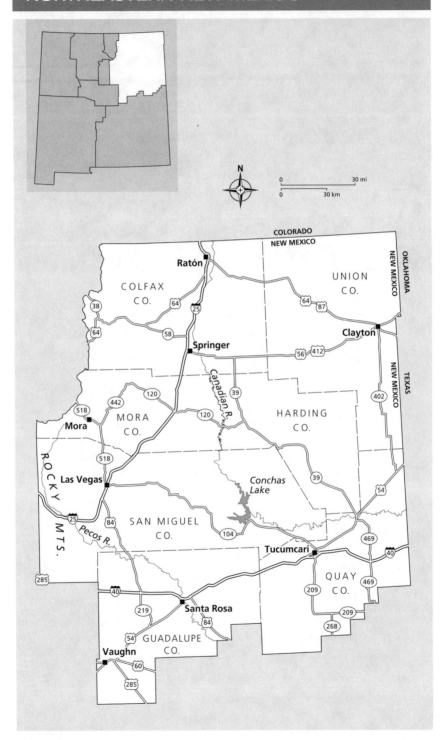

N

0   30 mi
0   30 km

COLORADO
NEW MEXICO

NEW MEXICO
OKLAHOMA

Ratón

COLFAX
CO.

UNION
CO.

38

64

64

25

64

87

58

Springer

Clayton

56

412

NEW MEXICO
TEXAS

442

120

Canadian R.

39

518

MORA
CO.

120

HARDING
CO.

402

Mora

518

R O C K Y

Las Vegas

Conchas
Lake

39

54

25

84

SAN MIGUEL
CO.

104

469

M T S.

Pecos R.

Tucumcari

40

285

40

QUAY
CO.

469

219

Santa Rosa

209

84

209

268

54

GUADALUPE
CO.

Vaughn

60

285

Colfax County

The quiet community of Springer, with its tree-lined main street, Maxwell Avenue, would seem more at home in the Midwest than in the plains of New Mexico. Here you'll find a slower pace, a couple of old antiques shops, and the **Santa Fe Trail Museum,** also known as the Springer Museum, housed in the old Colfax County Courthouse, which at first glance resembles a church.

Built in 1879, when Springer sat in the county seat before Ratón took over almost twenty years later, the Santa Fe Trail Museum served as a New Mexico reform school for boys, a public library, the town hall, and the city jail before townsfolk transformed it into a museum in 1967. It commemorates Colfax County's pioneers during the time when the Santa Fe Trail was an active route crossing the region.

The museum, which now also houses the Springer Visitor Center, is at 614 Maxwell Avenue; (505) 483–5554 (answered only during the summer). It's open Memorial Day through Labor Day daily from 9:00 A.M. to 4:00 P.M. Admission charges are $2.00 for adults, $1.50 for seniors and children.

STATE PARKS IN NORTHEASTERN NEW MEXICO
On the Web at: www.emnrd.state.nm.us/nmparks/

Cimarron Canyon State Park,
3 miles east of Eagle Nest,
(505) 377–6271

Clayton Lake State Park,
15 miles north of Clayton,
(505) 374–8808

Conchas Lake State Park,
34 miles northwest of Tucumcari,
(505) 868–2270

Coyote Creek State Park,
south of Angel Fire near Guadalupita,
(505) 387–2328

Morphy Lake State Park,
southwest of Mora near Ledoux,
(505) 387–2328

Santa Rosa Lake State Park,
7 miles north of Santa Rosa,
(505) 472–3110

Storrie Lake State Park,
6 miles north of Las Vegas,
(505) 425–7278

Sugarite Canyon State Park,
10 miles northeast of Ratón,
(505) 445–5607

Ute Lake State Park,
3 miles west of Logan,
(505) 487–2284

Villanueva State Park,
31 miles southwest of Las Vegas,
(505) 421–2957

As far as one-horse towns go, this one's got most others beat. It has its own livery stable—now known as the *Livery Stable Antiques*—which is a Springer landmark and houses a wonderful, cluttered mishmash of antiques for sale. Hidden treasures abound. Built in 1880, the stone stable is definitely from the horse-and-wagon days and is in excellent shape, considering its age and lack of restoration. Avoid this place if a little dust and dirt offend you. Livery Stable Antiques is at the corner of Maxwell Avenue and Third Street; (505) 483–2825. Open by appointment only.

For good food and lodging in Springer, check into the historic *Brown Hotel and Cafe Bed and Breakfast* downtown. Built during 1922–24, "the Brown," as it's known to locals, features eleven guest rooms furnished with antiques. Rates range from $40 to $73; 302 Maxwell Avenue; (505) 483–2269.

For the best New Mexican food in northeastern New Mexico, head over to *El Taco Cafe y Cantina* at 704 Maxwell Avenue in Springer (505–483–0402). Open for breakfast, lunch, and dinner, El Taco serves all New Mexican classics, plus fajitas and steaks for dinner. The cafe recently made the "top ten" list of Mexican restaurants in *Crosswinds* magazine. The cafe is open Monday through Saturday from 9:00 A.M. to 8:00 P.M., except on Monday, when it closes at 2:00 P.M. The cantina is open at least until midnight.

FAVORITE ATTRACTIONS/EVENTS IN NORTHEASTERN NEW MEXICO

Dinosaur Days,
April, Clayton
(505) 374–9253

Santa Fe Trail Heritage Days,
May, Las Vegas
(800) 832–5947

Capulin Volcano National Monument,
Union County
(505) 278–2201

Ft. Union National Monument,
Mora County
(505) 425–8025

Pecos National Historical Park,
San Miguel County
(505) 757–6032

Montezuma Castle,
United World College
campus, Las Vegas
(505) 454–4200

Ratón Historic District,
Ratón
(505) 445–3689/
(800) 638–6161

St. James Hotel,
Cimarron
(505) 376–2664

Philmont Ranch,
north of Cimarron
(505) 376–2281, ext. 46

Twenty-seven miles east of Springer you'll find the grand, thirty-six-room **Dorsey Mansion.** It's pure rustic opulence in the middle of New Mexico's high plains. The log-and-stone home was built by U.S. senator Stephen W. Dorsey of Arkansas in 1880. An addition several years later produced the castle-like structure with likenesses of the faces of Dorsey, his wife, and his brother carved in stone on the tower.

In addition to his role as a politician, Dorsey was a railroad financier and up-and-coming cattle baron who liked to throw elaborate parties at his mansion, now listed on the National Register of Historic Places. Highlights of a tour include the black marble fireplace from Italy, the cherrywood staircase brought from Chicago, and the artificial pond with three islands, one of which once boasted a gazebo.

The mansion, currently owned by a couple from California, is protected by caretakers Ernesto and Ernestine Romero. Though it had a brief stint as a bed-and-breakfast in the late 1980s, it's now open only by appointment for tours; (505) 375–2222; www .dorseymansion.com.

newmexicotrivia

The Santa Fe Trail Museum in Springer boasts New Mexico's first and only electric chair.

To get there, take U.S. Highway 56, proceeding 24 miles east of Springer (just past the first roadside rest area) and then going north on the dirt road for 12 miles; it's a good idea to call ahead for road conditions. There's a $3.00 per person charge for tours, children under age six, $1.00, with a minimum charge of $5.00; open Monday through Saturday from 10:00 A.M. to 4:00 P.M. and Sunday from 1:00 to 5:00 P.M.

Just 7 miles south of the Colorado border, the city of **Ratón** evolved along the Santa Fe Trail around three main influences: coal mining, railroading, and ranching. The days of the first two are pretty much in the past. Ratón's Spanish mission revival–style depot, built in 1903, served the city well until 1990, when Amtrak suspended its last scheduled stop (en route to Albuquerque from Chicago).

Nevertheless the depot is the focal point of the **Ratón Historic District,** which centers on First Street just across from the railroad tracks. Listed on the National Register of Historic Places since 1977, the district includes some seventy buildings. Businesses originally sprang up in this area in the 1880s to serve the needs of railroad workers. Today this strip is a great place to check out antiques shops and admire the diverse architecture. You can also travel back in time at the **Ratón Museum,** which chronicles the area's history of mines, rails, and cattle through artifacts and photographs.

The Ratón Museum is located in the old Coors Building at 216 South First Street; (505) 445–8979. It's open Tuesday through Saturday from 10:00 A.M. to 5:00 P.M., Memorial Day through Labor Day, and Thursday through Saturday from 10:00 A.M. to 3:00 P.M. the rest of the year. There's no admission charge.

Just a block away, at 131 North Second Street (505–445–4746), the restored *Shuler Theatre* continues to stage theatrical productions. It opened in 1915 and was named for Dr. J. J. Shuler, Ratón's mayor when the grand structure was built. The theater's exterior, described as European rococo architecture, pales in comparison with its interior, with its ornate woodwork, sky-painted ceiling, and gold-trimmed box seats. Eight Works Progress Administration (WPA) murals commissioned by the federal government during the Great Depression enhance the lobby and trace Ratón's history.

The theater welcomes visitors during office hours—call ahead, as they vary—and on weekends when a show is scheduled. There's no cost for a look or a snapshot.

The *Heart's Desire Inn Bed and Breakfast* opened in 1998, replacing the Red Violet Inn, which closed, as the only bed-and-breakfast in Ratón. Located in the heart of historic downtown Ratón, the 1885 Victorian-style home is the perfect setting for a romantic getaway to northeastern New Mexico. Innkeeper Barbara Riley pampers her guests by welcoming them with fruit baskets in their rooms, providing evening hors d'oeuvres such as fresh-baked breads and cheeses, and preparing breakfasts tailored to her guests' preferences. Six theme rooms (such as the Lodge Room, Blue Willow Room, and Victorian Room), each with its own sink, are appointed with antique furnishings, as is a suite, with kitchen, private bath, and living area.

The Heart's Desire doubles as an antiques shop, with antiques and collectibles featured throughout the inn's first floor. It's open to the public Monday through Friday, 8:00 A.M. to noon, and Saturday and Sunday, 9:00 A.M. to 6:00 P.M.

The Heart's Desire Inn is located at 301 South 3rd Street; (505) 445–1000. Room rates range from $69 to $90. (Discounts are offered for seniors and government employees.)

From Ratón, head 38 miles southwest on U.S. Highway 64 to discover the hidden Old West romance of *Cimarron* (roughly meaning "wild" or "unbroken" in Spanish). In fact, this *is* Marlboro Country in all its rugged, wide-open glory. Those famous cigarette ads were photographed on the CS Cattle Company ranch near Cimarron. All of Old Cimarron is ripe for exploring and centered on Santa Fe Trail (that's the name of the street here; it's also the trail, though it becomes Highway 21 south of town).

The *St. James Hotel* in Cimarron once bedded the famous and infamous of the Wild West. Located on the Santa Fe Trail, the St. James to this day reeks of mystery and intrigue reminiscent of its past. Built in 1873 by Henri Lambert, a former cook for Ulysses S. Grant and Abraham Lincoln, the stately, pale-pink adobe hotel was once considered one of the finest in the West. Jesse James, Black Jack Ketchum, Wyatt Earp, Buffalo Bill Cody, Annie Oakley, and Zane Grey were among the hotel's early patrons. The hotel was restored and reopened in 1985 by its current owners, Ed and Pat Sitzberger.

The entire hotel, including lobby, guest rooms, and dining area, is outfitted with authentic Victorian furnishings, mounted game, and large paintings. Individual rooms are now named after some of the celebrated figures who stayed in them. Every old hotel worth its salt has a resident ghost, and legend

Along the Santa Fe Trail

Interstate 25 on the east side of the Sangre de Cristos runs through a landscape so empty that it has fewer off-ramps in the whole 114 miles between Las Vegas and the Colorado state line than it has in Albuquerque, and pronghorn antelope outnumber humans by a wide margin. Driving across all that lonely, grassy grandeur invites the mind to drift. When I take this trip, my mind often wanders back to the days of the old Santa Fe Trail, the busiest route across the West in the early nineteenth century. I imagine what it must have been like to make the trip from Old Franklin, Missouri, to Santa Fe—a distance of roughly 800 miles one way—in a horse-drawn wagon along a rutted track that followed the Arkansas River across the prairies of Kansas and eastern Colorado before splitting at Ratón into the main trail around the southern tip of the mountain range and the Cimarron Cutoff shortcut. Looking ahead at the distant horizon, I can imagine what it must have felt like to go for many days without meeting another person.

Unlike later pioneer trails across the West, the Santa Fe Trail didn't carry wagon trains of settlers. Instead, it was a lucrative trade route between the United States and Mexico. During the entire Spanish colonial era, Anglo-Americans were prohibited from setting foot in Spanish territory. But in 1821, Mexico won its independence from Spain, and the rules changed. Although Americans still were not normally allowed to take up residence in Mexico, trade between the two countries flourished in the northernmost Mexican city, Santa Fe, which was also the end of El Camino Real, the "royal road" from Mexico City.

Traders from the United States carried factory-made goods—especially fabrics and clothing, as well as other items from pots and pans to telescopes—to Santa Fe to barter in exchange for coins and bullion from the gold and silver mines of Mexico. (No gold had yet been discovered in what is now the United States.)

Another valuable commodity Americans obtained from the Santa Fe trade was mules. The Spanish and Mexicans had long kept a closely guarded secret of the fact that mules, which could not reproduce, were a cross between horses and donkeys, so all the mules used by farmers and the military in the first half of the nineteenth century had to be imported from Mexico along the Santa Fe Trail. That's why mules are associated with Missouri, the eastern terminus of the trail where all mules arrived for sale.

has it that the St. James was not shortchanged—no clues, though, as to who the chandelier shaker might be. Evidence of the hotel's rough-and-tumble past is apparent in the bullet holes visible in the pressed-tin ceiling of Lambert's, the hotel's restaurant (previously Lambert's Saloon and Gambling Hall). Instead of red-eye, Lambert's now serves up continental cuisine such as Shrimp Provençale and Red Rock Filet au Dijon, as well as pasta, beef, chicken, and veal entrees, though the menu changes seasonally. Lambert's is open nightly from 5:00 to 8:00 P.M., except Tuesday when it's closed.

The St. James is on Highway 21, just north of U.S. Highway 64 in the center of Cimarron's historic district; (505) 376–2664; www.stjamescimarron .com. Room rates range from $75 to $125.

Just down the lane, across from the St. James, you'll spot the **Old Mill Museum,** guarded by the thick rock walls of the Aztec Mill. The mill was built in 1864 by Lucien B. Maxwell, who, with his 1.7 million acres, was the single largest landowner of all time in the Western Hemisphere. Maxwell brought an engineer, a millwright, and a chief mason from back East to take on the $50,000 project. In its time, the mill could turn out 300 barrels of flour per day. Though the three-story building was converted to a museum in 1967, the stone structure itself is just as impressive as its contents, which include exhibits chronicling late nineteenth-century northern New Mexico.

The museum is open Monday through Saturday from 9:00 A.M. to 5:00 P.M. and Sunday from 1:00 to 5:00 P.M., May through September. Admission is $2.00 for adults and $1.00 for seniors, children age eleven or younger, and scouts in uniform (read on and you'll understand). There's no phone at the mill, but the museum's curator, Buddy Morse (505–376–2913), will be glad to answer any questions.

About 5 miles south of the St. James on Highway 21 you'll find the headquarters to the vast **Philmont Ranch,** now owned by the Boy Scouts of America (BSA). Here's where the buffalo really do roam and the deer and the antelope are known to play. The jewel of the 137,493-acre ranch is **Villa Philmonte,** the Spanish Mediterranean–style mansion built as a summer home by Oklahoma oilman Waite Phillips, of Phillips 66.

Phillips gave the ranch to the BSA in 1938 "for the purpose of perpetuating faith, self-reliance, integrity, and freedom, the principles used to build this great country by the American Pioneer." And each summer since, thousands of scouts have convened at Philmont for the ultimate camping adventure.

But nonscouts too can enjoy Philmont. Tours of Villa Philmonte are given daily during summer. The home and most of its furnishings have been restored to their original grandeur. In addition to the living room, with its custom-built piano, the most impressive room is the trophy room, highlighted by the huge buffalo mounted above the fireplace.

The **Philmont Museum** and **Seton Memorial Library** (both 505–376–2281), just past the driveway that loops around the mansion, are also open to visitors. The museum displays exhibits of those persons who influenced this area—cowboys, Indians, miners, mountain men, and settlers. The library contains the books, art, and natural history collection of Ernest Thompson Seton, an author, artist, and naturalist and the first chief scout of the BSA. The museum and library are open daily from 8:00 A.M. to 5:00 P.M. June through August and Monday through Friday from 8:00 A.M. to 5:00 P.M. the rest of the year. There's no admission charge; tours cost $3.00 for adults, children under age twelve are free.

Seven miles south, in Rayado, you'll find another feature of the Philmont Ranch, the **Kit Carson Museum.** It's built in the adobe hacienda style and finished with 1850s period furnishings. Tours are given daily from June through August; call the Philmont Museum number for specific schedules.

If you're no Boy Scout and the St. James is booked, consider **Casa del Gavilan** ("House of the Hawk") bed-and-breakfast for a weekend hideaway. The inn was built in the early 1900s by the eastern industrialist J. J. Nairn, who often hosted famous artists and writers in his gleaming white adobe home tucked into the foothills of the Sangre de Cristo Mountains. Only those with confirmed reservations are allowed on the premises, though, because guests' privacy is highly regarded here. Casa del Gavilan is 6 miles south of Cimarron on Highway 21; (505) 376–2246; www.casadelgavilan.com. Rates range from $75 to $130, which includes breakfast.

Heading west on U.S. Highway 64 from Cimarron, you'll come across the community of Eagle Nest—along with its attractive namesake lake—and the village of Angel Fire. Between these two towns you'll find a delightfully comfortable inn, **Monte Verde** ("Green Mountain") **Ranch Bed and Breakfast.** The inn comprises most of innkeeper Sally Lebus's 1930s ranch house, which was constructed out of native granite and pine. With views of Eagle Nest Lake to the north and mountains to the east, guests enjoy total comfort at Monte Verde.

Sally is certainly no uptight innkeeper. She allows guests free run of her spacious home, including a glassed-in living area with a fireplace and a huge kitchen with a wood-burning stove. Some of the guest rooms also have fireplaces, with plenty of wood available. On cool mornings an eerie mist forms over Eagle Nest Lake, adding to the setting's magic. Sally reports that the inn has become quite popular as a setting for family reunions and weddings.

Monte Verde is located just off U.S. Highway 64 between mile markers 279 and 280; (505) 377–6928; www.monteverderanch.com. Monte Verde is open year-round. Rates are $85 to $110.

The meadows meeting the mountains in the countryside surrounding **Angel Fire** give new meaning to the enchantment of New Mexico. Atop a small hill you'll find the country's first memorial dedicated to all Vietnam veterans. Originally built in 1971 by Dr. Victor Westphall in memory of his son, who was killed in the war, the memorial was expanded and taken over by the Disabled American Veterans in the early 1980s; however, the memorial disaffiliated with the DAV in 2000.

The small, nondenominational chapel at the **Vietnam Veterans National Memorial** at Angel Fire is breathtakingly simple as it sits in harmony with the land. The tallest wing of this dovelike structure rises 64 feet, gracefully curving downward to the ground. The accompanying visitor center is just as contemporary and displays banners and poster-size photographs of wide-ranging scenes from the war.

Completed years before the celebrated memorial in Washington, D.C., the Angel Fire structure differs in the feeling it leaves within when visitors depart. There is no turbulence or divisive political statement associated with this memorial. Though powerful in the emotions it elicits, the memorial allows visitors to come away with their own reactions, rather than forcing any particular ones.

The Vietnam Veterans National Memorial is just off U.S. Highway 64 at the Angel Fire turnoff; (505) 377–6900; www.angelfirememorial.com. From Memorial Day through Labor Day, the visitor center is open daily from 9:00 A.M. to 7:00 P.M. The remainder of the year, it's open daily from 9:00 A.M. to 5:00 P.M. The chapel never closes, and there's no admission charge.

Union County

What's now a perfectly cone-shaped mountain rising from the plains was once a fiery volcano that last erupted some 10,000 years ago. What's left is known as **Capulin Volcano** and is a national monument about 30 miles east of Ratón. As one of the most remote and undiscovered of the nation's national monuments, Capulin rarely gets crowded.

A road from the visitor center winds 1,000 feet up the mountain to the edge of the mouth of the volcano. From here you can hike several trails. You can see four states—New Mexico (obviously), Texas, Colorado, and Oklahoma—if you hike the Crater Rim Trail. Another trail actually leads you inside the volcano—one of the few places in the world where you can do this. (Go try this in Hawaii!) Though Capulin hasn't erupted in 10,000 years, it's considered dormant, not extinct. Scientists say volcanoes 25,000 years old or less are potentially active, so no one knows if Capulin will ever erupt again. Not knowing—for certain, anyway—adds to the thrill.

To get to Capulin Volcano National Monument from Ratón, take U.S. Highway 64/87 east for about 30 miles to the community of Capulin, and then head north on Highway 325 for a few miles to the monument; (505) 278–2201; www.nps.gov/cavo. The visitor center is open daily from 8:00 A.M. to 4:00 P.M. Labor Day through Memorial Day; during summer, hours are 7:30 A.M. to 6:30 P.M. Admission is $5.00 per carload and $3.00 per person for motorcycles and bicycles; Golden Age Passports are accepted for seniors.

In extreme northeastern New Mexico (mere miles from the Oklahoma and Texas borders), you'll find the thriving community of *Clayton,* Union County seat and regional trading hub—and home base for exploring several notable area attractions, including Capulin Volcano, Clayton Lake, Rabbit Ear Mountains, authentic dinosaur tracks on an ancient mud flat, and Folsom Falls.

Along the Dry Cimarron River, 4 miles northeast of the small community of *Folsom* on Highway 456, you'll find *Folsom Falls,* a natural spring-fed water-fall on the river, which forms a favorite fishing spot as well as a great place for a picnic. The community of Folsom boasts the Folsom Museum, which offers information on the prehistoric Folsom Man, as well as artifacts from the area's pioneer history. Folsom was named for President Grover Cleveland's bride, Frances Ruth Folsom, for whom the Baby Ruth candy bar was also named.

newmexicotrivia

Notorious outlaw Black Jack Ketchum is buried in the Clayton Cemetery in Clayton.

Back in Clayton, be sure to check out the landmark *Eklund Hotel Dining Room and Saloon* (505–374–2551), which celebrated its centennial in 1992. Specializing in Union County beef (steaks), the Old West ambience includes a well-worn wooden bar and bullet holes in the pressed-tin ceiling. The restaurant is open daily from 10:00 A.M. to 9:00 P.M.

Mora County

Fort Union National Monument is at its best when visited on a crisp, sunny autumn day. Though it's quite isolated, Fort Union is easily accessible via Interstate 25, which brings a steady stream of visitors during summer. When approaching the remains of the fort, the vision of redbrick and adobe ruins jutting up from the grassy plains is at once attractive and a little odd. Once you get to the fort site along the Santa Fe Trail, with its incredibly expansive views, you sense why this spot was chosen.

Established in 1851 by Lieutenant Colonel Edwin V. Sumner to protect the Santa Fe Trail and the New Mexico Territory from Indian raids, Fort Union was the largest military depot in the Southwest. There were actually three Fort Unions, the last of whose ruins constitute the park. The fort was abandoned in

Ruins at Fort Union National Monument

1891, after which residents from nearby communities scavenged most of its usable materials, thereby hastening its deterioration.

The visitor center provides a walking-tour map to help interpret the fort's layout. If you visit on a sunny day, follow the trail to the fort's sundial, just across from the quartermaster's quarters. It's still intact and quite accurate. The park service has done a great job preserving the frontier feeling and dignity of the fort. Interpretive audio stations at selected stops along the trail emit dialogues indicative of the situation, that is, soldier to commander, soldier to soldier. And recorded bugle calls sporadically echo across the grounds from loudspeakers hidden by the adobe walls. Fort Union is also one of the best places to see the wagon-wheel ruts of the Santa Fe Trail; those wagons last cut through the plains more than a century ago.

To get to Fort Union, take Interstate 25 north of Las Vegas to exit 366, then head north on Highway 161, which dead-ends at the fort after 8 miles; (505) 425–8025; www.nps.gov/foun. A tree-shaded picnic area is available. The park is open daily from 8:00 A.M. to 6:00 P.M. Memorial Day through Labor Day and 8:00 A.M. to 4:00 P.M. the remainder of the year. The admission price is $3.00

per person, with those age sixteen or younger admitted free. Golden Age and Golden Access passes are accepted.

Just east of the village of Cleveland, northeast of Mora, you'll come across the *Cleveland Roller Mill Museum.* Like other, earlier flour mills in the area, the Cleveland Roller Mill, built in 1901, helped satisfy the growing demands for wheat flour in the region around the turn of the century. The two-story adobe mill was the last of its kind to be built in northern New Mexico—and the last to cease operations around 1954; as such, it's the only roller mill in New Mexico of any size to have its original milling works intact. The mill's restoration began in 1979, when it was placed on the National Register of Historic Places and the New Mexico Cultural Properties Register. Providing a glimpse into the agricultural past of the area, the museum features historical and cultural exhibits focusing on the Mora Valley. On Labor Day weekend, the museum hosts Millfest, during which the operation of the mill is demonstrated. The usual food, fun, and frolic round out the event.

The museum is open weekends only from Memorial Day weekend through the end of October. Hours are 10:00 A.M. to 3:00 P.M., but subject to change, so please call ahead. Admission is $2.00 for adults and $1.00 for children ages seven to sixteen. The grounds are always open; (505) 387-2645.

Just outside the community of Mora, you'll encounter *La Cueva Mill,* another beautifully rustic old structure now part of Mora County's Salman Ranch. The mill was built by Vicente Romero in the 1870s, partly in response to the heavy demand for flour, owing to the establishment of Fort Union and to the steadily increasing Santa Fe Trail traffic. Though Mora County is now one of New Mexico's most economically depressed areas, during the late 1800s it was one of the most prosperous.

The old adobe and stone buildings of the mill are not accessible, for safety reasons; nevertheless, you can pull off the road for an exterior look at one of New Mexico's more impressive old water-driven mills. The cold, clear water from the acequia (constructed ditch) still flows around the mill, though it's now diverted from the wheel.

Though the mill has not been used for grinding wheat and generating electricity since 1949, during late summer through early fall *Salman Ranch* sets up shop at the mill to sell its produce, including vegetables, herbs, cut flowers, and, most notably, farm-fresh raspberries. You can also stock up on the ranch's prized raspberry jam. And its raspberry vinegar is perfect for dressing a salad. They also have a cafe.

The mill is located 6 miles south of Mora near the junction of Highway 518 and Highway 442. In-season produce sale hours are generally 9:00 A.M. to 5:00 P.M. daily. For more information, call the ranch at (505) 387-2900.

San Miguel County

Often confused with the glitzier and much younger gambling capital of Nevada, the community of **Las Vegas,** New Mexico, has a charm all its own. During its railroad heyday in the 1880s, Las Vegas ("The Plains") was the largest and most exciting city in New Mexico. Today, Las Vegas has mellowed into a captivating community enhanced by a rich architectural heritage—half the state's registered historic buildings, more than 900, are located here.

To get a sense of Las Vegas's past, stop by the **City of Las Vegas Rough Riders Museum,** which is named for the heroic group of men Teddy Roosevelt organized for his acclaimed Cuban campaign during the Spanish-American War. Many of the volunteers came from New Mexico, and the Rough Riders later held a reunion in Las Vegas every year from 1899 (when the event was attended by Roosevelt while he was governor of New York) until 1967, when it was attended by only one veteran, Jesse Langdon, who died in 1975. In Las Vegas, Roosevelt even announced his candidacy for president and twice stayed at the Plaza Hotel (see below).

The museum began with mementos brought home by the Rough Riders and now includes a great variety of artifacts relating to Las Vegas's history and New Mexico's past. The museum is located at 725 Grand Avenue; (505) 454–1401. It's open Monday through Friday from 9:00 A.M. to noon and 1:00 to 3:00 P.M.; from May through October, the museum is also open on Saturday from 10:00 A.M. to 3:00 P.M. and Sunday from noon to 4:00 P.M. There's no admission charge, but donations are appreciated.

Many native New Mexicans consider Las Vegas's Old Town Plaza the most beautiful plaza in the state because of its large size, abundance of trees, and gazebo. Anchored by the historic **Plaza Hotel,** the streets around and adjacent to the plaza are dotted with shops and restaurants.

More than a century after it originally opened, and following a $2-million renovation, the Plaza Hotel reopened in 1982 to its former Victorian grandeur. From the worn hardwood of the lobby floor to the towering twin staircases connecting the lobby to the second floor, the Plaza Hotel has an air of history and elegance. Except for the modern comforts of queen-size beds and new bathrooms, the high-ceilinged guest rooms are appointed in period antiques with wall and window treatments consistent with the Victorian era. As a welcome change from many historic hotels, the guest rooms are surprisingly well insulated and are thus quiet, each offering its own thermostat.

Byron T's, the lobby bar, is named after former Plaza Hotel owner Byron T. Mills, who's also the hotel's resident ghost. It's a comfortable place to have a drink while enjoying a street-level view of the plaza. The hotel's restaurant,

Adelia's Landmark Grill, features New Mexican dishes as well as beef, seafood, and chicken entrees, including shrimp scampi, filet mignon, and Piñon Trout. Pasta specialties like Pollo Pesto Linguini round out the menu.

The hotel is located at 230 on the Old Town Plaza; (505) 425–3591; www.plazahotel-nm.com. Room rates range from $96 to $146.

For a more intimate overnight adventure in Las Vegas, consider a stay at the ***Carriage House Bed & Breakfast.*** The inn is housed in a three-story Queen Anne–style mansion built in 1893, one of the many architectural gems found throughout Las Vegas's inner core of historic districts. The inn was totally renovated in the mid-1990s and has five guest rooms, three of which have private baths. The Carriage House is located at 925 Sixth Street; (505) 454–1784. Room rates range from $75 to $95.

Head out of Las Vegas about 6 miles on Hot Springs Boulevard (which borders the streetside corner of the Plaza Hotel) and you'll be in the small community of ***Montezuma*** at the mouth of Gallinas Canyon. The imposing ***Montezuma Castle*** looms on a hilltop as the focal point for Armand Hammer United World College of the American West (505–454–4221). Built in 1884 as a showpiece resort by the Santa Fe Railroad, Montezuma Castle was abandoned as a hotel during the financial depression at the turn of the century. The castle was purchased in 1981 by the late Dr. Armand Hammer—billionaire phi- lanthropist and former chairman of Occidental Petroleum Corporation— with the intent of starting the college. The small college now has more than

Plaza Hotel

200 students from more than sixty nations. Students conduct free tours on some Saturdays—call ahead for a recording of specific dates and times.

While you're on campus, don't miss the opportunity to visit the **_Dwan Light Sanctuary._** The unusual and striking building is the result of a collaboration between conceptualizer Virginia Dwan, artist Charles Ross, and architect Laban Wingert. The project grew out of Dwan's dream of creating a quiet space for contemplation for people of all beliefs. According to Dwan, the sanctuary

A Sampling of Movies Filmed in New Mexico

All the Pretty Horses (2000).
Matt Damon, Penelope Cruz
(Santa Fe, Las Vegas).

Butch Cassidy and the Sundance Kid (1968).
Paul Newman, Robert Redford, and Katharine Ross (Taos, Chama).

The Cheyenne Social Club (1970).
James Stewart, Henry Fonda, and Shirley Jones (Santa Fe).

City Slickers (1991).
Billy Crystal, Jack Palance, and Daniel Stern (Ghost Ranch, Santa Fe, Abiquiu, Nambe Pueblo, Santa Clara Pueblo).

The Cowboys (1972).
John Wayne, Bruce Dern, and Colleen Dewhurst (Chama, Galisteo, Santa Fe).

Hang 'Em High (1968).
Clint Eastwood, Inger Stevens, and Ben Johnson (Las Cruces).

Lonesome Dove (1989).
Robert Duvall, Tommy Lee Jones, Danny Glover, and Angelica Huston (Santa Fe, Angel Fire).

The Milagro Beanfield War (1988).
Ruben Blades, Sonia Braga, and Daniel Stern (Truchas).

Contact (1997).
Jodie Foster and Matthew McConaughey (Socorro County).

My Name Is Nobody (1973).
Henry Fonda and Terence Hill (Acoma Pueblo, Mogollon).

Silverado (1985).
Kevin Kline, Danny Glover, Kevin Costner, Rosanna Arquette, and Linda Hunt (Galisteo, Abiquiu, Santa Ana Pueblo).

Superman (1978).
Christopher Reeve and Margot Kidder (in and around Gallup).

Wyatt Earp (1993).
Kevin Costner, Dennis Quaid, and Gene Hackman (Santa Fe, Rancho de las Golondrinas, Chama, Las Vegas, and Zia, Tesuque, and Santa Clara Pueblos).

Young Guns (1988).
Emilio Estevez, Charlie Sheen, Lou Diamond Philips, Kiefer Sutherland, Terence Stamp, and Jack Palance (Cerrillos, Galisteo, Ojo Caliente, Rancho de las Golondrinas).

Source: New Mexico Film Commission.

"revolves around the spiritual and temporal universality of the number twelve." Integral to her vision, the Light Sanctuary incorporates twelve angles of light within its circular space, and twelve large prisms in the apses and ceiling create a progression throughout the year of unique spectrum events. In addition, the sanctuary's orientation and geometry were constructed so as to align the prisms of the building to the sun, moon, and stars, as well as to capture their light rays from sunrise to sunset. The interacting spectrums create broad, moving ribbons of color on the walls, ceiling, and floor of the sanctuary. *(NOTE: The United World College is a closed campus; guests are asked to register at the Administration Building upon arrival.)*

Just past the castle on Hot Springs Boulevard (Highway 65) are the **Montezuma Hot Springs,** nondescript holes that dot the banks of the Gallinas River. Located on the property of the United World College, these natural hot tubs are fed from mineral springs that bubble up from the ground. The springs are a great place to relax and enjoy the view—Montezuma Castle, the river, the rock cliffs—especially when it's a little nippy outside. A brown sign, hot springs baths, marks the spot. There's no charge to enjoy the therapeutic waters, but it's a first-come, first-soak arrangement. Early morning and late night are the best times to find them vacant. You may encounter naked people milling about, so if this offends you, consider yourself warned.

About ½ mile farther on Highway 65 toward the mountains, veer left on a gravel road and you'll immediately come across **Gallinas Pond,** or City Pond, as it's also known. During most times of the year, the pond is nothing more than a small body of water bordered by shimmering, sheer cliffs on one side. But during the dead of winter, when the water has frozen and the ice skates have been brought out, the pond turns into a winter wonderland reminiscent of the Northeast and Midwest. It's one of only a few places open to the public in New Mexico where you can pond-skate.

The **Star Hill Inn,** 10 miles north of Las Vegas, is the perfect getaway for stargazers and ardent astronomy buffs alike. Several modern cabins constitute the inn, which was founded by former Dallas resident Phil Mahon. Mahon, who has led astronomy seminars at Abiquiu's Ghost Ranch (see page 73), concluded that rural New Mexico, with its clear, pitch-black nights, was the perfect place for an inn catering to the cosmically inclined.

The cabins are comfortably outfitted with custom-designed furnishings and individual kitchens. A library and warming house contains three telescopes that may be wheeled out onto an outside observation deck. The inn's largest telescope—6,000 millimeters in focal length—is kept in an adjoining structure with a rollback roof. When the sun is out, guests take advantage of the inn's natural surroundings—almost 200 acres of ponderosa pine forest, perfect for hiking and photography.

Moonless nights are most popular with guests because of increased visibility. Major meteor showers are also peak times for the inn. The best shows occur in the second half of the year: the Perseids in August, the Orionids in October, the Leonids in November, and the Geminids in December.

Rates range from $165 to $375 (for a three-bedroom house), with a two-night minimum. Call (505) 425–5605 for reservations and directions; www .starhillinn.com.

Heading south from Las Vegas, plan a stop at *Pecos National Historical Park,* near the community of Pecos. The park boasts one of the most attractive visitor centers (Spanish hacienda-style, with impressive woodwork) and the friendliest park rangers in the state. The monument preserves the ruins of the abandoned Cicuye Pueblo. Before you start exploring, be sure to view the short film—narrated by actress Greer Garson, who owned the surrounding ranch and left it to the National Park Service in her will—which dramatically presents the history of the pueblo site. The film will put you in the right frame of mind to better appreciate what you'll see later. It's screened every twenty minutes or so.

newmexicotrivia

Tom Mix shot his silent Westerns in the Las Vegas, New Mexico, area.

The park includes a walking tour as well as a museum containing artifacts relating to the Indians, the Spanish, and the Anglo pioneers who lived at or affected the monument site. While exploring the trails that wind among the ruins, you can climb down a ladder into a restored kiva (ceremonial chamber) and see the sipapu, the small hole in the ground believed to connect to the spirit world in the center of the earth. To see evidence of the Spanish colonial influence, you can walk through the remains of a mission church. The scenery is inspiring as it varies from plains, mesas, and mountains in the distance.

The historical park also encompasses the 10,000-acre Forked Lightning Ranch along the Pecos River and the Glorietta Pass Battlefield from the Civil War. These areas are only open to the public on ranger-guided tours, which can be scheduled by calling the visitor center at least two weeks in advance.

To get to the park from Las Vegas, take Interstate 25 south to the Pecos exit and proceed on Highway 63; (505) 757–6414. From Memorial Day through Labor Day, the monument is open daily from 8:00 A.M. to 6:00 P.M., otherwise, the park is open daily from 8:00 A.M. to 5:00 P.M. The admission charge is $3.00 per person.

A Glimpse of Northeastern New Mexico: Impressions of Las Vegas

When I was researching the first edition of this book, a northeastern New Mexico excursion brought me to the town of Las Vegas for the first time. The city's renaissance was just getting under way, when I found myself staying at the then newly remodeled Plaza Hotel, just off the plaza. (See entry earlier in this chapter).

I'd been looking forward to staying at the gracious old hotel, wondering if I'd have any run-ins with its resident ghost, Byron T. Mills—the former owner and namesake of the hotel's lobby bar, Byron T's. Unfortunately (or fortunately, depending on how you look at it), I did not, but the hotel's imposing presence did captivate me. There's something about staying in a grand old hotel that makes you feel a bit grander and more gracious yourself.

My visit reminded me of my job, during college, as a doorman of another historic hotel. And I remembered seeing the same relaxed feeling expressed on the faces of its guests that I myself felt at the Plaza: well-rested, hospitably attended to, and ready to head out and explore the world. Las Vegas's downtown business district has slowly come back to life with an even greater array of shops, restaurants, and galleries—but there's still the welcoming feel of a small town and a city in transition. Some may say it's no Santa Fe or Taos, but I say nor should it want to be. With its vast quanitity of Victorian homes, many on historic registers, and quiet, tree-lined streets, Las Vegas is a pleasant town to explore on foot—after a wonderful night spent in the cradling comfort of the Plaza Hotel.

Harding County

The **Kiowa National Grasslands** (505–374–9652) preserves thousands of acres of short prairie grasses on New Mexico's northeastern plains and stands in stark contrast to the more popular mountainous areas of the state. Though there are two regions of the preserve (the eastern section lies east of Clayton), the western section, which comprises most of northwest Harding County, is more impressive because of its proximity to the Canadian River Canyon. Highway 39 bisects the grasslands and thus serves as a convenient route for a road tour, from which you just may encounter grazing pronghorn antelope, among other wildlife.

One of the most impressive and remote areas of the federal preserve is **Mills Canyon,** named for a once-prosperous farmer, lawyer, and businessman named Melvin Mills, who tended thousands of fruit and nut trees in the late 1800s, before he was wiped out by the great flood of 1904. Mills's misfortune and eventual financial ruin ultimately led to his farm becoming public lands. If you've got a sturdy, high-clearance vehicle (four-wheel-drive recommended, just in case) and want to explore one of the most remote, hidden river valleys in the state, then a hiking or camping trip to Mills Canyon may be just what you're looking for. After you turn off the highway, psych yourself up for the 2-mile, 800-foot descent into the rugged Canadian River valley. In addition to the natural beauty of the area, you'll also see the ruins of the great Mills estate—including a few of the more hardy fruit trees that have barely survived decades of inattention and the unforgiving extremes of New Mexico weather.

newmexicotrivia

Five New Mexico counties were named for U.S. presidents: Harding, Grant, Lincoln, Roosevelt, and McKinley.

To get to Mills Canyon, take the Wagon Mound exit off Interstate 25 north of Santa Fe/Las Vegas; head east on Highway 120 to Roy, then north on Highway 39 for 10 miles until a sign at the turnoff.

Guadalupe County

Just southeast of downtown Santa Rosa, you'll find northeastern New Mexico's most fascinating hidden jewel: Santa Rosa's city-owned **Blue Hole,** a true oasis. Well known in scuba-diving circles across the country as the diving mecca of the Southwest, the Blue Hole is a tiny, bell-shaped lake prized among divers for its clarity.

Selected New Mexico Authors

N. Scott Momaday,
author of *House Made of Dawn*

Leslie Marmon Silko,
Laguna Pueblo author of *Ceremony*

Tony Hillerman,
author of many murder mysteries

Mark Medoff,
playwright, author of *Children of a Lesser God*

Luci Tapahonso,
Navajo poet

Oliver LaFarge,
Pulitzer Prize winner for *Laughing Boy*

John Nichols,
The Milagro Beanfield War

Robert Creeley, poet

D. H. Lawrence, author

Traditional Food of New Mexico

Biscochitos

(Anise-flavored shortbread cookies)

Traditionally enjoyed around the Christmas holiday, the biscochito also has the distinction of being designated New Mexico's official state cookie.

6 cups flour

¼ teaspoon salt

3 teaspoons baking powder

1 pound (2 cups) lard

1½ cups sugar

2 teaspoons anise seeds

2 eggs

¼ cup brandy

¼ cup sugar

1 tablespoon cinnamon

Sift flour with baking powder and salt. In a large mixing bowl, cream lard with sugar and anise seeds until fluffy. Beat in eggs one at a time. Mix in flour and brandy until well blended. Turn dough out onto floured board and pat or roll to ¼- to ½-inch thickness. Cut into shapes. (The fleur-de-lis is traditional.) Dust with mixture of sugar and cinnamon. Bake 10 minutes at 350° F or until lightly browned. Makes approximately 5 dozen cookies.

With a mere 60-foot diameter (though it widens to 130 feet across the bottom), yet 81-foot depth, the Blue Hole is truly more of a hole than a lake. The crystal-clear water, which appears to glow a turquoise color with the light reflecting from the stones below, is replaced every six hours, at a rate of 3,000 gallons per minute, by a subterranean river. Often called Nature's Largest Fishbowl because of its wide variety of fish, snails, plants, and sands, the Blue Hole remains a constant sixty-four degrees.

If you're a diver, avoid the crowds by visiting during the week. If you just want to see what all the fuss is about, you'll see the most action on weekends. The Santa Rosa Dive Center (505–472–3370) rents equipment next to the Blue Hole. You'll need to buy a permit ($10 per week) at the dive shop or at the Santa Rosa City Hall (505–472–3404) if you want to dive, and you must be certified or accompanied by a certified, insured instructor.

If your travels take you through the crossroads town of *Vaughn* (37 miles southwest of Santa Rosa via Highway 54) and your stomach is grumbling for some good grub, make sure to stop in at **Penny's Diner.** The squeaky-clean eatery's 1950s rock-and-roll theme is reflected in the decor and music, and its menu includes American diner classics such as burgers and roast beef, as well as fajitas and several New Mexican dishes. A friendly wait staff and a smoke-free environment round out the appeal. What more could you want? Penny's Diner is affiliated with adjacent Oak Tree Inn and is located at the junction of Highways 54, 60, and 285; (505) 584–8733, ext. 2; it's open daily, twenty-four hours.

Quay County

The town of **Tucumcari** is the gateway to New Mexico from the east. But if you've driven through New Mexico along Interstate 40 from the west, chances are your curiosity has been piqued about Tucumcari because of the stark red billboards exclaiming Tucumcari Tonight—1,500 Hotel Rooms, along with the mileage from the sign to this model Route 66 town. The town, named after nearby Tucumcari Mountain, is proud of its abundance of lodging.

While in Tucumcari, check out the **Tucumcari Historical Museum.** As far as New Mexico's community-based museums go, this is one of the finer ones. It contains thousands of old relics, including such large-scale ones as a nineteenth-century windmill and a 1926 fire truck. Several "reenactment" exhibits are featured, such as a 1920s hospital room, an early post office, a cowboy room complete with barbed wire and gun collections, and an old moonshine still. The museum also has a worthy collection of musical instruments.

The museum is located at 416 Adams Street; (505) 461–4201. From June 2 through September 2, it's open Monday through Saturday from 8:00 A.M. to 6:00 P.M. and Sunday from 1:00 to 5:00 P.M.; during the rest of the year, it's open Tuesday through Saturday from 8:00 A.M. to 5:00 P.M. Admission charges are $2.11 for adults and 53 cents for children ages six to fifteen.

Where to Stay in Northeastern New Mexico

COLFAX COUNTY

St. James Hotel,
Highway 21,
Cimarron,
(505) 376–2664

Brown Hotel,
302 Maxwell Avenue,
Springer,
(505) 483–2269

Monte Verde Ranch Bed and Breakfast,
just off U.S. Highway 64,
Angel Fire,
(505) 377–6928

Casa del Gavilán,
Highway 21,
south of Cimarron,
(505) 376–2246

Best Western Sands Motel,
300 Clayton Road,
Ratón,
(505) 445–2737/
(800) 528–1234

UNION COUNTY

Super 8 Motel,
1425 South First Street,
Clayton,
(505) 374–8127

Angel Fire Chamber of Commerce,
P.O. Box 547,
Angel Fire, 88710;
(505) 377–6661/(800) 446–8117;
Web site: www.angelfirechamber.org

Cimarron Chamber of Commerce,
104 North Lincoln Avenue,
P.O. Box 604, Cimarron, 87714;
(505) 376–2417/(888) 376–2417;
Web site: www.cimarronnm.com

Clayton/Union County Chamber of Commerce,
P.O. Box 476,
Clayton, 88415;
(505) 374–9253/(800) 390–7858;
Web site: www.claytonnewmexico.org

Eagle Nest Chamber of Commerce,
P.O. Box 322,
Eagle Nest, 87718;
(505) 377–2420/(800) 494–9117;
Web site: www.eaglenest.org

Las Vegas/San Miguel County Chamber of Commerce,
513 Sixth Street,
Las Vegas, 87701;
(505) 425–8631/(800) 832–5947;
Web site: www.lasvegasnm.org

Logan/Ute Lake Chamber of Commerce,
P.O. Box 277,
Logan, 88426;
(505) 487–2722;
Web site: www.utelake.com

Ratón Chamber of Commerce,
100 Clayton Road,
P.O. Box 1211, Ratón, 87740;
(505) 445–3689/(800) 638–6161;
Web site: www.raton.info

Red River Chamber of Commerce,
P.O. Box 870,
Red River, 87558;
(505) 754–2366/(800) 348–6444;
Web site: www.redrivernewmex.com/

Santa Rosa Chamber of Commerce,
486 Parker Avenue,
Santa Rosa, 88435;
(505) 472–3763/(800) 450–7084;
Web site: www.srnm.org

Springer Chamber of Commerce,
P.O. Box 323,
Springer, 87747;
(505) 483–2998;
Web site: www.springernm.us

Tucumcari/Quay County Chamber of Commerce,
404 West Route 66,
P.O. Drawer E, Tucumcari, 88401;
(505) 461–1694/(888) 664–7255;
Web site: www.tucumcarinm.com

**Best Western
Kokopelli Lodge,**
702 South First Street,
Clayton,
(505) 374–2589/
(800) 392–6691

Holiday Motel,
Highway 87 North,
Clayton,
(505) 374–2558

SAN MIGUEL COUNTY

Plaza Hotel,
230 Old Town Plaza,
Las Vegas,
(505) 425–3591

Comfort Inn,
2500 North Grand,
Las Vegas,
(505) 425–1100/
(800) 716–1103

Inn on the Santa Fe Trail,
1133 Grand Avenue,
Las Vegas,
(505) 425–6791/
(888) 448–8438

Regal Motel,
1809 North Grand Avenue,
Las Vegas,
(505) 454–1456

HARDING COUNTY

Mesa Hotel,
downtown,
Roy,
(505) 485–2661

GUADALUPE COUNTY

Best Western Adobe Inn,
1501 Will Rogers Drive,
Santa Rosa,
(505) 472–3446/
(800) 528–1234

Ramada Limited
1701 Will Rogers Drive,
Santa Rosa,
(505) 472–4800/
(800) 272–6232

Oak Tree Inn,
Junction of Highways 54, 60,
and 285,
Vaughn,
(505) 584–8733

QUAY COUNTY

**Best Western Discovery
Inn,**
200 East Estrella Avenue,
Tucumcari,
(505) 461–4884/
(800) 528–1234

**Best Western Pow
Wow Inn,**
801 West Route 66,
Tucumcari,
(505) 461–0500/
(800) 527–6996

Holiday Inn,
3716 East Route 66,
Tucumcari,
(505) 461–3780/
(800) 335–3780

Royal Palacio Motel,
1620 East Route 66,
Tucumcari,
(505) 461–1212

Where to Eat in Northeastern New Mexico

COLFAX COUNTY

Brown Cafe,
Main Street,
Springer,
(505) 483–2269.
Inexpensive. Fare: Small-
town eclectic.

El Taco Cafe,
704 Maxwell Avenue,
Springer,
(505) 483–0402.
Inexpensive to moderate.
Fare: New Mexican.

Domingo's,
1903 Cedar Street,
Ratón,
(505) 445–2288.
Inexpensive to moderate.
Fare: American and Mexican
dishes.

Ice House,
945 South Second Street,
Ratón,
(505) 445–2339.
Inexpensive to moderate.
Fare: Steaks, seafood,
burgers, etc.

El Matador,
1012 South Second Street,
Ratón,
(505) 445–9575.
Inexpensive. Fare: New
Mexican.

UNION COUNTY

**Eklund Hotel Dining Room
and Saloon,**
15 Main Street,
Clayton,
(505) 374–2551.
Inexpensive to expensive.
Fare: American, featuring
steaks and seafood, and
New Mexican.

La Palomita Restaraunt,
1022 South First Street,
Clayton,
(505) 374–2127.
Inexpensive. Fare: Mexican.

Rabbit Ear Cafe,
402 North First Street,
Clayton,
(505) 374–9912.
Inexpensive. Fare: Mexican.

El Nicho Restaurant,
Highway 518,
Mora,
(505) 387–9297.
Inexpensive. Fare: Traditional
New Mexican.

Hatcha's Cafe,
Highway 518,
Mora,
(505) 387–9299.
Inexpensive. Fare: Traditional
New Mexican.

SAN MIGUEL COUNTY

Adelia's Landmark Grill,
Plaza Hotel,
230 Old Town Plaza,
Las Vegas,
(505) 425–3591.
Moderate to expensive. Fare:
American and Southwestern.

El Alto Supper Club,
706 Saltillo Street,
Las Vegas,
(505) 454–0808.
Inexpensive to moderate.
Fare: Steaks, seafood,
Mexican food in an old,
romantic New Mexican
atmosphere.

El Rialto,
141 Bridge Street,
Las Vegas,
(505) 454–0037.
Inexpensive to moderate.
Fare: New Mexican.

Hillcrest Restaurant,
1106 Grand Avenue,
Las Vegas,
(505) 425–7211.
Inexpensive to moderate.
Fare: American.

HARDING COUNTY

Martha's Cafe,
downtown,
Roy,
(505) 485–2661.
Inexpensive. Fare:
American.

GUADALUPE COUNTY

**Joseph's Restaurant
& Cantina,**
865 Will Rogers Drive,
Santa Rosa,
(505) 472–3361.
Inexpensive to moderate.
Fare: New Mexican.

Mateo's Restaurant,
500 Coronado West,
Santa Rosa,
(505) 472–5720.
Inexpensive to moderate.
Fare: New Mexican.

Silver Moon Restaurant,
3501 Will Rogers Drive,
Santa Rosa,
(505) 472–3162.
Inexpensive to moderate.
Fare: American.

Penny's Diner,
Junction of Highways 54, 60,
and 285,
Vaughn,
(505) 584–8733.
Inexpensive. Fare: American.

QUAY COUNTY

El Toro Cafe,
107 South First Street,
Tucumcari,
(505) 461–3328.
Inexpensive to moderate.
Fare: American and
New Mexican.

Del's,
1202 East Route 66,
Tucumcari,
(505) 461–1740.
Inexpensive. Fare: American,
with salad bar.

Branding Iron,
3716 East Route 66,
Tucumcari,
(505) 461–3780.
Inexpensive to moderate.
Fare: American and New
Mexican.

Pow Wow Restaurant,
801 West Route 66,
Tucumcari,
(505) 461–2587.
Inexpensive to moderate.
Fare: American and New
Mexican.

**La Cita Mexican
Restaurant,**
812 South First Street,
Tucumcari,
(505) 461–0949.
Inexpensive to moderate.
Fare: New Mexican and
American.

Lena's Home Cooking,
116 East Smith Street,
Tucumcari,
(505) 461–1610.
Inexpensive to moderate.
Fare: American and
New Mexican.

Southeastern New Mexico

Probably the most diverse region of the state, southeastern New Mexico can't be pigeonholed. Its varying landscape ranges from the harshness of the high desert and the glistening dunes of White Sands to the cool peaks of the Sacramento Mountains and the evergreen-laden Lincoln National Forest. Fertile river basins like the Hondo Valley produce pastoral scenes of horses grazing on green fields of oats, as well as vistas of orchards teeming with crisp, red apples. And vast areas of rich, irrigated cropland help feed the nation, thanks in part to the legendary Pecos River (as in "the law west of the Pecos").

De Baca County

De Baca County is **Fort Sumner** and Fort Sumner is **Billy the Kid.** Without a doubt, the Kid is New Mexico's most famous legend who actually lived. Though only twenty-one when he died, William Bonney, also known as Billy the Kid, created a legacy and a legend that just won't die. And the community of Fort Sumner is one of several locales in New Mexico where the Kid left his mark. It's also where his remains remain.

In the **Old Fort Sumner Cemetery,** you can visit the grave of Billy the Kid. Graves are few and scattered in the small mil-

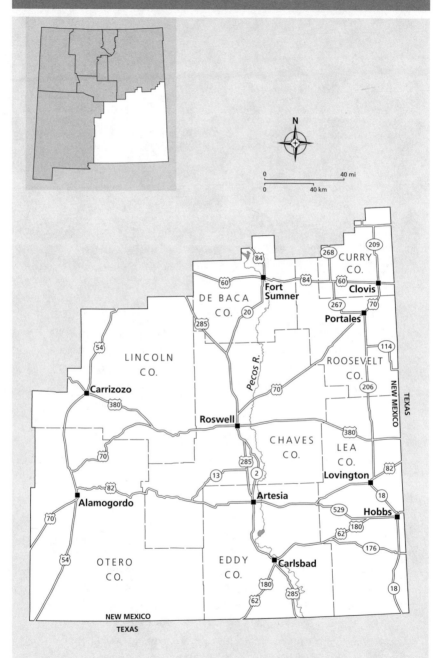

N

0   40 mi
0   40 km

209

268   CURRY CO.

84

60   Fort Sumner   84   60   Clovis

DE BACA CO.   20

267   70

285   Portales

114

54   LINCOLN CO.   Pecos R.   ROOSEVELT CO.

206   NEW MEXICO   TEXAS

Carrizozo   70

380

Roswell   CHAVES CO.   380

70   285   LEA CO.   82

13   2   Lovington

82   18

Alamogordo   Artesia   529   Hobbs

70   62   180

176

54   OTERO CO.   EDDY CO.   Carlsbad   18

180

62   285

NEW MEXICO
TEXAS

STATE PARKS IN SOUTHEASTERN NEW MEXICO
On the Web at: www.emnrd.state.nm.us/nmparks/

Bottomless Lake State Park,
16 miles southeast of Roswell,
(505) 624–6058

Brantley Lake State Park,
12 miles north of Carlsbad,
(505) 457–2384

Living Desert State Park,
in Carlsbad, (505) 887–5516

Oasis State Park,
6 miles north of Portales,
(505) 356–5331

Oliver Lee Memorial State Park,
10 miles south of Alamogordo,
(505) 437–8284

Sumner Lake State Park,
16 miles northwest of Fort Sumner,
(505) 355–2541

itary cemetery, but the most prominent site is encaged in metal—it's a three-person grave, Billy's alongside those of two of his pals, Tom O'Folliard and Charlie Bowdre.

The Kid's tombstone has a history of its own. It was first stolen in 1950, and its whereabouts remained a mystery until 1976, when Joe Bowlin, owner of the Old Fort Sumner Museum adjacent to the cemetery, recovered it in Granbury, Texas. Several years later it was stolen again, but this time it was recovered within days, in California. The Kid's tombstone, now shackled in iron for protection, has an epitaph that reads THE BOY BANDIT KING/HE DIED AS HE HAD LIVED.

Each summer during the second weekend in June, Fort Sumner hosts Old Fort Days. Here a favorite event is, appropriately enough, the World's Richest Tombstone Race, wherein participants run while carrying a replica of Billy's tombstone.

To get to the cemetery (which is just behind the Old Fort Sumner Museum), head east on U.S. Highway 60/84 from Fort Sumner for 3 miles and then take a right onto Billy the Kid Road (Highway 272), proceeding for 4 miles. There's no admission charge to enter the cemetery, and it's always open.

The *Old Fort Sumner Museum* (505–355–2942), in front of the Old Fort Sumner Cemetery, contains artifacts from the town's past. Historical paintings line the walls, and Billy the Kid newspaper clippings and photos are posted on easels throughout. If you have time on your hands, you can learn a lot about the Kid by reading the news items. Otherwise, check out the barbed-wire collection and the old Apache moccasins and articles of Indian ceremonial dress. The museum also has items that were purchased from La Paloma Museum when it closed down in Lincoln many years ago.

FAVORITE ATTRACTIONS/EVENTS IN SOUTHEASTERN NEW MEXICO

Old Fort Sumner Cemetery,
Fort Sumner
No phone

Lincoln,
New Mexico
(505) 653-4372

Smokey Bear Museum,
Capitan
(505) 354-2298

Carlsbad Caverns National Park,
Eddy County
(505) 785-2232

White Sands National Monument,
Alamogordo
(505) 479-6124

Smokey Bear Stampede,
July, Capitan
(505) 354-2748

UFO Encounter,
July, Roswell
(888) 767-9355

Old Lincoln Days,
August, Lincoln
(505) 653-4025

Old Fort Sumner Museum is open daily from 9:00 A.M. to 5:00 P.M. during summer (roughly Memorial Day through Labor Day) and from 10:00 A.M. to 4:00 P.M. the rest of the year (although it may open late and/or close early during the winter, so consider yourself advised). Admission is $3.00 for adults, $2.00 for young people ages seven to fourteen, and free for children age six or younger. Group rates are available.

About ¼ mile down the gravel road in front of the museum, you'll find *Fort Sumner State Monument* (505–355–2573). It's here that the town gets its name, because the monument's grounds include the ruins of the old military fort. A small visitor center tells the story of Fort Sumner and showcases items excavated from the fort. Late autumn is a great time to visit, for instead of seeing other people you'll get to take a gander at the migratory birds making patterns in the blue sky above nearby Bosque Redondo, the 16 miles of wooded wetlands along the Pecos River.

Fort Sumner was created because of a horrible experiment that failed. During the Civil War, settlers in New Mexico and Arizona, feeling they were in constant danger from the non-Pueblo Indians living in the territory, built the fort as part of a new reservation on which to relocate the Mescalero Apaches and the Navajo. For five years 9,000 Indians were confined to the reservation, after having been forced to walk hundreds of miles from their homelands. Because disease and shortages of food and firewood plagued the reservation, General William T. Sherman sent the Indians home in 1868. At the monument you'll see a shrine dedicated in 1971: a small pile of rocks carried from different parts of the Navajo Nation in northwestern New Mexico and northeastern Arizona to commemorate "The Long Walk."

The fort site is also where Billy the Kid was gunned down by Lincoln County sheriff Pat Garrett on July 14, 1881, years after the 1869 abandonment of the fort.

The monument is open daily from 8:30 A.M. to 5:00 P.M. Admission charge is $3.00, with youths age sixteen or younger admitted free.

Back in the modern-day community of Fort Sumner, you'll come across the most fun of this off-the-beaten-track area's unique spots. If you're a true lover of the legend, you might just satiate your hunger for Kid artifacts and lore at the **Billy the Kid Museum.** The privately owned facility was opened as a one-building museum in 1953 and now rambles both indoors and out through several structures.

You can spend several enjoyable hours strolling among the more than 60,000 relics—some historic, some pure kitsch—collected over the years by Ed Sweet, former owner of the museum, and his wife, Jewel. This place just plain smells old, a wonderfully sentimental scent, as if hundreds of grandmothers' houses were combined.

Kid artifacts include his guns, a jail-cell door that imprisoned the outlaw, and even locks of his hair saved by a Las Cruces barber. There's also an original Billy the Kid "wanted" placard signed by territorial New Mexico governor Lew Wallace (author of the novel Ben Hur). In addition, you can view a fine selection of antique cars (some of which are usually parked out front, for effect), as well as fossilized dinosaur droppings.

The museum is located at 1601 East Sumner Avenue, 2 miles east of downtown; (505) 355–2380. It's open daily from 8:30 A.M. to 5:00 P.M. May 15 to October 1 and Monday through Saturday (same hours) the remainder of the year, with the exception of Sundays, when it's open from 11:00 A.M. to 5:00 P.M., and January 1 to January 15, when it closes. Admission is $4.00 for adults, $3.50 for seniors, $2.00 for children ages six to eleven, and free for kids age five or younger.

Lincoln County

No other town in New Mexico has preserved its past more meticulously than the community of **Lincoln,** nestled in the Bonito Valley. History buffs of the Southwest will want to spend the whole day in Lincoln, because the entire town is a National Historical Landmark, thus making visible commercialism absent. As Bob Hart, formerly of the Lincoln County Heritage Trust, notes, "You will find no rubber tomahawks here." Much of the one-street town constitutes the *Lincoln State Monument* and other museums.

As with many old, remote New Mexico towns, Lincoln has definitely seen its wilder days. The former county seat achieved its notoriety as the site of one of the Wild West's bloodiest events: the Lincoln County War of 1878. The war was the culmination of a dispute between opposing factions vying for political and economic control—especially of the city's lucrative mercantile business, which included nearby Fort Stanton. Billy the Kid got his infamous start during the conflict, in which he sided with one of the factions. Eventually he became a fugitive and, much later, after being captured, made his daring escape from the Lincoln County Courthouse in 1881—only to be tracked down in Fort Sumner by Sheriff Pat Garrett (see De Baca County entry). The two-story courthouse is part of the Lincoln State Monument. It's said that Billy's gun is responsible for a bullet hole visible in the wall at the foot of the stairwell.

A single ticket, available at the Lincoln County Historical Center along U.S Highway 380, provides access to all the historical sites in town. Though everything is open daily from 8:30 A.M. to 4:30 P.M., two of the five sites are not accessible during the off-season (basically winter). Tickets are $3.50 for adults and free for young people age sixteen or younger. Call (505) 653–4372 for more information.

The most distinctive lodging in the area can be found at *Casa de Patrón,* a bed-and-breakfast along Lincoln's main street. The primary part of the inn was built in the mid-1800s as the home of Juan Patrón, the youngest speaker of the house in New Mexico's territorial legislature. A gracious host, Patrón entertained the likes of pre-outlaw Billy the Kid and territorial governor Lew Wallace in his home. Today, the old adobe home continues to delight persons who find themselves in this isolated part of New Mexico.

Hosts Jeremy and Cleis Jordan escaped the stress—and humidity—of Houston in the early 1980s to settle into the laid-back—and dry—landscape of Lincoln. Jeremy, an engineering consultant, and Cleis, a classical musician, occasionally treat their guests to "salon evenings" based on a particular theme,

newmexicotrivia

ABC newsman Sam Donaldson owns a ranch in Lincoln County.

newmexicotrivia

Former New Mexico Territorial governor Lew Wallace wrote his acclaimed novel *Ben Hur,* which was first published in 1880, in Lincoln County.

such as "An Evening in Vienna," in which an elegant dinner is combined with a concert performed by Cleis on the inn's grand piano.

For those who want to enjoy a longer stay or have a place to themselves, the Jordans offer two cabins as part of their inn: Casita Bonita and Casita Paz ("Small Pretty House" and "Small Peace House," respectively). In addition, in the mid-1990s, two new luxury guest rooms were added to the complex. The inn's grounds are the most handsome patch of green in Lincoln—a comforting contrast for the eyes.

Casa de Patrón is on U.S. Highway 380; (505) 653–4676 or (800) 524–5202; www.casapatron.com. An ever-changing breakfast, complete with freshly ground coffee, is included in the daily rate of $77 to $117.

The **Wortley Pat Garrett Hotel** is another fine place to stay in Lincoln, and it's the only public place to get a meal for miles. The original structure was built in 1874 but burned to the ground in the 1930s. The current replica was constructed some thirty years later and is open from April 28 through October 15. Because the hotel, formerly known simply as the Wortley Hotel, was briefly owned by Sheriff Pat Garrett in 1881, the current owner expanded the name in 1999.

The small, comfortable rooms are simply done in period furnishings reflecting Lincoln's heyday in the late 1800s. Each of the seven rooms has an antique brass bed, fireplace, and private bath. For a great diversion on a lazy Lincoln afternoon, settle into one of the many old rockers on the porch spanning the Wortley's facade and close your eyes as the creak-creak lulls you back to Lincoln's colorful past.

The hotel's restaurant is open daily, during the season from 8:00 A.M. to 6:00 P.M. The family-oriented restaurant features classic Americana comfort foods.

Wortley Pat Garrett Hotel porch

The Wortley is situated along U.S. Highway 380 in Lincoln; (505) 653–4300 or (877) 967–8539 (toll-free; www.patgarrethotel.com). Rates range from $65 to $75.

The picturesque mountain resort town of **Ruidoso,** along Highway 70 just north of the Mescalero Apache Indian Reservation, provides a beautifully polished place to kick back and relax. There's no shortage of lodging here—from luxury condos to rustic cabins and everything in between—and you'll find plenty of fine restaurants, art galleries, and interesting shops. **Ski Apache Ski Area** is also nearby and provides excellent downhill skiing.

If you're planning to spend time in Ruidoso and happen to be a horse fan, be sure to head a few miles farther east on Highway 70 to the community of **Ruidoso Downs** (known for the racetrack of the same name, home of the world's richest quarter-horse race) and stop by the **Hubbard Museum of the American West,** formerly known as the Museum of the Horse. This relatively new museum pays tribute to an animal the museum claims has played a dramatic role in the exploration and expansion of the cultures of the world throughout history. The museum houses the collection of Anne C. Stradling, a woman born into a wealthy East Coast family who developed a lifelong passion for horses and anything horse-related. Starting with a worn-out stirrup and bit, her collection eventually grew to more than 10,000 pieces—now housed in the handsome museum. Gracing the entrance of the museum, *Free Spirits at Noisy Water* is billed as the world's largest equine sculpture. *Free Spirits* is the creation of American sculptor Dave McGary and includes replicas of eight horses, representing all popular breeds, running through a meadow amid falling water. The sculpture is a marvel of engineering, with five of the horses each balanced on one hoof.

newmexicotrivia

At 12,003 feet, Sierra Blanca Peak near Ruidoso is the highest point in the southern United States.

The museum is open daily from 10:00 A.M. to 5:00 P.M. Admission is $6.00 for adults, $5.00 for seniors and active military personnel with ID, $2.00 for young people ages six to sixteen, and free for children age five or younger. The museum is located 1 mile east of Ruidoso Downs racetrack, on Highway 70; (505) 378–4142 or (800) 263–5929; www.hubbardmuseum.org.

In the placid Hondo Valley east of Ruidoso, you'll find one of the most tranquil, unaffected spots in southern New Mexico: the tiny community of **San Patricio,** along the Rio Ruidoso.This is a place of horse ranches and apple orchards. It's also a thriving arts community—a well-hidden fact because of its low-profile location. It's neither promoted nor pretentious. San Patricio is where some of the surviving members of the Wyeth-Hurd creative dynasty continue to paint. Though the family tree has many branches of artists, some of the most celebrated members are N. C. Wyeth, Andrew Wyeth, Peter Hurd, and Henriette Wyeth.

The most imposing and beautiful brick structure in San Patricio houses the very polished **Hurd–La Rinconada Gallery** (505–653–4331). Built by Mike Hurd, the gallery features the art of members of the Wyeth-Hurd family, including that by Peter Hurd and Henriette Wyeth. The gallery is open Monday through Saturday from 9:00 A.M. to 4:00 P.M. and Sunday from 10:00 A.M. to 4:00 P.M., with the exception of Labor Day through Memorial Day, when the gallery is closed on Sunday.

Farther east on U.S. Highway 70 you'll come across the tiny town of **Tinnie.** The focus here is the **Tinnie Silver Dollar**—restaurant, bar, old-time mercantile, and gallery. The red-roofed adobe structure with its wooden bell tower dominates the landscape and provides a wonderful time-travel experience inside.

Alternately a private residence, mercantile company, and post office dating from 1882, the building became a restaurant in 1959 and was later reconditioned to become the polished gem of southeastern New Mexico. The Silver Dollar's authentic Brunswick bar in its lounge and the hand-beveled glass, fine art, and exquisite antiques galore provide a visual feast for diners. Especially notable is the Victorian Room, which hosts special one-sitting dinners featuring a custom predetermined menu. Selections from the regular menu include a full range of steaks, chicken, pasta, and seafood, most notably Tinnie's Choice-Cut Ribeye, Margarita Chicken, Pasta Diablo (shrimp sautéed with tomatoes, basil pesto, crushed red pepper, and white wine, served atop green chile fettucini).

During summer the Silver Dollar hosts various bands and serves drinks on its long veranda. The colorful and carefully landscaped backyard that slopes toward the Rio Hondo adds to this establishment's charm—and its appeal as a site for weddings.

In addition to the high-society glamour of territorial New Mexico it provides for its ordinary customers, the Silver Dollar is patronized by some of New Mexico's most powerful economic and political players who like to keep a low public profile.

newmexicotrivia

The tiny village of San Patricio has been home to the following famous New Mexicans: Billy the Kid, actress Helen Hayes, and artists Paul Horgan, Peter Hurd, and Henriette Wyeth.

Adjacent to the restaurant and bar, you'll find a mercantile/gallery that sells everything from flour to Arabian horses, including a selection of locally made gifts. The manager explains that the store stocks things for the community residents, not tourists, adding, "If we don't have it, you don't need it."

The Silver Dollar is on U.S. Highway 70 near the intersection of Highway 368; (505) 653–4425. It is open daily from 11:00 A.M. to 11:00 P.M.

The favorite son of the village of **Capitan** wasn't even human. He was none other than Smokey Bear. (No one knows where that pesky middle name "the" came from, but for the record it's not Smokey the Bear.) Yes, it's a fact, the national symbol of forest-fire prevention really did exist, and he lived right here in the Capitan Mountains. And the legendary story of Smokey's life is amazingly accurate.

In May 1950 a fire crew rescued a badly singed black bear cub that had been clinging to a charred pine tree after devastating human-caused fires destroyed much of the Lincoln National Forest near Capitan. After recuperating at a veterinary hospital in Santa Fe, Smokey was flown to the National Zoo in Washington, D.C., where he "spoke out" for forest-fire prevention until his death in 1976. He was buried in Capitan in the **Smokey Bear Historical State Park** (505–354–2748; www.smokeybearpark.com), which also has a fine visitor center filled with Smokey memorabilia. The visitor center is open daily from 9:00 A.M. to 5:00 P.M. His legacy and his message live on. According to the USDA Forest Service, the Smokey Bear fire-prevention campaign is the longest-running public-service-announcement campaign in the history of the Ad Council. Admission to the park is $1.00 for adults, 50 cents for children ages seven to twelve.

Adjacent to the park you'll find the **Smokey Bear Museum,** which documents Smokey's story. The museum contains several scrapbooks filled with photographs and news clippings on Smokey's life and times. The fact that a museum would even make scrapbooks accessible to visitors is odd, but the effect is very personal, down-home, and nostalgic—a detail that adds to the sentimental feeling of this small log museum.

An exhibit of Smokey Bear toys, books, and comics from the 1950s and 1960s shows how popular culture was used to convey an important message to the youth of the era.

The museum is on Highway 380 in downtown Capitan; (505) 354–2298; www.smokeybear.org. It's open daily from 9:00 A.M. to 4:00 P.M. except during the summer, when it stays open until 5:00 P.M. There's no admission charge.

Farther north in Lincoln County you'll find the remains of New Mexico's most raucous mining town in the ghost town of **White Oaks.** One version of White Oaks's birth in the 1870s says that the discoverer of the North Homestake mine sold it to a friend for $40, a pony, and a bottle of whiskey. He probably lived to regret that decision when the mine eventually produced $500,000 in gold.

White Oaks Bar and Museum

Along came other mines with names like Rip Van Winkle, Large Hopes, Little Hell, and Smuggler, and the boomtown was under way with a population that swelled to 4,000. The town became a hangout for cattle rustlers and outlaws, including Billy the Kid. Saloons, gambling houses, and "houses of another sort" took hold as White Oaks entrepreneurs thought of quick ways to wheedle away the day's take from area miners.

White Oaks faded when a planned railroad link with El Paso went instead to the New Mexico town of Capitan. The gold played out at about the same time.

A simple historical marker, a cemetery, and many abandoned buildings are all that's left of old White Oaks. A few hardy folks have rediscovered the town, elevating its status to semighost town. An impressive building is Hoyle's Castle, a brick Victorian mansion that looms over the town from its hilltop site. A retired schoolteacher from Carrizozo lives in the structure, which resembles a classic haunted house out of an old movie. It's not open to visitors.

White Oaks does have a bar and a museum. They're one and the same, housed in the old post office, a tiny wooden shack near the center of town. It's not only an interesting place in which to look at relics from the mining days but also a fun, though eerie, place in which to grab a beer and play a game of pool in the back room.

Since the late 1990s White Oaks has become one of the state's newest artists' communities, featuring several nice galleries, which participate in a studio tour each April.

White Oaks is 9 miles off U.S. Highway 54 on Highway 349, 11 miles northeast of Carrizozo.

Otero County

Driving into Otero County from the north along U.S. Highway 54, observant motorists and spider fanciers should be on the lookout for the brave tarantulas that cross the highway on warm summer days. Highway department tarantula crossing signs wouldn't last out here, as less-than-honest souvenir seekers would pick them off as fast as they could be placed. Tarantulas aside, Otero County offers weekend adventurers several special spots. Though much of the county is off-limits (White Sands Missile Range, Fort Bliss Military Reservation, and the Mescalero Apache Indian Reservation), the parts that are accessible make up for it.

The missile range isn't the only place that's privy to the soft, snow-white gypsum dunes just southwest of the city of Alamogordo. Adjacent to the range is the *White Sands National Monument*—part of the largest gypsum dune field in the world—whose majesty you're welcome to explore.

This extremely stark park is the perfect place for uninhibited barefoot frolicking. It's also the place for people who are afraid of the water: lots of beach, no ocean. Pack plastic sleds and snowboards to slide down the up-to-60-foot-tall sand dunes. During the height of summer, the sand tends to get quite hot, but you wouldn't want to visit then anyway—tourists, you know. Plan a late autumn visit—or, better yet, camp out during a full moon (allowed at a backcountry campsite only; registration required). At night, the reflection of moonlight from the sand provides an unearthly adventure you won't soon forget—it's bright enough to read by!

A visitor center and museum explains how the dunes were formed and contains an exhibit on those species of plants and wildlife hardy enough to thrive in such a harsh environment. Still, it's the Dunes Drive, an 8-mile scenic loop, that forms the highlight of a visit to White Sands. The "sands" are almost like a living entity. Gusting winds cause them to shift, which makes keeping the roads clear a full-time chore. Occasionally, the Dunes Drive is closed because of missile-range testing, so call ahead.

White Sands National Monument is 15 miles southwest of Alamogordo, just off U.S. Highway 70/82; (505) 479–6124. It's open daily, with hours as follows: in summer (Memorial Day through mid-August), visitor center 8:00 A.M. to 7:00 P.M. and Dunes Drive 7:00 A.M. to 9:00 P.M.; in winter, visitor center 8:00 A.M. to 5:00 P.M. and Dunes Drive 7:00 A.M. to sunset. There's a $3.00 fee per person for the Dunes Drive, with children age sixteen or younger admitted free.

Just north of Alamogordo you'll find *Eagle Ranch Pistachio Groves,* producer of "Heart of the Desert" pistachio nuts. Though the bulk of domestic pistachio farming occurs in the fertile San Joaquin Valley in California, a new agricultural industry has emerged in this southern New Mexico town after a little research showed that climate and elevation were nearly perfect in Alamogordo for growing the fickle nut.

Never dyed red to appeal to consumers or cover blemishes, Eagle Ranch's off-white and green nuts are available only by mail or at the ranch store. The outlet recently introduced red chile pistachios for die-hard New Mexican chile-heads who need an extra kick to everything they eat.

Marianne Schweers, who owns the groves with her husband, George, shares an interesting bit of pistachio lore: When the Shah of Iran was overthrown in 1979, not only was the world oil market affected but the Middle Eastern country's other principal export also suffered when its markets were cut off. Yes, until that time Iran was the world's premier pistachio supplier. The situation was a big boost to U.S. pistachio production, and the timing couldn't have been better for fledgling Eagle Ranch. Marianne sums up the situation by saying, "The Ayatollah was the best friend that [U.S.] pistachio growers ever had."

newmexicotrivia

Ham, the first chimpanzee in outer space, and Minnie, the longest-surviving "astrochimp," are both buried at the International Space Hall of Fame in Alamogordo.

Though visitors are always welcome to look at the groves, guided tours are available only to groups of ten or more. The Eagle Ranch store, which also sells other southwestern food and gift items, is located 4 miles north of Alamogordo at 7288 Highway 54/70; (505) 434–0035 or (800) 432–0999; www.eagleranchpistachios.com. The store is open from 8:00 A.M. to 6:00 P.M. Monday through Saturday and 9:00 A.M. to 6:00 P.M. Sunday. Farm tours are available Monday through Friday at 10:00 A.M. and 1:30 P.M. June through August, 1:30 P.M. only the rest of the year.

In Alamogordo ("Fat Cottonwood"), you'll find the *New Mexico Museum of Space History* nestled in the foothills of the Sacramento Mountains. This shimmering, massive gold cube of a building houses four levels of museumlike exhibits in the International Space Hall of Fame (annual induction ceremony held the last Saturday in September).

You start on the top floor and work your way down ramps through exhibits like the "There's Space in New Mexico" room, which combines traditional New Mexico ambience—adobe walls, pine-planked floor, vigas (ceiling beams)—with the state's cutting-edge research and contributions to the nation's space program. You can also step inside the interactive "Space Station 2001" exhibit for an astronaut's view of space travel in the future, as well as examine a Skylab space suit and even Soviet space food.

For those who want to take a load off, the Space Center is also home to an Imax theater with a 2,700-square-foot screen, as well as to a high-tech planetarium system. Outside, on the grounds of the Space Center, you'll find the John P. Stapp Air and Space Park, which is filled with actual space hardware and rocket equipment. This is also a good place to get a broad view of White Sands in the distance.

To get to the Space Center, turn east on Indian Wells Road off U.S. Highway 54/70/82 in Alamogordo and follow the signs; (505) 437–2840; www.space frame.org. It's open daily from 9:00 A.M. to 5:00 P.M. Hall of Fame admission charges are $2.50 for adults, $2.25 for seniors and military personnel, and $2.00 for young people ages six to seventeen; theater admission charges are $6.00 for adults, $5.50 for seniors, and $4.50 for children ages four to twelve. There are also special combination and family rates. *(NOTE:* Admission for all attendees is free to the Hall of Fame on the day of the annual induction ceremony.)

newmexicotrivia

Alan Hale, codiscoverer of the much-celebrated Hale-Bopp comet, lives and watches the sky near Cloudcroft in the Sacramento Mountains of Otero County in southeastern New Mexico.

Highway 82, from Alamogordo to the village of **Cloudcroft,** is one of southern New Mexico's most beautiful drives. In just 16 miles you'll climb nearly 5,000 feet, passing through all the climatic zones from the Sonoran Desert region of Mexico to the Hudson Bay region of Canada. As the road winds through the forested Sacramento Mountains, you'll come across many scenic overlooks, as well as roadside stands selling apples, cider, and various other forms of produce. New Mexico's only highway tunnel is also on this route.

Once you experience the breathtaking setting of Cloudcroft high in the Sacramentos, you'll understand why getting here is worth the effort. The small town is a year-round playground where you can beat the heat in summer and marvel at the turning of the aspens in fall. And Cloudcroft's magical winters bring snow skiing at Ski Cloudcroft (see appendix, page 204), the southernmost ski area in the United States, and ice-skating at Sewell Skate Pond, one of only a few outdoor places in the state where you can pursue this sport.

Cloudcroft is also home to **The Lodge,** a romantic mountain getaway. This place has a history. Built as a railroad resort in 1899, the inn was reconstructed after the original lodge burned in 1909. Famous guests include Judy Garland and Clark Gable. Conrad Hilton, founder of the hotel chain that bears his name, owned the place in the 1930s.

A Glimpse of Southeastern New Mexico:Impressions of the Magnificent Caves

Without knowing it, I became an explorer of New Mexico more than twenty years ago during an out-of-state family vacation with my dad, mom, and older sister. I'd known little about Carlsbad Caverns, but the thought of any escape from the unbearable heat and humidity of another South Texas August was enough to get me excited.

Though our trip included running barefoot through the endless soft dunes of White Sands National Monument, escaping into the forests and mountains of Cloudcroft, and watching the horses run at Ruidoso Downs, it was the caverns that had begun to cast their spell on my nine-year-old imagination. My energy level increased on the final hours of the drive, and all I could do was fantasize about the darkness, the coolness, and the otherworldly, eerie silence that awaited me.

After parking, gathering gear, and trekking toward the entrance, we saw the mouth-shaped, giant cave entrance loom before us. As the opening swallowed us up on our descent, the air became cooler, and, now glad that my mom had made me bring along my blue windbreaker, I smiled as I blocked voices and other sounds from my mind. Confident I would not get lost, I broke away from the slow pace of my family and sped around a blind bend in the trail. I had begun chasing my first New Mexico adventure, and I was hooked.

The Lodge's European-style architecture, with its four-story copper tower, adds to a mood of romantic seclusion in a chalet high in the Alps. Inside, Victorian ambience takes over in the high-ceilinged guest rooms outfitted with antique furnishings and down comforters. Select a stay when your weary bones need a rest and you couldn't care less about roaming the byways for further adventure.

Because it's usually chilly at this altitude (9,200 feet), expect a cozy fire in the lobby fireplace any time of year. Just off the lobby is Rebecca's, the lodge's dining room, named after the ghost who is said to roam the inn's halls; Rebecca, the story goes, was a flirtatious, redheaded chambermaid who in the 1930s was killed by a jealous lover.

The Lodge is just off Highway 82 in Cloudcroft; (505) 682–2566 or (800) 395–6343; www.thelodgeresort.com. Room rates range from $89 to $319, depending on the particular room and season.

The ***National Solar Observatory at Sacramento Peak*** (505–434–7000; www.nso.edu) in the village of ***Sunspot*** offers visitors a chance to see why and how astronomers study the sun from their vantage point at 9,200 feet in the Sacramento Mountains. The observatory is open to the public between dawn and dusk for self-guided tours. Weekend-afternoon guided tours, beginning at 2:00 P.M. May through October, begin with a slide-show presentation about the observatory and the sun and a walk around the observatory, including a visit to the Vacuum Tower Telescope, the largest at the site. The observatory's visitor center, which has a gift shop, is generally open daily from 10:00 A.M. to 4:00 P.M., with extended hours during the summer. Even if you're not into astronomy, the drive through and the setting in the Lincoln National Forest are quite awe inspiring. In addition to the million-dollar views of the Tularosa Basin (including White Sands National Monument), you'll find plenty of hiking trails and remote picnic spots.

From Cloudcroft, take Highway 130 East to its junction with Highway 6563 (a designated scenic byway). Follow Highway 6563 to its end, about 15 miles, to Sunspot. Guided tours are $2.00 for adults and $1.00 for seniors and children; self-guided tours are free.

By planning ahead, you may combine your visit to the solar observatory with a tour of neighboring *Apache Point Observatory* (505–437–6822), which offers tours only by advance reservation. Unlike the former, the latter is oriented toward nighttime astronomical observation. Owned by a private consortium and operated by New Mexico State University, the observatory is home to the Sloan Digital Sky Survey, a project that is mapping 100 million celestial objects in one-quarter of the earth's sky.

Chaves County

The city of **Roswell** is one of those near-perfect all-American cities. Cited by national publications as one of the ten best small cities in the country, Roswell has also been included in the list of "Ten Peaceable Places to Retire" compiled by Money magazine. (Though lately the media cannot get enough coverage of Roswell as the "UFO capital of the world." See listing later in this section.) As the largest city in southeastern New Mexico, Roswell has its share of interesting sites and cultural diversions as well as the century-old New Mexico Military Institute. But the most impressive spot to visit is the **Roswell Art Center and Museum.** With twelve galleries in the grand adobe structure, the center focuses on art, history, and science.

Known for its excellent paintings of the Southwest, the center has the finest single collection of art in southeastern New Mexico. Featured New Mexico artists include Georgia O'Keeffe, Ernest Blumenschein, Henriette Wyeth, Andrew Dasburg, and Fremont Ellis. The museum's nationally acclaimed

Hurd Collection is the most extensive collection of Roswell native Peter Hurd's works.

A special wing of the center displays the actual engines and rocket assemblies developed by Dr. Robert H. Goddard, who worked in Roswell from 1930 to 1942. The Goddard Wing also has a replica of the early space scientist's laboratory, where he built the world's first liquid-fuel rockets. In addition, the **Robert Goddard Planetarium** on site presents various programs, for which fees are generally $2.00 to $5.00 per person.

newmexicotrivia

Actress Demi Moore was born in Roswell.

The museum is located at 100 West Eleventh Street; (505) 624–6744; www.roswellmuseum.org. It's open Monday through Saturday from 9:00 A.M. to 5:00 P.M. and Sunday and holidays from 1:00 to 5:00 P.M. There's no admission charge.

People take UFO sightings seriously in Roswell—people like Walter Haut, president of the **International UFO Museum and Research Center** (505–625–9495; www.iufomrc.org). He has reason to believe. In 1947 Haut made national headlines when, as a public relations officer from the former Roswell Army Air Field, he announced the recovery of a crashed flying saucer at a nearby ranch. The increasingly known museum features interesting displays and published accounts of reported UFO sightings from all over the world.

Though the army later denied that extraterrestrial matter was found from what is often known as "The Roswell Incident," claiming the debris came from a downed weather balloon, Haut remains convinced that aliens have visited earth. He wants museum visitors to decide for themselves, however. Volunteers staff the nonprofit museum to answer questions and help interpret displays. The museum, located at 114 North Main (Highway 70), now has a popular gift shop and is open daily from 9:00 A.M. to 5:00 P.M. There's no admission charge.

In the wake of Roswell's increased notoriety as a mecca for those who believe in UFOs—especially after the release of the 1996 sci-fi blockbuster film *Independence Day* and the acclaimed 1997 film *Contact,* plus an appearance by Roswell's mayor on *The Late Show with David Letterman*—the community now hosts the annual **Roswell UFO Encounter,** a festival held during, appropriately, the July Fourth weekend. The event includes talks by well-known conspiracy theorists and other UFOlogists, a fireworks display, a nighttime golf tournament (complete with glow-in-the-dark balls), an alien costume contest, and a UFO Crash and Burn Expo, a nonmotorized vehicle competition. For

newmexicotrivia

In 1933 the Bottomless Lakes area near Roswell was set aside as New Mexico's first state park.

information on the event—as well as for information regarding guided tours of the alleged crash site, complete with an area rancher as the unlikely guide—call the Roswell Chamber of Commerce at (877) 849–7679.

Other notable museums in Roswell include the **Gen. Douglas L. McBride Museum** (505–624– 8220), a U.S. military history museum located at the New Mexico Military Institute; open Tuesday through Friday from 8:30 to 11:30 A.M. and 1:00 to 3:00 P.M. Also the **Historical Center for Southeastern New Mexico,** formerly the Chaves County Historical Museum, can be found at 200 North Lea (505– 622–8333). It is open from 1:00 to 4:00 P.M. daily.

Eddy County

Eddy County should probably be called Cave County. In addition to containing the world-famous Carlsbad Caverns, the county has untold numbers of other caves, most of them patiently waiting to be discovered by some daring young spelunker. And if the name changed to Cave County, the county seat would undoubtedly be **Carlsbad Caverns National Park,** probably the single most-visited spot in New Mexico and certainly one of the best known.

Despite its name, the park is located not in Carlsbad but, rather, 26 miles southwest of the city. Actually, it's closer to **Whites City,** named after Jim White, who discovered this underground fantasyland in 1901. Because you'll be underground in a constant-temperature (read: quite cool) environment during most of your visit, pleasant weather is not a major factor for enjoyment. Therefore, it's a good idea to avoid the crowds of summer, when the above-ground temperatures can soar.

From late May through October the park offers visitors the fun of viewing mass bat flights. After dusk, almost a million Mexican free-tailed bats swirl out of the cave's entrance for their nightly escapades and insect-feeding frenzies. The bat flight is preceded by informative—and humorous—talks by rangers about the tiny winged mammals. Though it's true that these same bats are in the cave during the day, don't worry: The caverns are enormous, and you won't even notice the slumbering bats.

Though the park is decidedly remote, access is no problem. Of course, after making the significant trek to the park, you'll undoubtedly want to view the famed stalactites and stalagmites decorating the grand chambers of the main

Carlsbad Cavern, but as a true adventurer you'll also be drawn to its other less accessible caves, such as Slaughter Canyon Cave, Spider Cave, Lower Cave, and Hall of the White Giants.

These alternative caves preserve some of the thrill cavers experience when exploring a new find. Guided-lantern tours take you through the undeveloped caves in all their eerie, dark splendor. You'll need to bring along a flashlight, water, and nonslip shoes. Advance reservations are required; call The National Park Service at (800) 967–2283. Tour fees range from $7 to $25. (NOTE: Don't attempt this type of cave adventure unless you're in reasonably good physical shape.)

In a remote section of the park is the deepest cave in the United States: **Lechuguilla Cave,** whose magnitude was discovered only in 1986. It's designated a "wild" cave and open just to experienced cavers in organized expeditions (park permit required). Neither does the National Park Service plan to develop Lechuguilla; it, along with several other wild caves, may be designated the world's first cave wilderness.

The park entrance is located just west of Whites City on Highway 7; (505) 785–2232 or (800) 967–2283. Though Carlsbad Cavern is open daily with continuous self-guided tours, other caving experiences are limited and often

The Goodnight-Loving Trail

Nineteenth-century cattle trails were just about as important to the settlement of the American West as were the celebrated commerce trails like the Santa Fe Trail and the Oregon Trail. The Chisolm Trail may have more name recognition as a cattle trail, but it was the trail with the soothing name that made its mark on southeastern New Mexico.

The Goodnight-Loving Trail adventure began because two particularly ambitious ranchers, like many southern ranchers, had experienced problems selling "recovered" cattle (those that had scattered during the Civil War) in war-ravaged markets. In 1886 Charles Goodnight and Oliver Loving set out from the northwest-Texas frontier to blaze a trail that would allow them to seek out more lucrative markets to the west. The Goodnight-Loving Trail led for hundreds of miles, looping up into New Mexico near present-day Carlsbad and Roswell, and ended in Fort Sumner, where Goodnight and Loving separated. Loving continued north to Colorado and Goodnight returned to Texas for another herd of cattle.

That lucrative first trip started a new industry in New Mexico. Cattle ranching and beef processing continue the legacy of the Goodnight-Loving Trail in eastern New Mexico to this day.

require reservations. Fees vary widely, from $6.00 for adults ($3.00 for children ages six to fifteen, kids age five or younger are free) for the normal self-guided tour to $20 for select guided tours. The park hours are 8:00 A.M. to 7:00 P.M. daily in summer, until 5:00 P.M. the rest of the year; hours for self-guided tours are 8:30 A.M. to 3:30 P.M.

Closer to the city of Carlsbad, you'll find *Living Desert State Park.* This unique park atop the Ocotillo Hills combines botanical gardens and a zoo in a natural setting. It concentrates on plants and animals indigenous to the Chihuahuan Desert. You'll see mountain lions, bobcats, buffalo, antelope, and the endangered Mexican wolf, as well as an excellent collection of exotic cacti and succulents from around the world. The views of Carlsbad and the Pecos River valley from parts of the trail are spectacular.

The park is located just off Highway 285 at 1504 Miehls Drive on the northwest edge of Carlsbad; (505) 887–5516. It's open daily from 8:00 A.M. to 8:00 P.M. (last tour at 6:30 P.M.) Memorial Day through Labor Day and from 9:00 A.M. to 5:00 P.M. (last tour at 3:30 P.M.) the rest of the year. Admission is free; tours cost $3.00 per person.

The small southeastern community of *Artesia* often gets short-changed due to its convenient location halfway between the larger and more well-known cities of Roswell and Carlsbad. It's here, however, where you'll find authentic small-town hospitality and a leisurely pace. If you're passing through and looking for good eats, check out the classic *La Fonda Restaurant* at 206 West Main (505–746–9377); open daily from 11:00 A.M. to 9:00 P.M.

Following in the path of unusual locations of public buildings—Artesia boasts the first underground elementary school, built as a bomb shelter—is the town's first bed-and-breakfast inn. The *Heritage Inn Bed & Breakfast* is at once one of the most likely places for a small-town inn—in the oldest building on Main Street, built in 1905—yet also in one of the most unlikely: It's perched above a computer store. But you won't even be aware of the steady business of a retail store below as you enjoy the well-insulated country Victorian atmosphere of the inn, with its old 8-foot-high windows, gleaming hardwood floors, and colonial American furnishings and decor. In addition to eleven guest rooms, each with a queen-size bed and its own bathroom, the inn provides a parlor/lounge for its guests, complete with TV/VCR and a small library. Though the building may be old, the inn is not. The space was completely renovated in the mid-1990s, so you can expect the conveniences of a modern hotel: remote-control TVs, telephones, and modem hookups in every room, with fax services available.

You'll find the inn at 209 West Main; (505) 748–2552. Rates range from $50 to $65.

Lea County

The Llano Estacado, or "Staked Plains," makes up a large part of the landscape of New Mexico's southeasternmost county, one of the last major land areas in the continental United States to be settled. Homesteading and open-range ranching were a way of life on this often-harsh land during the early part of this century. For the most part, working cowboys have given way to rodeo cowboys in these parts. In fact, Lea County has produced more professional rodeo champions than any other county in the United States, starting with Henry Clay McGonagill in 1901. He was the first professional rodeo cowboy. In 1978 the county's heritage was honored with the founding of the *Lea County Cowboy Hall of Fame and Western Heritage Center* in the county's largest city, Hobbs.

The result of the dream of Dale "Tuffy" Cooper, the Hall of Fame captures the essence of the early days and the pioneers of Lea County. It honors county residents who have distinguished themselves in rodeo, as ranch cowboys, or as pioneer or present-day women on ranches. In contrast to many museums, the chronologically displayed exhibits are glimpses of history depicting entire scenes rather than just labeled artifacts. Complete portrayals of a pioneer bedroom and kitchen look as though someone might return any minute. Memorabilia of all inductees are also displayed in the Hall of Fame.

Traditional Food of New Mexico

Classic Gold Margarita

This *comida* (food) is actually a *bebida* (drink) and is the perfect accompaniment or prelude to a traditional New Mexican meal.

1 oz. any premium gold tequila
½ oz. Cointreau (or triple sec, a less expensive orange liqueur)
1 oz. fresh-squeezed lime juice
¼ oz. fresh-squeezed lemon juice
margarita or kosher salt (coarser than table salt)
1 wedge lime and/or 1 wedge lemon

Make a slice in a lime wedge and run the edge around the rim of a glass (in order to dampen the edge). Dip dampened glass edge in salt. Fill a large cup with ice and add remaining ingredients. Shake gently. Pour ice and drink into the salt-rimmed glass for your margarita "on the rocks"; for a margarita "neat," strain out the ice. *¡Salud!* Makes 1 Margarita.

The Hall of Fame is on the campus of New Mexico Junior College, 5317 Lovington Highway, in Hobbs; (505) 392–5518. It's open Monday through Friday from 10:00 A.M. to 5:00 P.M. and Saturday from 1:00 to 5:00 P.M. There's no admission charge.

Other notable museums in the area include the **Confederate Air Force Museum** (no phone; call the Hobbs County Chamber of Commerce at 505–397–3202) at the Lea County Airport on Highway 180 in Hobbs and the **Lea County Museum** (505–396–4805) at 102 South Love in the town of Lovington (northeast of Hobbs via Highway 18). This local-history museum, situated in a former landmark hotel, built in 1918, displays exhibits of pioneer families. It's open from 1:00 to 5:00 P.M. Tuesday through Friday and 10:00 A.M. to 5:00 P.M. on Saturday; admission is 50 cents per person.

Roosevelt County

North of the city of **Portales**—the home of Eastern New Mexico University— you'll come across one of the most significant archaeological sites in North America: Blackwater Draw. And the **Blackwater Draw Museum** is on hand to help interpret exactly why this spot is so important. (The Blackwater Draw site is actually a little northwest of the museum, but visit the museum first.)

On this site in 1932, A. W. Anderson of nearby Clovis discovered the oldest evidence of human existence in the New World—from 11,000 years ago. Spear points, bones, and fossilized remains of woolly mammoth, saber-toothed tiger, camel, and bison have been recovered from the sprawling maze of canyons. At one time Blackwater Draw was a large pond used as a watering hole for animals and, subsequently, as an ambush site for the early human inhabitants. The pond dried up 7,000 years ago, eventually forcing the hunter-gatherers to move on.

Though the museum displays some of what has been discovered at the site, archaeological excavations continue. Over the years, the digs have been funded by the likes of the Carnegie Institute, the National Geographic Society, and the Smithsonian Institution.

The museum is located 7 miles northeast of Portales on U.S. Highway 70; (505) 562–2202. From Memorial Day through Labor Day, the museum is open Monday through Saturday from 10:00 A.M. to 5:00 P.M. and Sunday from noon to 5:00 P.M.; during other times of the year, hours remain the same except that the museum is closed on Monday. Visits to the archaeological site are by appointment only. Admission is $2.00 for adults, $1.00 for seniors and young people ages six to fifteen, and free for children age five or younger. A single ticket allows visits to both museum and site. (*NOTE:* On the fourth Sunday of each month, a "free" day is held, on which no admission fees are charged.)

What with the huge *scientific* brain trust in New Mexico (Sandia and Los Alamos National Laboratories, White Sands Missile Range, Intel), it's only fitting that the genre of science fiction would earn a place of respect here as well—and it did, with the opening and dedication of the *Jack Williamson Science Fiction Library* in 1982 on the campus of Eastern New Mexico University in Portales. Combine that with all the renewed attention focused on "the Roswell incident" of 1947 (see International UFO Museum, earlier in this chapter), and you'd imagine the public interest in this little-known specialty library is bound to increase.

Begun in 1967, when Dr. Williamson—noted pioneer science-fiction writer, teacher, student, and benefactor—first donated his personal collection of materials, the library has grown to house one of the top science-fiction collections in the world, now including more than 13,000 volumes. Among the collection are the manuscripts and papers of noted authors Edmond Hamilton and Leigh Brackett, thousands of issues of science-fiction "pulps," dating back to the early 1900s, and an original copy of Gene Roddenberry's pilot script for the *Star Trek* television series. Among authors designedly collected are Isaac Asimov, Edgar Rice Burroughs, Harlan Ellison, Robert Heinlein, Robert Silverberg, Spider Robinson, Ursula LeGuin, and Gordon Dickson. And the best part is, most of the books can be borrowed, with the exception of autographed or fragile editions.

The library is open Monday through Friday from 8:00 A.M. to 5:00 P.M.; (505) 562–2636.

Curry County

Clovis, the largest city in Curry County and trade center for nearby Cannon Air Force Base, holds a place in rock-and-roll history with its *Norman Petty Recording Studios.* The old studio is now a shrine to Buddy Holly, the pioneering rock-and-roller who propelled such hits as "That'll Be the Day" and "Peggy Sue" to the top of the charts in the 1950s—hits that were recorded right here at the then state-of-the-art studio.

The studio was founded by the late producer-arranger-musician Norman Petty, who died in 1984, and his wife, Vi, who later cleaned and restored the studio to its former glory and personally led tours through the place before her death in 1992. She'd point out the drink machine where Holly would buy Cokes, Holly's microphone and Fender guitar amplifier, the room where Holly and other studio guests stayed, all its furniture intact. Besides Holly, the studio drew other musicians from West Texas and New Mexico, most notably Roy Orbison.

Kenneth Broad, an area minister and executor of the Pettys' estate, feels it's important to keep the restored studio open as a shrine for Holly's fans. Broad and other locals would like to open the studio for regular tours as well as turn it into a working recording studio again. In the meantime, however, the little gray building on Seventh Street in downtown Clovis is officially open only during the four-day ***Clovis Music Festival*** held each July as an annual tribute to Petty and local musicians. During other times, anyone wanting to see the place must call at least one month in advance (505–356–6422) to arrange for a tour. There's no admission fee, but donations are accepted.

Like many sizable towns across America, Clovis has a historic theater on its Main Street, 411 Main to be precise. A tall, rather ordinary facade, with that familiar vertical neon spelling out LYCEUM in an art-deco typeface, belies the grand interior of the town's ***Old Lyceum Theatre.*** Built during 1919–20 as a theater that would be used for both live performances and films, the Lyceum's huge screen was tailor-made to reflect the glory of early Hollywood, including Tom Mix cowboy movies and films starring Shirley Temple. The vision of the theater's founder, Eugene F. Hardwick, was to create the best performing stage west of Kansas City. Many folks at the time believed that he succeeded.

The Lyceum closed in 1974, and later a group of locals formed to "Save the Lyceum!" and ended up purchasing it for $40,000. A nonprofit group then began restoring and, eventually, operating the theater. At present, the restored Lyceum serves as the town's performing arts center. Guided tours are available upon request; (505) 763–6085.

Where to Stay in Southeastern New Mexico

DE BACA COUNTY

Coronado Motel,
309 West Sumner,
Fort Sumner,
(505) 355–2466

Billy the Kid Country Inn,
1704 East Sumner,
Fort Sumner,
(505) 355–7414

Fisherman's Hideaway,
Sumner Lake
(call for directions),
Fort Sumner,
(505) 355–2629

LINCOLN COUNTY

Casa de Patrón,
U.S. Highway 380,
Lincoln,
(505) 653–4676

Wortley Pat Garrett Hotel,
U.S. Highway 380,
Lincoln,
(505) 653–4300/
(877) 967–8539 (toll-free)

Best Western Swiss Chalet Inn,
1451 Mecham Drive,
Ruidoso,
(505) 258–3333/
(800) 477–9477

Forest Home Cabins,
436 Main Road,
Ruidoso,
(505) 257–4504/
(800) 678–7647

Holiday Inn Express,
400 West Highway 70,
Ruidoso,
(505) 257–3736/
(800) 257–5477

Shadow Mountain Lodge,
107 Main Road,
Ruidoso,
(505) 257–4886/
(800) 441–4331

OTERO COUNTY

The Lodge,
just off Highway 82,
Cloudcroft,
(505) 682–2566

Inn of the Mountain Gods
(resort and casino),
Mescalero Apache
Reservation,
(505) 257–5141/
(800) 545–9011

Satellite Inn,
2224 North White
Sands Boulevard,
Alamogordo,
(505) 437–8454/
(800) 221–7690

White Sands Inn,
1020 South White
Sands Boulevard,
Alamogordo,
(505) 434–4200/
(800) 255–5061

CHAVES COUNTY

**Best Western
El Rancho Palacio,**
2205 North Main Street,
Roswell,
(505) 622-2721/
(800) 528–1234

Holiday Inn Express,
2300 North Main,
Roswell,
(505) 627–9900/
(800) 465–4329

Days Inn,
1310 North Main Street,
Roswell,
(505) 623–4021/
(800) 329–7466

Budget Inn,
2101 North Main Street,
Roswell,
(505) 623–6050/
(800) 752–4667

EDDY COUNTY

**Heritage Inn Bed
& Breakfast,**
209 West Main,
Artesia,
(505) 748–2552/
(800) 594–7392

Best Western Pecos Inn,
2209 West Main,
Artesia,
(505) 748–3324/
(800) 676–7481

Best Western Stevens Inn,
1829 South Canal Street,
Carlsbad,
(505) 887–2851/
(800) 730–2851

Carlsbad Super 8,
3817 National Parks
Highway,
Carlsbad,
(505) 887–8888/
(800) 800–8000

Holiday Inn,
601 South Canal Street,
Carlsbad,
(505) 885–8500/
(800) 465–4329

Best Western Cavern Inn,
17 Carlsbad Caverns
Highway,
Whites City,
(505) 785–2291/
(800) 228–3767

LEA COUNTY

Innkeepers of New Mexico,
309 North Marland
Boulevard,
Hobbs,
(505) 397–7171

**Hobbs Howard
Johnson Inn,**
501 North Marland,
Hobbs,
(505) 397–3251

Sands Motel,
1300 East Broadway,
Hobbs,
(505) 393–4442

ROOSEVELT COUNTY

Morning Star Inn
(bed-and-breakfast),
620 West Second,
Portales,
(505) 356–2994

**Classic American
Economy Inn,**
1613 West Second,
Portales,
(505) 356–6668

Super 8 Motel,
1805 West Second,
Portales,
(505) 356–8518/
(800) 800–8000

CURRY COUNTY

Best Western La Vista Inn,
1516 Mabry Drive,
Clovis,
(505) 762–3808/
(800) 528–1234

Clovis Inn,
2912 Mabry Drive,
Clovis,
(505) 762–5600/
(800) 535–3440

Holiday Inn,
2700 Mabry Drive,
Clovis,
(505) 762–4491

SELECTED CHAMBERS OF COMMERCE/ VISITOR BUREAUS IN SOUTHEASTERN NEW MEXICO

Alamogordo Chamber of Commerce,
1301 North White Sands Boulevard,
Alamogordo, 88310;
(505) 437–6120, (800) 826–0294;
Web site: www.alamogordo.com

Artesia Chamber of Commerce,
P.O. Box 99,
Artesia, 88211;
(505) 746–2744/(800) 658–6251;
Web site: www.artesiachamber.com

Capitan Chamber of Commerce,
P.O. Box 441,
Capitan, 88316;
(505) 354–2273;
Web site: www.villageofcapitan.com

Carlsbad Convention & Visitors Bureau,
P.O. Box 910,
Carlsbad, 88220;
(505) 887–6516/(800) 221–1224;
Web site: www.carlsbadchamber.com

Cloudcroft Chamber of Commerce,
P.O. Box 1290,
Cloudcroft, 88317;
(505) 682–2733;
Web site: www.cloudcroft.net

Clovis/Curry County Chamber of Commerce,
215 North Main Street,
Clovis, 88101;
(505) 763–3435/(800) 261–7656;
Web site: www.clovisnm.org

Fort Sumner Chamber of Commerce,
P.O. Box 28,
707 North Fourth Street,
Fort Sumner, 88119
(505) 355–7705
Web site: www.ftsumnerchamber.com

Hobbs Chamber of Commerce,
400 North Marland,
Hobbs, 88240;
(505) 397–3202; (800) 658–6291;
Web site: www.hobbschamber.org

Portales/Roosevelt County Chamber of Commerce,
200 East Seventh,
Portales, 88130;
(505) 356–8541/(800) 635–8036;
Web site: www.portales.com

Roswell Convention & Visitors Bureau,
912 North Main Street,
Roswell, NM 88201;
(505) 624–7704/(888) ROSWELL;
Web site: www.roswellcvb.com

Ruidoso Valley Chamber of Commerce,
720 Sudderth,
P.O. Box 698,
Ruidoso, 88355;
(505) 257–7395/(877) 784–3676;
Web site: www.ruidoso.net/

Where to Eat in Southeastern New Mexico

DE BACA COUNTY

Fred's Restaurant & Lounge,
1408 East Sumner,
Fort Sumner,
(505) 355–7500.
Inexpensive.
Fare: American.

Sprout's Cafe,
1701 East Sumner,
Fort Sumner,
(505) 355–7278.
Inexpensive to moderate.
Fare: American.

Fisherman's Hideaway,
Sumner Lake
(call for directions),
Fort Sumner,
(505) 355–2629.
Inexpensive to moderate.
Fare: American.

Sadie's Frontier Restaurant,
Highway 60 West,
Fort Sumner,
(505) 355–1461.
Inexpensive to moderate.
Fare: New Mexican.

LINCOLN COUNTY

Café Rio,
2547 Sudderth Drive,
Ruidoso,
(505) 257–7746.
Inexpensive to moderate.
Fare: Pizza, sandwiches, as well as Greek, Portuguese, and Cajun classics.

El Paisano Restaurant,
442 Smokey Bear Boulevard,
Capitan,
(505) 354–2206.
Inexpensive to moderate.
Fare: New Mexican cuisine.

Tinnie Silver Dollar,
U.S. Highway 70,
Tinnie,
(505) 653–4425.
Moderate to expensive. Fare: American and Southwestern.

Smokey Bear Restaurant,
316 Smokey Bear Boulevard,
Capitan,
(505) 354–2253.
Inexpensive. Fare: American.

OTERO COUNTY

Western Restaurant and Bar,
Burro Avenue,
Cloudcroft,
(505) 682–2445.
Inexpensive. Fare: New Mexican and American.

Spring Mountain Chuck Wagon BBQ,
Highway 82,
Cloudcroft,
(505) 682–4550.
Inexpensive to moderate.
Fare: Southwestern American, known for BBQ catfish.

Memories,
1223 New York Avenue,
Alamogordo,
(505) 437–0077.
Moderate. Fare: Steak, seafood, pasta.

CHAVES COUNTY

Cattle Baron,
1113 North Main Street,
Roswell,
(505) 622–2465.
Inexpensive to moderate.
Fare: Steaks, seafood, etc.

Claim Restaurant & Saloon,
1310 North Main Street,
Roswell,
(505) 623–6042.
Inexpensive to moderate.
Fare: Steaks, etc.

El Toro Bravo Restaurant,
102 South Main Street,
Roswell,
(505) 622–9280.
Inexpensive to moderate.
Fare: New Mexican cuisine.

Nuthin' Fancy,
2103 North Main Street,
Roswell,
(505) 623–4098.
Inexpensive to moderate.
Fare: Homemade comfort food including meat loaf, chicken, and wonderful vegetables.

Pasta Cafe,
4501 North Main Street,
Roswell,
(505) 624–1111.
Inexpensive to moderate.
Fare: Authentic Italian entrees and New York–style hand-thrown pizza.

EDDY COUNTY

La Fonda Restaurant,
210 West Main,
Artesia,
(505) 746–9377.
Inexpensive to moderate.
Fare: New Mexican.

Flume Restaurant,
1829 South Canal Street,
Carlsbad,
(505) 887–2851/
(800) 730–2851.
Moderate to expensive.
Fare: Prime rib, steaks, etc.

Sirloin Stockade,
710 North Canal Street,
Carlsbad,
(505) 887–7211.
Inexpensive to moderate.
Fare: Steaks, etc.

Lucy's Mexicali Restaurant,
701 South Canal Street,
Carlsbad,
(505) 887–7714.
Inexpensive to moderate.
Fare: New Mexican,
steaks, etc.

Bamboo Garden,
1511 South Canal Street,
Carlsbad,
(505) 887–5145.
Inexpensive to moderate.
Fare: Chinese.

LEA COUNTY

Cattle Baron,
1930 North Grimes,
Hobbs,
(505) 393–2800.
Inexpensive to moderate.
Fare: Steaks, seafood, etc.

La Fiesta Restaurant,
604 East Broadway,
Hobbs,
(505) 397–1235.
Inexpensive to moderate.
Fare: New Mexican.

North 40 Restaurant,
408 West Bender
Boulevard,
Hobbs,
(505) 392–8178.
Inexpensive to moderate.
Fare: American.

ROOSEVELT COUNTY

The Cattle Baron,
1600 South Avenue D,
Portales,
(505) 356–5587.
Inexpensive to moderate.
Fare: Steaks, seafood, etc.

Something Different Grill,
805 West Second Street,
Portales,
(505) 356–1205.
Inexpensive. Fare: Eclectic
deli-sandwiches, salads.

Juanito's,
813 South Avenue C Place,
Portales,
(505) 359–1860.
Inexpensive to moderate.
Fare: New Mexican.

CURRY COUNTY

Juanito's,
1608 Mabry Drive,
Clovis,
(505) 762–7822.
Inexpensive.
Fare: New Mexican.

Leal's Mexican Food
Restaurant,
3100 East Mobry Drive,
Clovis,
(505) 763–4075.
Inexpensive. Fare: New
Mexican and American.

Poor Boy's Steakhouse,
2115 North Prince,
Clovis,
(505) 763–5222.
Inexpensive to moderate.
Fare: Steaks, etc.

China Star,
1221 North Main,
Clovis,
(505) 762–8489.
Inexpensive to moderate.
Fare: Chinese.

Appendixes

NEW MEXICO INDIAN PUEBLOS

(Listed by county where most of the reservation is located)

BERNALILLO COUNTY

Isleta Pueblo
P.O. Box 1270
Isleta, NM 87022
(505) 869–3111

CIBOLA COUNTY

Acoma Pueblo
P.O. Box 309
Acomita, NM 87034
(505) 552–6604/(800) 747–0181

Laguna Pueblo
P.O. Box 194
Laguna, NM 87026
(505) 552–6654

MCKINLEY COUNTY

Zuni Pueblo
P.O. Box 339
Zuni, NM 87327
(505) 782–4481

RIO ARRIBA COUNTY

San Juan Pueblo
P.O. Box 1099
San Juan, NM 87566
(505) 852–4400

Santa Clara Pueblo
P.O. Box 580
Española, NM 87532
(505) 753–7330

SANDOVAL COUNTY

Cochiti Pueblo
P.O. Box 70
Cochiti, NM 87072
(505) 465–2245

Jemez Pueblo
P.O. Box 100
Jemez, NM 87024
(505) 834–7359
Web site: www.jemezpueblo.org

Sandia Pueblo
Box 6008
Bernalillo, NM 87004
(505) 867–3317
Web site: www.sandiapueblo.nsn.us/

San Felipe Pueblo
P.O. Box 4339
San Felipe, NM 87001
(505) 867–3381

Santa Ana Pueblo
2 Dove Road
Bernalillo, NM 87004
(505) 867–3301
Web site: www.santaana.org

Santo Domingo Pueblo
P.O. Box 99
Santo Domingo, NM 87052
(505) 465–2214

Zia Pueblo
Pueblo of Zia
Administration Building
135 Capital Square Drive
Zia Pueblo, NM 87053
(505) 867–3304

SANTA FE COUNTY

Nambé Pueblo
Route 1, Box 117–BB
Santa Fe, NM 87501
(505) 455–2036

Pojoaque Pueblo
Route 11 Box 71
Santa Fe, NM 87501
(505) 455–2278

San Ildefonso Pueblo
Route 5, Box 315-A
Santa Fe, NM 87501
(505) 455–2273

Tesuque Pueblo
Route 5, Box 360T
Santa Fe, NM 87501
(505) 983–2667

Taos County
Picuris Pueblo
P.O. Box 127
Peñasco, NM 87553
(505) 587–2519

Taos Pueblo
P.O. Box 1846
Taos Pueblo, NM 87571
(505) 758–1028
Web site: www.taospueblo.com

NON-PUEBLO INDIAN TRIBES IN NEW MEXICO
(Listed by county where most of the reservation is located)

Navajo Nation
Tourism Department
P.O. Box 663
Window Rock, AZ 86515
(928) 871–6436
Web site: www.navajo.org
(San Juan and McKinley Counties in
New Mexico but also in northeast
Arizona and southeast Utah)

Alamo Chapter (Navajo)
Alamo Route
Magdalena, NM 87825
(505) 854–2686
(Socorro County)

To'hajiilee Chapter (Navajo)
P.O. Box 3398
To'hajiilee, NM 87026
(505) 836–4221
(Bernalillo County)

Ramah Chapter (Navajo)
P.O. Box 308
Ramah, NM 87321
(505) 775–7140
(Cibola County)

Jicarilla Apache Tribe
P.O. Box 507
Dulce, NM 87528
(505) 759–3242
(Rio Arriba County)

Mescalero Apache Tribe
P.O. Box 176
Mescalero, NM 88340
(505) 671–4494
(Otero County)

NEW MEXICO WINERIES

Anasazi Fields Winery
26 Camino de los Pueblitos
Placitas, NM 87043
(505) 867–3062
Web site: www.anasazifieldswinery.com

Anderson Valley Vineyards
4920 Rio Grand Boulevard NW
Albuquerque, NM 87107
(505) 344–7266

Arena Blanca Vineyards
7320 U.S. Highway 54/70 North
Alamogordo, NM 88301
(505) 437-0602/(800) 368-3081
Web site: www.pistachiotreeranch.com

Balagna Winery
223 Rio Bravo Drive
Los Alamos, NM 87544
(505) 672–3678

Black Mesa Winery
1502 Highway 68
(mile marker 15)
Velarde, NM 87582
(800) 852–6372
Web site: www.blackmesawinery.com

Blue Teal Tasting Room
1720 Avenida de Mesilla
Las Cruces, NM 88005
(505) 524–0390
Web site: www.blueteal.com

Casa Rondeña Winery
Rondeña Way
733 Chavez Road NW
Albuquerque, NM 87107
(505) 344–5911
Web site: www.casarondena.com

Corrales Winery
6275 Corrales Road
Corrales, NM 87048
(505) 898–5165
Web site: www.corraleswinery.com

Gruet Winery
8400 Pan American Freeway NE
Albuquerque, NM 87113
(505) 821–0055/(888) 857–9463
Web site: www.gruetwinery.com

Jory Winery
San Pedro Avenue
Albuquerque, NM 87113
(505) 858–0074/(800) 632–8059
Web site: www.jorywinery.com

La Chiripada Winery
Highway 75/P.O. Box 191
Dixon, NM 87527
(505) 579–4437/(800) 528–7801
Web site: www.lachiripada.com

La Viña Winery
4201 South Highway 28
La Union, NM 88021
(505) 882–7632

Los Luceros Winery
P.O. Box 110
Alcalde, NM 87511
(505) 852–1085

Mademoiselle de Santa Fe Vineyards at Blue Teal Tasting Room
1720 Avenida de Mesilla
Las Cruces, NM 88005
(505) 524–0390

Madison Vineyards and Winery
Star Route 490
Ribera, NM 87560
(505) 421–8028

Milagro Vineyards
985 West Ella
P.O. Box 1205
Corrales, NM 87048
(505) 898–3998
Web site: www.milagrovineyards.com

Ponderosa Valley Vineyards and Winery
3171 Highway 290
Ponderosa, NM 87044
(505) 834–7487
Web site: www.ponderosavineyards.com

Sandia Shadows Winery
(physically in Truth or Consequences)
P.O. Box 92675
Albuquerque, NM 87199–2675
(505) 856–1006
Web site: www.sandiawines.com

Santa Fe Vineyards
Route 1, Box 216A
Española, NM 87532
(505) 753–8100

Sisneros-Torres Winery
23 Winery Road
Bosque, NM 87006
(505) 266–3370

St. Clair Winery
1325 De Baca Road
Deming, NM 88030
(505) 546–9324

Tularosa Vineyards
23 Coyote Canyon Road
Tularosa, NM 88352
(505) 585–2260
Web site: www.tularosavineyards.com

Willmon Vineyards
2801 Sudderth Drive
Ruidoso, NM 88345
(505) 630–9463

NEW MEXICO SKI AREAS

As part of the southern reaches of the Rocky Mountains, New Mexico's mountain ranges are home to many downhill and cross-country ski areas. During ski season, which is roughly late November or early December to mid-March or early April, most ski areas are open from 9:00 a.m. to 4:00 p.m. For New Mexico road conditions, call 827–5213 or (800) 432–4269 (out of state); and for detailed or updated information on the downhill ski areas listed below, or for information on cross-country ski areas, please call Ski New Mexico at (505) 982–5300; www. skinewmexico.com. (*NOTE:* Lift fees are included for comparison purposes only; they are subject to change from season to season. Fees for half-day lift tickets and those for children and seniors are lower.)

Angel Fire (Angel Fire, NM)
(800) 633–7463
Web site: www.angelfireresort.com
Accommodations:
(800) 633–7463
Number of trails: 68
Adult full-day lift ticket: $48

Pajarito (Los Alamos, NM)
(505) 662–5725
Web site: www.skipajarito.com
Accommodations:
(800) 444–0707
Number of trails: 37
Adult full-day lift ticket: $39

Red River (Red River, NM)
(505) 754–2223
Web site: www.redriver skiarea.com
Accommodations:
(800) 331–7669
Number of trails: 58
Adult full-day lift ticket: $46

Sandia Peak (Albuquerque, NM)
(505) 242–9052
Web site: www.sandiapeak.com
Accommodations:
(800) 473–1000
Number of trails: 25
Adult full-day lift ticket: $38

Ski Santa Fe (Santa Fe, NM)
(505) 982–4429
Web site: www.skisantafe.com
Accommodations:
(877) 737–7366
Number of trails: 44
Adult full-day lift ticket: $45

Sipapu (northern New Mexico)
(800) 587–2240
Web site: www.sipapunm.com
Accommodations:
(800) 587–2240
Number of trails: 31
Adult full-day lift ticket: $34

Ski Apache (Ruidoso, NM)
(505) 336–4356
Web site: www.skiapache.com
Accommodations:
(800) 253–2255
Number of trails: 55
Adult full-day lift ticket: $47

Ski Cloudcroft (Cloudcroft, NM)
(505) 682–2333
Accommodations:
(505) 682–2733
Number of trails: 21
Adult full-day lift ticket: $25

Taos Ski Valley (Taos, NM)
(505) 776–2291/(800) 347–7414
Web site: www.skitaos.org
Accommodations:
(800) 776–1111
Number of trails: 72
Adult full-day lift ticket: $51

Indexes

GENERAL INDEX

ART GALLERIES

BED-AND-BREAKFASTS

OTHER LODGING

MUSEUMS

About the Author

Former tour guide Richard K. Harris has written or cowritten twenty-nine other guidebooks, including *Hidden Southwest* (Berkeley: Ulysses Press), *Getaway Guide to the American Southwest* (Oakland: RDR Books), and *National Trust Guide: Santa Fe* (New York: John Wiley & Sons). He has also served as contributing editor on guides to Mexico, New Mexico, and other ports of call for John Muir Publications, Fodor's, Birnbaum, and Access guides. He is past president of PEN New Mexico and president of the New Mexico Book Association. Richard writes and lives in Santa Fe, New Mexico.